SHADES

LIVING WITH MENTAL ILLNESS

NIKKI LANGDON

Dear Mike,
Together — one
story at a time —
we will end
the stigma

[signature]

nikkilanagdon.com

Photography by Andrea Norberg
Cover and text design by Streetlight Graphics
Contact: nikkilangdonauthor@gmail.com

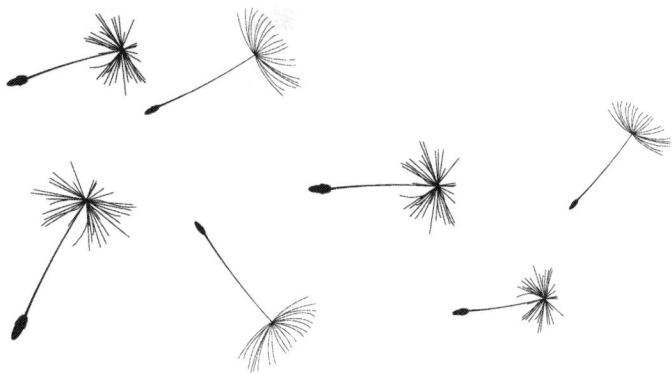

Thank you Richard and Jen, Eric and Lisa,
Michael and Lindsay, and Liz and Yvond
for loving me unconditionally, supporting
me, and never judging me
through all the Shades.

TABLE OF CONTENTS

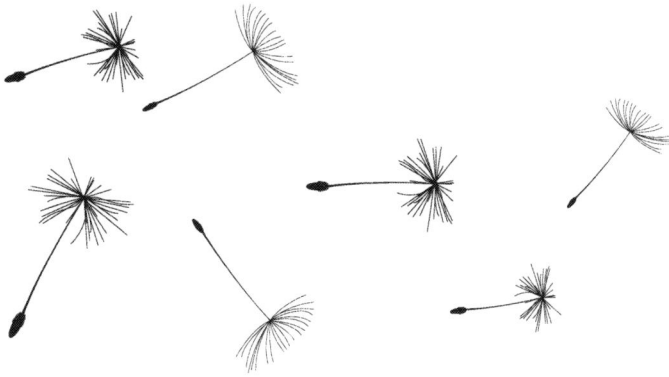

A dandelion can endure almost any living condition. They represent overcoming every hardship by standing strong and proud. They are a symbol of emotional healing. Often viewed as a pest or out of place in the expanse of a beautiful lawn, they are warriors who don't care how different they are. They grow, survive and shine their bright yellow beauty and then become delicate and fly, granting wishes to those who believe.

SHADES

Gradients
On a continuum
Obsession to interest
Eating disorder to healthy diet
Overreactions to acceptable boundaries
Terror to reasonable fear
Fury to appropriate anger
Paranoia to danger
Sadness to immobility
Sensitive to fragile

Where is the tipping point?
Where is "normal?"
Where is socially acceptable?
When is a reaction correct and when is it illness?

This is how I live

Grading, weighing, evaluating ... Is this
illness? Is my reaction warranted?
Illness never questioned this. The path to wellness does.
I embrace my work toward wellness, but now I
must maneuver the gradients. The shades.

FORWARD

I ASK YOU, MY DEAR READER, as you join me on my walk through my past fifty-nine years, to consider from your perspective where does each incident fall on the continuum? What shade is it? This is written from my perspective and each character within may, and likely does have, a different interpretation and analysis. What do you see, my valued reader? What is your interpretation? What do you perceive as "normal"? What is illness? Or what is somewhere in between?

For Book Clubs, please find questions at the back of the book for discussion as you read through this memoir together.

I have divided my journey loosely into three parts:

1. Everything was normal to me; illness wasn't a consideration. This was all real and my life.

2. Everything became suspect as being illness-based. Nothing that caused deep feelings of any kind was a shade of well. Everything had to be from illness, and therefore, treated and responded to accordingly.

3. Theoretically being from a place of wellness brought about via a multifaceted treatment plan that enabled me to discern more clearly wellness versus illness, and thereby determine an appropriate action and reaction. But is it? Or is the illness just craftier, trickier, and more able to manipulate me?

I leave you to decide, dear reader. What shade do you see?

PART ONE
PRE-DIAGNOSIS
THE DARKNESS

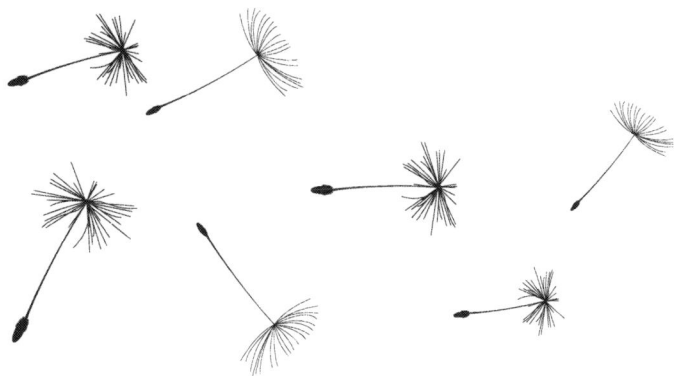

1.

I KNEW THE APARTMENT HAD A demon, an entity, an evilness within. I knew it at my core. But I couldn't tell anyone. It would hurt me, hurt my husband if I spoke of IT. I had to live silently with IT tormenting me.

It was one of the worst winters in many, many years. Weeks of freezing weather, with wind chills in the negative forty and fifty degrees Celsius range. Brutal. And we were flat broke. Worse than broke. Our expenses exceeded my husband's income every month, and I couldn't find work in this small town. I would walk the streets and through the small mall when I was able to leave the apartment, looking for dropped change to buy us a banana or a bit of cheese to add to our sparse macaroni diet.

We had no money for gas, so every day, my husband would walk to work in the frigid temperatures, the windchill ripping at him.

I felt guilt. I felt useless. I would spend the days I wasn't able to leave the apartment, which were many, pacing between the tiny living room and kitchen. The TV was on at all times, broadcasting one of the two channels we received. I only stopped pacing and stood in the middle of the living room during a cooking show that aired mid-afternoon every day. I salivated as I watched the food created. When it ended, I would pace again.

Often, I would put on my coat, my mittens, my hat and get as far as the door. Wanting, no, needing, to leave. To get away from the demon. But IT wouldn't let me. I would freeze as I reached for the doorknob. Unable to touch it. And I knew I was not allowed freedom that day.

I hated to go to the bathroom and would hold off as long as I could. To get to the bathroom, I had to walk by IT. The room with the demon.

We had a two-bedroom apartment. That was all that was available in this small town where my husband got his job. It cost too much and we didn't need that much room, but that was all there was for rent. The bedrooms were across from each other, the bathroom at the end of the hall. One bedroom was ours; the other was ITs.

I had to keep the TV on at all times, otherwise I could hear IT, and that was terrifying. But at night, when it was dark and quiet, there was nothing to drown IT out. IT was in my head. A buzz, a hum, a noise, a feeling. I couldn't label or define it, but IT was there. IT would communicate with me and IT knew I could hear.

I didn't share any of this with my husband. He was working so hard and I already felt like such a burden. A useless weight in his life. I couldn't help with finances; I did nothing each day; I felt lazy and meaningless all the time. I couldn't tell him about the pacing. I couldn't tell him that I was physically unable to leave the apartment most of the time. I couldn't tell him that IT, or maybe THEM, lived in the room across the hall from ours. I was already a liability. He was so stressed. How could I make things worse? I had no right to and I wouldn't.

I met my husband at university, both of us studying Agriculture. I was terrified when my parents dropped me off in the dormitory and drove away. It was bone dread terror. Not a little scared or nervous, but a deep fear that completely immobilized me. Paralyzed me. I was away from home for the first time and had just turned seventeen years old. I recalled feeling similar on the first day of high school, too terrified to leave the truck that my father drove me to the new school in. I was sobbing both times. I was unable to breathe both times. Why was I so weak?

My parents said I was terribly bored at home when very young, and they had taken me to the school board to take a test to see if I would be allowed to start my formal education a year early. I recall thinking how ridiculous the test was as the examiner, and I went through it. I decided shortly into the assessment that it was simple and stupid. Things like hiding an eraser and I was to find it? I remembered thinking the examiner needed to be much quieter, and how badly he would suck at hide and seek. He was so noisy hiding the eraser anyone would easily find it.

I passed the test and started school a year earlier than I was scheduled to, so I graduated high school shortly after my seventeenth birthday. And that's why I was dropped off at a university two and half hours away from my family at that young age. Most left home at eighteen. But would that have made a difference for me? I was so weak, so sensitive, so helpless, so unable to manage life like others. Would another year have helped? Likely not. My parents always told me I needed to toughen up or the world would eat me alive, and they were correct. I just didn't know exactly how to do it.

It started a long time ago...

2.

THE CURTAIN DREAMS. FROM THE time I could remember. The curtain dreams haunted me.

There were bright orange vinyl curtains in my childhood bedroom. I was asleep but awake, or at least thought I was awake. All of a sudden, the room would grow huge around me, and I was so tiny on my small bed in this massive, expanding room. There were no doors, no pictures, no closet, nothing in this room except a tiny bed in the centre. And I could see myself, so small on that bed, clutching my blankets, trying to hide. I could see my wide-eyed terror.

The orange curtains would slowly fade to black. The window they covered would vanish. They looked like tar. Thick gooey tar, just like in the barrel on our farm. Then they would come alive and slowly expand. They would stretch, then thicken, stretch and thicken. They oozed thickly from the rod they hung on, reaching for the corner of the room furthest from me. When they connected with that corner, they would slowly drip down, pooling into a solid blob on the floor at the base. They looked like a massive, black, oily drape pulled from the middle of the wall with a sash to hang heavily in the corner.

Then the blob on the floor would grow. It would slowly flatten and expand, inching along the floor and sliding up the walls it was adjacent to, defying nature by oozing thickly upward to fill the entire corner of the room. It crept to the ceiling, blackening it with the shiny goo, as with the floor, inching toward me, fanning out from the corner. I watched myself scramble off the bed and scurry to the corner opposite the ooze. It continued expanding agonizingly slowly but still coming. Stretching, thickening, stretching, thickening. It was alive, breathing, reaching, growing. Occasionally, a section that slid along the floor would lift as if someone lifted a throw rug a little to peek under. That lifted piece would search for me, slowly scanning the environment, rippling across its width, from one side to the other to find me. Then it would flatten again and begin its terrifying advance. It was slowly filling the space between us, inch by inch, covering the room with thick, black, shiny death.

I knew if it touched me, I would die. I knew it planned to slowly ooze over my legs and climb my body just as it had climbed the walls. It knew it was going to slowly smother me. And I knew I wouldn't be able to get free. It was going to surround me, trap me. The bed was gone. It was just me in the room, trying to make myself as small as I could in the corner, and the ooze coming to kill me. All I could do was scream soundlessly as the blackness stretched and thickened, stretched and thickened.

I clawed helplessly at the wall behind me, but never took my eyes from the ooze. The room continued to expand and the black death surged to fill it. The room was massive, and I watched myself helplessly from outside of my body, seeing tiny me curled into the corner of an endless room with black slime pulsing, breathing, as it got nearer and nearer. I could see my eyes wide and my mouth open in terror. Then I was inside of me. I was simultaneously outside and inside of me, and I could see me as it approached my toes, and I could feel it, hear it, smell it. I felt myself pulling my toes in, my knees in, trying to get smaller, trying to stay alive.

I could hear a sound, but only inside my head. It was almost a laughter, a dry cackle, mixed with the sound of stale, dry air being laboriously inhaled and exhaled. It was most definitely not human. It grew louder and louder the closer it got to me. I felt its excitement at being able to get me. It reached for me, but I couldn't get smaller. Just as it was about to touch me, with me pressing my tiny body into the corner, my mind racing and soundlessly sobbing inside and my outside self screaming, "No, no, no!" I would wake. I would find myself shaking and crying in my bed, struggling to breathe. Gasping. Searching. Where was it? It was here. Where was it hiding? I could still hear it. I could feel it. Even though I couldn't see it, I knew it was coming.

And then I would remember my little brother. He had the same curtains and I had to save him. I would scramble out of my bed and run across the hall, terror filling me. And each night I would find him safe. But I had to make sure. So each night, I would stand in the doorway of his room for hours. Waiting. I would wake sometime later on the floor of his doorway and then, shivering, I would make my way back to my room and crawl under my blankets to warm. I would fall into a heavy, dreamless sleep, knowing we had both once again survived. Knowing, also, that one night we wouldn't.

I remember having these dreams from the time I was four years old. Not every night but several times a week. They may have been with me prior but I don't have a memory of that. Other than that, I have very few memories of my childhood, almost none in fact. But these dreams are clear, vivid, and continued long into my life.

When I was about ten years old, we moved and left the orange curtains. I felt such relief that I would stop having those dreams. But that was not to be. The dreams followed. I no longer ran to my brother's room to check on him as, somehow, I knew he was safe because the ooze wasn't attached to the curtains; it was attached to me. It was coming for me and only me, and I always knew when the black ooze got me not only would I die, I would burn for eternity. The ooze had told me and that made it happy.

3.

THE ABSOLUTE KNOWING OF THIS was confirmed for me at age thirteen. It started with Bible study at my aunt's house. My aunt was a born-again Christian and wanted to make sure that everyone she knew would be saved. I knew I was invited as I was one who needed saving. The black ooze had shown me and I knew. But I also knew this was a chance at redemption. I believed in my heart that this was the way I could be saved from the black ooze, that darkness that was coming for me.

I was nervous upon arrival but was filled with hope. I was led into my aunt's good living room, so I knew this was important. We never socialized as a family in the good living room. Everyone seated in chairs and on couches around the room was much older than I, and all were holding well-worn bibles and singing together. They were wonderful and welcoming, and all stood and took turns hugging me warmly. But I felt uneasy and out of place. I didn't have a Bible or know the songs, and I felt embarrassed and ashamed by my lack of knowledge. All of a sudden, I felt heat filling me and I was struggling to breathe evenly. I tried to concentrate on just taking air into my body.

Everyone stood and I tried to make myself rise on wobbly legs. I made it upright, but felt a little unsteady and slightly dizzy.

Suddenly, noise filled the room. It came from everywhere. It was deafening, crushing. I noticed all the women had their hands lifted and were rocking side to side. They were making sounds, not words, just sounds. Endless, crushing sounds filled me inside and out. My head started to ache. My dizziness increased and things became blurry. I felt like I had to get away from these noises. I just needed out, away from this cacophony. I needed to run. Immediately! Leave! And I tried but was unable to move. I physically could not move my body. I was paralyzed, frozen to the spot. I felt hot tears rolling down my face. It was getting harder and harder to breathe. My heart felt like it was going to explode. My body went from being on fire to ice cold and I began shaking.

Then someone noticed me.

"Don't worry, honey. When you receive the Lord into your heart, you too will speak in tongues. That's how we will know... That's how we will know..." she repeated softly over and over. She put her arm around my shoulder, her Bible in the other hand lifted to the sky.

"And we will know because we can interpret what you are saying. We will know when Our Lord enters your heart." She said this louder, passionately, eyes focused on her raised Bible. I heard endless murmurs around me, "Amen. Yes Jesus. Amen Jesus. Yes Jesus. Yes. Yes. Yes." Everyone was speaking hushed, whispery words and now those words were closing in on me, suffocating me. They were worse than the loud voices prior. They were filling my airways, my lungs, like heavy smoke, slowly flowing into me, suffocating me, and I would die if I didn't get away.

Someone was touching me. I was pushed or fell backwards into my chair. Someone else said they were going to pray over me. Then I heard the group raise their voices, still talking over each other, words, sounds, filling my brain. Taking my breath from me. I knew I was going to die.

I have no recollection of how long I sat. My next memory was of my head being held between my knees. I was gulping for air, sobbing. As my eyes focused, I could see my tears falling to the carpet. My head was released, and I raised it and looked into a sea of expectant faces. They kept exchanging looks and then someone said, "Just try, child."

Try what? Breathing? I was trying! My body felt like it was spasming, violently hitching as I sobbed and tried desperately to get air into my lungs.

"We felt the Lord enter your heart! Speak child! Speak in tongues!" Someone cried out.

I opened my mouth but nothing came out. I was simply unable to form any words or sounds. Nothing, either English or "tongues" would come out of my mouth. I was mute. And terrified. And I knew deep in my heart why their prayers had failed.

I was afraid they would see the evil that haunted me and blocked their prayers. I was afraid they would shun me. But they didn't. Maybe they couldn't see it? Maybe they were protected from it as Jesus lived in them. They were incredibly kind to me and continued to assure me that it would happen and to be patient.

But I knew it wouldn't. I knew I was cursed. The black ooze was right.

That night the ooze's cackle was brittle. I could now identify the sounds it made. It was the same dry, whispery sounds the women made earlier that day. Not the same words, no words at all, but the same sounds. And those sounds were suffocating. They filled my airways and I struggled to breathe.

It let me know how much joy it felt that I failed earlier in the day. Just before it touched me it whispered into my mind that now I had only one chance remaining to save myself. I had a chance earlier in the day but had failed, just as it knew I would. But there was one more thing I could try, it said, whispering so softly I could barely hear. Be perfect. Suddenly thousands of voices whispered over and over. I heard and felt them speaking over each other, just as the women had earlier in the day.

"Jesus couldn't live in your heart, so now you need to be a perfect human being." The voices all breathed into my mind how that was my only hope.

Then I was surrounded by brittle, whispered laughter coming from everywhere. It sounded like a person who smoked many packages of cigarettes a day for sixty years and was unable to laugh but still tried to do so. A brittle, breathless cackle was surrounding me and then filling me. At the same time, thousands of dry voices whispered that I was too broken to succeed. That I was too broken to be perfect. And that I was going to Hell. I felt its joy in my terror as the whispers and laughter filled my lungs to the point I was no longer able to get air into my body. I was suffocating. I was dying.

Then I jolted awake, drenched in sweat, sobbing and struggling once more to take air into my lungs.

Two years later it was confirmed. I was going to Hell.

4.

I WAS IN THE BATHROOM STALL at school, doubled over, writhing in pain. The pain had been getting worse and worse over time. I was dying. I knew the time had come. I had messed everything up. I had done all I could think to do, but clearly, it wasn't enough. I had near-perfect grades. I did endless chores for my parents, begging to be helpful, trying to be the perfect daughter. I had insisted on taking over as much meal preparation as possible and insisted that I do all the family laundry every weekend. When I wasn't doing chores, I studied or danced. I had started dancing lessons when I was six years old and had never practised at home, but since the ooze had told me I needed to be perfect, I practised as many hours as I was able to. I had read my Bible, attended Bible study, attended my confirmation classes, attended church regularly, and never learned to speak in tongues. I failed. I tried everything I knew to be a perfect person, but I failed, and now, this is how I would die, on the floor of the high school bathroom. And it was my fault.

Leading up to this moment, I was practising ballet even more so than in the past, preparing to perform a high-level examination. I was also practising other forms of dance and running every day. I believed the pain that had been slowly increasing in my body to be a muscle strain that was just not healing, so I didn't mention it to my parents. And besides, they would have told me to rest and I had no time to rest. I had to be perfect. My parents knew of my obsessive behaviours, my all-consuming need to be perfect and achieve, but didn't understand it. They had never asked this of me or in any way expected me to be this way to win their love or acceptance. I was even aware it exasperated them sometimes. But I knew. It was the only way I would survive. And I couldn't explain this to them.

They would ask me to rest, to eat, to engage in whatever recreation people my age engaged in, and I did try, as pleasing my parents was also part of being perfect. But I had so much to maintain. If I slipped, if I stopped being vigilant, it would happen. The worst would happen. So I needed to strive for perfection. I needed to earn my right to exist and if I didn't ... Well, it was happening. I hadn't earned my existence and now I was dying on that bathroom floor.

Then, somehow, I was with my mother. I hadn't recalled her arriving but I was no longer on the bathroom floor. Great! Now I was causing her stress. It seemed I just couldn't mess up enough.

She said we were going to a doctor. A gynecologist. My mother was very pale, with bright red spots on her cheeks. My parents were and are such amazing people and here I was, causing trouble. They were such hard workers, had four of us in five years (I was the oldest), and always provided the necessities and the extras for us such as my dancing. They didn't deserve such a shitty daughter. I wanted to say I was sorry to them. They didn't need to take me to the doctor; it was a pulled muscle and it would heal. But the pain was so intense I had trouble speaking.

The gynecologist examined me. The pain was unbearable. He stated I had a tubal pregnancy and had to get to a hospital immediately. Pregnant? What? No! I had never been intimate with anyone. A perfect daughter would never do such a thing. So this was my punishment. I had fallen short and my world was crashing. I earned this.

At the hospital, both my parents, on either side of me, worried. I could see the strain on them. How could I do this to them? I felt stiff sheets, pain, shaking. I heard words drifting over me, "emergency surgery," "pregnancy," "urgent," "we don't know." I heard my father telling the doctor there was no way I was pregnant. He was firm with his words. I felt some relief. Thank goodness they knew. I hated hurting them, worrying them, but at least they knew that much was true.

The pastor of our church was suddenly in my eyeline. Where were my parents? He was leaning over me. I smelled his sour breath. This was bad. I must have done something very wrong. I couldn't think clearly. There was the pain and the medication. But I needed to focus. I had to figure out what I had done and I had to try to fix it. Or was it too late?

"What would you say to Jesus to get into His heaven if you met Him today?"

My brain screamed. This was it. I hadn't spoken in tongues. I wasn't perfect. The toaster not being wiped clean before I put it away, the 87 percent on the biology test, that dance step I missed over and over, the dusting not done well, the rug after I vacuumed and I accidentally stepped on it and spoiled the perfection of the nap all going the same way ... I hadn't fixed it! Any of it! All of those things and more flashed in my mind. That's where I messed up. And now I was dying, and I was going to meet Jesus, and I needed a password or I was going to Hell. The ooze had finally gotten me!

I saw my hand grabbing the lapel of his tweed jacket. I felt the coarseness. I noticed an IV in the hand that held fast to the fabric. I heard my voice, raspy, begging, far away. "Tell me, tell me, tell me ... Please, please, please ... Tell me."

He asked the question again. I searched my mind for an answer.

The answer. I felt the tears burning my cheeks, pooling in my ears. "You have to tell me!"

A detached hand pried mine from the lapel of the pastor's jacket. I was moving. "Tell me … Please … Tell me!" I tried to yell but only a whisper came out.

The ceiling in the elevator … I was dying and I couldn't get into Heaven. I failed. And this was it.

I opened my eyes, my dad on one side, my mom on the other. "Tell ME!" I croaked.

"Shush, shush, You're OK," my dad.

"It's OK, honey. Just rest. It's OK," my mom.

Words … "A cyst … The size of a grapefruit … Ruptured … Lucky to be on the table or we would have lost her … Lost the ovary … Endometriosis … Trouble having children … Maybe more to come … Lucky girl."

"NO! Heaven? Jesus? TELL ME!"

"Just rest, love."

"Tell me …"

In a hospital room. Hours later? Days? I asked the question as it had been asked of me and begged for the answer. Dad's brow furrowed. He was angry. I knew that look. So angry. Angry with me? I apologized. I was sorry for having a cyst. "No," he said, not with me. And, at some point, I overheard him tell mom he was going to talk to our pastor. It didn't sound like it was going to be a friendly talk. He also told me the answer that day, the password. "By Your Grace." I had many more surgeries after that but knew the password now, just in case.

Six weeks later, I performed and passed that ballet exam. My parents said it was too soon after the surgery, but I had to do it. I had to be perfect. I narrowly escaped once but that didn't mean I got to relax.

5.

WE WERE LINED UP FOR our breakfast the first day. I watched a group of dancers, recognizable by their leotards, leg warmers, and heavy bags, walk by the eggs, bacon, and sausage. Some stopped at the fruit station; many just grabbed coffee and loaded it with sugar. The other camp attendees, those carrying instruments and such for other forms of art, loaded their plates heavily.

I was lucky to be able to come to this Summer School of the Arts for these three weeks. I knew it cost my parents a lot of money, and I knew I needed to work hard and do my best to learn. When my turn came to load my plate, I too walked by the warm food piled high in steaming pans and instead took an apple. Like the others before me, I filled a cup of coffee. I looked at the sugar but thought twice. Sugar made a person fat, and I had already noticed I was bigger than those dancers and I didn't want to increase that. I had never had coffee before. It was bitter and tasted horrible. But if that is what the dancers did, I would do it too.

I found my way to my first session and again noticed how thin the dancers were. I was not. I needed to fix this. Over the next three weeks, I danced for eight and ten hours each day. In between sessions, I would grab a cup of black coffee and continue to the next.

When I arrived home, I continued with my new diet regime. I noticed some of the horrible darkness had receded from my life, and I knew why: because I had something to think about every single moment. I was obsessed with what I ate, what I would eat, or what I had eaten. What would I eat tomorrow? How would it feel in my mouth? How would I chew it? Every time the darkness and fear crept in at night, I would feel my rib cage, running my hands along the ridges pushing through my skin and feeling every bump from my sternum to the side of my body. I would let my hands drop off the edge of my ribs to the hollow of my sunken belly. I let my hands slide down to my hip bones, protruding like blades, feeling the dip between those bones, and I knew if I kept focused, I could soon be thin. And then I would think about food and the curtain wouldn't come, not that night.

I allowed myself as much coffee as I wanted, several cups a day. I would eat an apple one day, a half a tuna sandwich another. I thought constantly about what my food would be the next day. I timed my food carefully and made sure my parents saw me eat the one item I allowed myself a day. I also ran and danced every day to make sure that I burned the calories I had taken in. One Sunday, I had a pancake after church. I ran an extra mile that day, furious with myself for my weakness.

"OH … MY … GOD!" I froze, my hoodie lifted above my head, ready to pull over my body. My mother's voice. "What? Your bones? I can see every rib! Your hips!"

I quickly pulled the heavy sweater that I wore every day over my body. But I was too late. Mom was upset. She was freaking out. I upset her again. Would I ever learn?

And then we were on our way to a doctor, again.

When I left for camp earlier that summer, I weighed one hundred ten pounds and was four feet nine inches tall. Almost four months later at the doctor's office, I weighed sixty-seven pounds. Eating disorders weren't discussed or part of mainstream knowledge at that time. So I was examined for an illness that could have caused weight loss, was pronounced well, and was sent home to eat. I was made to eat. That was it.

No more hoodie, and instead of the wandering, constantly snacking act I believed I had perfected, I was required to sit at the table with the family and I was to eat. Period. It was extremely difficult. I gagged and had trouble swallowing. I was terrified of getting fat again. I was on my way to thinness and now I was being forced to eat. I had finally gained control over something in my life. But now I was being forced to give up that control. Forced to give up the one thing I was starting to succeed at. I was obligated to put food into my mouth. I was made to keep it in my mouth. I was monitored as I chewed and swallowed, retching throughout. It made me feel sick for the longest time. But that is what a perfect daughter would do, so I did it. And the curtain dream was back.

6.

ALONE. IMPOSSIBLE. NEVER. CAN'T DO it. I. WILL. DIE.
This is a specific alone. It's not by myself as in running
by myself, practicing dance by myself, studying by myself. It's not
when someone is in the house or waiting at home. This is alone
without choice. This is everyone out and just me. Alone when I had
only my company and couldn't find someone to interact with and
distract me. This was not being occupied with activity that kept
the thinking at bay. Alone as in alone with my brain. Alone as in
me with me.

I could not be alone. If no one was in the house when I was,
that was the bad alone. And for the most part, I didn't have to be.
Someone was usually home, so it was OK. But on that rare occasion
when no one was around, when I was at home alone for thirty
minutes or so, I would wind up sobbing and unable to breathe. I
would be filled with all-consuming terror. The moment I realized I
was alone, my chest would restrict, my lungs would struggle to drag
air in, my heart would race, my eyes would blur, and I wouldn't
be able to think or process thought. I was consumed with fear.
Nameless, reason-less, paralyzing fear. It came from within; I think.
It wasn't an outside threat, so it must have been from within. I think
I ran around sometimes. I think I hid somewhere sometimes. I

don't really know as I am not able to think and therefore remember during these episodes. So I simply had to avoid alone. And I did so at all costs.

I had no ability to hide what happened to me when I was alone; it was a well-known family fact, "Nikki can't be alone." I know it was viewed as ridiculous and overreactive. And obviously, it was. I just didn't know how to not be ridiculous and overreactive.

In fact, that was pretty much a lifetime theme.

"Nikki is so sensitive and overreacts all the time."

"She's completely terrified to be alone for even five minutes."

"She thinks people are watching her and judging her all the time."

"She can't get under ninety-five percent on her report card without coming unglued."

"She can't watch certain TV programs."

"She is so needy. She is terrified of her own shadow. She needs to grow up and cut the umbilical cord already."

"She gets something in her head and that is all she can focus on for days."

"She thinks there are ghosts and she has crazy nightmares."

"She is just too sensitive and needs to toughen up or life will eat her alive."

All true. And this was not meant in a mean-spirited way. This was caring. This was worrying. And this was fact. And life did eat me alive.

And so, as best able, I made sure I was never alone. I never lived alone or spent any time alone. I knew I would not survive aloneness, so I worked hard to ensure that never happened.

Until I was alone all day every day in a small town in the middle of winter with a demon living in the next room.

7.

THE DARKNESS SURROUNDED ME, LIVED in me, lived all around me. I was deep in a hole, a blackness, and I couldn't get out. I couldn't tell my husband. He was working so hard and had so much responsibility and had the burden of me. He never once complained. And he didn't know I was hiding the darkness from him. I would lay awake at night next to him and listen for the demon. I felt the blackness all around me, ready to consume me. The curtain was gone and there was only darkness. Emptiness. Nothingness.

When I was able to sleep, I would dream only of death.

One night, I dreamt of a very distant aunt. Not even really an aunt, a person who had married a great uncle of mine late in life. I think I met her once. In my dream, she was at an old dinette set, the ones with the chrome legs from the sixties, sitting in a chair, her back to the counter in an equally dated kitchen. She sat on a chair that matched the chrome dinette in the very centre of one of the long sides of the table. She had her head resting on her hand on the table. Beside her head was a plate of half-eaten food. It looked like chicken, bones stripped and placed on the table beside the plate. A bottle of beer sat in front of the plate and several matching bottles were all over the table. It was like she had fallen asleep while eating.

But her head was odd. It was facedown, not sideways as one might lay their head on their hand. Facedown, forehead on the back of her hand. It troubled me, as did all the other nightmares. Something to add to the racing thoughts that plagued me every day as I paced the tiny apartment.

A few days later, my mother called for our weekly check-in. I would share bits of the darkness, the endless thoughts, the exhaustion, and the nothingness. I frustrated them. I had insisted on getting married very young, at the age of nineteen. I had left university, without completing my degree, to move to this small town four months after my marriage as I missed my husband terribly and didn't want to continue my education living apart from him. I had made these decisions against their advice, so my complaining would annoy them. And I understood. They would tell me I was being too sensitive, letting my imagination run wild, over-thinking, and I simply needed to stop. And I knew they were correct.

During the call, I mentioned my dream. There was a long pause.

"Uh ... Where did you hear that?" My mother finally spoke softly, haltingly.

I didn't hear it. She and dad were the only people I ever spoke to besides my husband. "I dreamt it," I stated.

She paused again, then shared quietly with me that this distant aunt was found exactly as I described after choking on a chicken bone while eating a plate of wings. There was some suspicion alcohol was involved. I felt a chill and my mind went to the demon. We changed the subject and subconsciously agreed that we would never discuss this again. When I ended the call, I felt a true, bone-chilling terror. IT was now controlling my thoughts, day and night.

I can't recall much of the time in that small town after that. I don't know what happened day-to-day. I have flitting, disjointed memories of it all. The same as most of my childhood, there are flashes of things but nothing concrete or in sequence. I know at one point, when it was warming a bit in the spring, I found a church close to our apartment. I thought it would help me to feel better, to battle the demon.

It was an energetic church where people lifted their hands, swayed back and forth, and sang heartily. I attended twice. I was watched, appraised, judged. Eyes narrowed. Whispers were shared. I still didn't speak in tongues and knew I didn't belong here. No one spoke to me. I sat alone in the back corner. Heads turned at intervals to watch me try to find the songs in a book they all seemed to know by heart. Sighs, slow, barely discernible head shakes of disgust. I never went back. I knew there was no help for me there. Maybe the demon had taken me too far. Maybe there would never be help again.

Days and nights blurred, save one, and I remember the details clearly.

8.

ONE SATURDAY, MY PATIENT HUSBAND came to me. He somehow had five dollars. Where had he come upon such a sum? We had no money at all and five dollars felt like a million. He proposed a "date." It was one of the first warmer days of the year, the sun bright and melting the snow and ice. The smell in the air was glorious, the smell of winter being pushed away. The smell of newness and rebirth.

He took me to the car, long since parked in the lot as we had no money for fuel. He was able to start it and drove to a gas station and put four dollars of gas in the tank. Then he drove to the local ice cream store and purchased a small milkshake. He popped in a Johnny Horton cassette and cranked it up. We rolled our windows down and drove all over that tiny town until our fuel ran low again, sharing that milkshake and singing loudly along. The darkness was pushed aside. The demon at bay. I laughed; I felt joy. For a moment in time, life was better. I believed this was the beginning of something better. I felt hope.

Shortly after, my husband was able to secure a new job and it was coincidentally in my hometown. I was going home! I was leaving the possessed apartment! I was going to be OK! The darkness was behind me and I had people to talk to. People to engage with. I wouldn't be so alone. I could get a job and not be a burden. I had survived the worst and life would be good.

9.

A BABY. A TINY LIFE WAS coming. I was elated and terrified. I didn't know children and hadn't interacted with children very much. They were foreign and scary to me. But I was soon to be a mom.

It's so hard to explain how I felt all the time. So much was going on below the surface that no one could see—that I couldn't allow anyone to see. I felt like an actor playing the part of Nikki. I knew the character. She needed to be perfect, happy, funny, a great homemaker, soon to be a great mother, and she needed to do everything correctly. And I knew what "correctly" meant but wasn't able to define it in words or lists or actions. I also knew what "incorrectly" meant, and so many times I behaved incorrectly. In fact, "incorrectly" seemed to be my norm. My face felt like a thin, brittle shell, a mask, hiding the imperfections and wrongness that ran beneath. I couldn't allow people to see under or through the mask. There was chaos and destruction and nothing but ugliness and damage under it. And for the most part, I believed I kept that mask in place and was hiding things well. I had to; there was no other option.

I liken how I felt at this time to how I perceive our Earth. The surface is magical and filled with life and beauty. There is a feeling of solidness and stability as we walk on it. We experience the stunning landscapes from heavy vegetation to desert, depths of water to layers of ice, and every variation within, all able to take our breath away. We interact with what we see, perceiving it to be the whole, not thinking of it as any more than a thin crust. We feel we know and trust our Earth. We build on it and believe we own it. But that stability is an illusion. Just below the surface exists layers of hot, dark, fractured, unpredictable things. Many we know nothing about. Molten lava, a vast buried ocean, shifting tectonic plates with the ability to damage and destroy in a moment. Complex, unpredictable, savage, wild things.

That's what it feels like to be me. I keep the brittle shell in place as best as possible. The surface. But underneath is chaos, savagery, emptiness, darkness, the ability to cause irreparable damage with no warning. As we busy ourselves, building our things, doing what we do, working on a project, we can forget the chaos that exists under our feet until it makes itself known and wreaks havoc on all we have done. And as the surface of the Earth can shift and cause damage, so could my surface, my thin mask. If the outside surroundings tilted, changed, strained, or became difficult, then the surface would crack and some of the bad would leak out. Like an earthquake or volcano, damage would be done, unpredictable and wild. And other times, under the surface, there was nothing. Vast emptiness. No feeling. No anything. A void with a shell on it. But I never knew what was under the thin mask at any given moment, so I had to be vigilant. Just as we humans have no real control over the landmass we live on, I had no real control over me.

My body had been in and out of labour for days. Braxton Hicks they said. I had been in the hospital two weeks prior and was two centimetres dilated. "Any day now," they uttered cheerfully. I guess we were still waiting for "Any day." I was beyond frustrated. I was convinced this baby would never come. I analyzed each feeling in my body, I focused for hours on what my body was or was not doing. Was that a contraction? Was that real? Fake? How will I know what to do and when to do it? I was driving myself and everyone else around me crazy.

My husband was exhausted by trying to deal with me day in and day out. I could see it on his face as he walked through the door after work every day. Never knowing what he was walking into. Guarded. Waiting for my endless report, my complaining, my ranting, or my crying.

One beautiful, warm spring evening, my husband suggested we go for ice cream. I had lived through another long day of regular contractions, ten minutes apart, meaning nothing, and he was trying so hard to keep my spirits up, to help us both manage what seemed like an endless wait.

I hoisted my heavy body up into his new half-ton, and we drove to the local ice cream parlour. We decided I would wait in the truck, he would get the ice cream, and we would eat in the vehicle. So much easier for me. When I started to eat again after the summer of my self-imposed, restricted diet, I grew another two inches in height, so I was a whopping four feet eleven inches tall, and very, very pregnant. Getting in and out of a normal-sized half-ton was a lot of work and was especially hard with those damned fake contractions. My husband returned and handed my ice cream cone to me through the open window of the vehicle. At that moment, I felt a snap and a whoosh. I was sitting in a pool of warm water. It was pouring down my legs. "What the fuck?" my mind screamed. And then the fear washed over me. I had ruined my husband's new truck. I would never forgive myself. This was not what a good wife did.

My husband got into the driver's side and saw my face first, then saw the mess. I started crying and apologizing. "I must have peed or something. I'm so, so sorry. I'll wash it. I'm so, so sorry," I blurted, repeating my words over and over.

I don't recall him saying anything, but I know he didn't yell at me, and he wouldn't have. It was me who judged me at all times. Not him. He might have said something, but it wouldn't have been harsh or judgemental. That all came from within. But I heard nothing, registered nothing. I was too panicked to think straight and could only hear myself babbling.

We went into the house and the liquid kept coming out. It wasn't stopping and then I knew my water had broken. We learned of this in birthing class. But I didn't think it was supposed to be so much! I was soaked from the waist down as if I had been standing in a pool. And then something gripped my body with such intensity I crumbled and fell to my knees. Oh, this was a contraction! I headed to the bedroom to change my clothes and another contraction ripped through me. I folded in half over the bed, gripping it with white knuckles. The pain was excruciating. When the agony released, I looked across the room to my husband, who was gathering towels, and screamed, "I CAN'T DO THIS!" My body wrenched again, and I was once more crumpled to the floor. I cried out, "I can't … Please … I can't." This was far worse than I had imagined, and I knew it was just the beginning. I had hours of this ahead of me. How would I survive? My husband helped me out of my wet clothes between the rhythmic spasms ripping at my body. He tried to reason with me as he helped me into dry clothes, telling me I had to have the baby. There was no choice.

"I CAN'T!" I screamed.

The baby was coming and now I didn't want it to. I didn't want to be pregnant. I didn't want to have a baby. I wanted it to stop. I didn't have the ability to do this. I screamed at him as I soaked through another pair of pants. "I'VE CHANGED MY MIND! I CAN'T DO THIS!" But nature stops for no one, so whether I liked it or not, I was going to do it.

We got to the hospital. I heard phrases like, "head wasn't engaged" and "dry labour." It was hard to focus when, every two minutes, my body would try to tear itself in half. I was vomiting, walking, lying, trying to survive, trying to breathe as we had been taught. Nothing was working. I was slowly being ripped apart.

This was a time of medication-free childbirth, and for the next three and half hours, those transition contractions—so a nurse called them—continued, from two minutes apart until it was just one continuous, endless rending. At some point, I was wheeled into a delivery room. It was sterile and terrifying. They transferred me to a bed so narrow I was afraid my thrashing body would fall to the floor. I needn't have worried as they strapped me down. I was flat on my back with my feet in stirrups and then was instructed to push. I pushed and pushed. I felt like my head would burst open as I pushed with everything I had. I pushed until I felt exhausted but continued as best I could. I remembered when I would dance through exhaustion and made myself do the same now. But I felt myself starting to slip away as I tried to do what I was told.

I turned to my left and saw a picnic table in a beautiful forest. My tie-down straps loosened, and I got off the delivery table and walked over to it. I felt its rough wood with my hand. I hoisted my heavily pregnant body onto it and felt my open-backed gown fluttering slightly in a gentle warm breeze as I lifted my knee to the tabletop. It felt like a heavenly caress. I struggled and shifted to lie down on my back on this rustic table. I felt the roughness on my bare skin where my gown didn't close. The table was so warm, having been baking in the sun. It felt so good. I breathed deeply, closing my eyes, inhaling the scent of warm pine. I let the sun warm me, flow into me, and I felt at peace. I opened my eyes and saw the clear blue sky directly above me. The warmth filled me as I lazily watched the occasional cloud drift over the opening the trees had provided for my table. All of my senses were absorbing this beautiful, safe space. A warm, woodsy smell filled my nostrils. I heard the birds, the bugs, and the small forest animals moving within the space. I felt the hardness of the table beneath me and the warmth of the sun warming me. I could finally rest. And I closed my eyes and did just that.

I heard someone from deep in the forest. "Forceps, C-section, or we cut." There was tension in the voice—firmness, demanding a response.

Without warning, I was back on the delivery table and in incredible pain. I heard my voice, "No forceps."

"Then we section or cut. We can try to cut first and if it doesn't work, we need to section."

"Cut."

Metal clanging, sharp pain, I heard my scream, then I was back on my picnic table. I sighed with relief and then deeply inhaled the smells once more. I closed my eyes and let all the warmth fill me.

I heard a baby through the trees. I turned my head to find the source of the noise and was instantly back on the delivery table. A baby boy! He was here! They showed him to me and he was beautiful! Then they took him somewhere. I looked back to my picnic table across the room, but it was gone.

I was told I had pushed for almost two hours and had a large episiotomy that needed extensive work. I was informed he was a large baby for my small pelvis, and they were very close to sending me to the OR for a C-section. I wasn't really listening. Words flowed around me. I didn't care; I had a baby! And he was beautiful! And everything was OK. I had done it. I had a baby!

The next day I started to think about my picnic table in the delivery room and realized it couldn't have been real. But it had felt so real. I can still see it clearly in my mind. My brain knew there was no way a picnic table in a forest was in that sterile delivery room. Yet for me, it was as real as the other items in that room, and I knew I had lain on it. I could still feel the rough wood on my back where my hospital gown opened. It was there and I was on it. But it wasn't, and I couldn't have been.

I put it out of my mind and focused on learning how to care for this new person we created.

We brought the baby home five days later. When we walked in, I saw a beautiful hand-made wooden cradle. It was intricately crafted, it rocked, and it shone with several layers of varnish. It took my breath away. While I had been recovering in the hospital and learning to feed and care for this tiny new person, my husband had been working hours to create this beautiful piece of furniture. I wept, so humbled by this man. What a wonderful father this baby had! I went to put some items in the freezer that the hospital had sent home to help manage the pain in my bottom. That tragic mess felt as though it would never recover. I opened the freezer door and saw my ice cream cone sitting there, wrapped, waiting for me, and I cried harder. What a wonderful husband I had. He was so good to me, and I vowed to be the best mother and the best wife I could be.

But that was a hard, hard promise to keep.

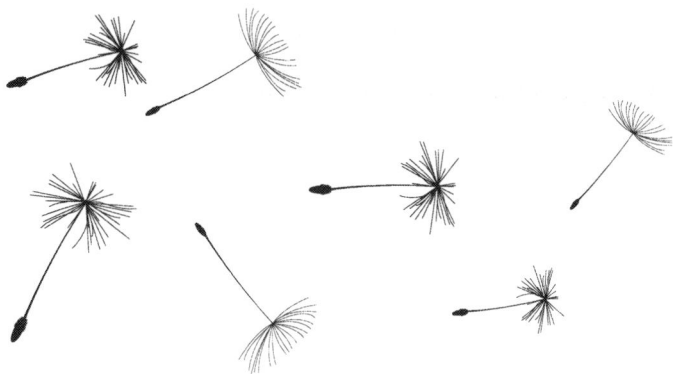

10.

THE DAYS BECAME NIGHTS. TIME blurred. There was only the
baby. I had to make the baby happy.

He cried so much of the time. If I was able to get him to sleep,
he only slept for twenty minutes at a stretch. He would regurgitate
and spit up every feed. I was a horrible mother. I wasn't able to
make my baby happy. I read all the books I could find and nothing
I tried worked. I had a simple job: feed, care for, and sustain a tiny
human. Women had been doing this for thousands of years and
without the luxuries I had. Yet, I was unable to do this.

Then I got mastitis. I marvelled at how I could actually be so
terrible at this. The nurse said I was holding my baby wrong as I
nursed and had caused this infection. Could I still feed my baby?
Why had I done this? Why hadn't I listened better in the hospital?
I was so focused on the pain in my bottom and the pain in my
bleeding nipples that I hadn't listened properly. Selfish, selfish,
selfish!

I was able to continue to nurse my child through the infection,
but the pain was intense. I had to nurse my child. I expected it of
myself. I couldn't process any other options in my exhausted brain.
I had to do this right. I had to be perfect.

Everything blurred. Night and day ran together. Nothing was

in order. I had to protect this baby. I became completely obsessed with this little person. I became filled with fear that something would happen to him. Somehow, someway, I would fail. I needed to watch, to be vigilant at all times. Nothing else mattered in my world. Nothing else existed. Only this little being and making sure he was OK.

One night, in the wee hours of the morning, once again a failure, I couldn't soothe the baby. His dad came and took him from my arms. I recall getting up from the rocking chair, walking slowly to the plant behind the chair, uprooting it, and throwing it across the room. I did this calmly and with no feeling or emotion. I watched the soil fall from the roots as the plant travelled through the air, and I thought, "Hmm … That's a mess." I knew I needed to clean it up, and I wondered why I would do something like that. There was no frustration, no anger, no emotion at all. I just passively observed the dirt strewn through the living room. I walked to my rocking chair, brushed it off, and wandered into our bedroom. I laid down and listened to my husband try to comfort the baby. The baby whose mother was incapable of caring for.

Our son was five months old when my husband received a promotion. We were moving to another small town, a five-hour drive from our current home. I was terrified but said nothing. The last time we lived away from my family, away from my support system, was horrible. What if it happened again? I couldn't manage being alone. I wanted to beg him not to take the job, not to make us go. But I knew that was selfish and ridiculous. I needed to support my husband. I was an adult, a mother, and I needed to grow up. Why was I so weak?

In no time, as expected, the darkness descended again, and the constant fear returned. We relocated at the beginning of winter. Horrible, isolating, cold winter. But this time, I had a baby and the baby needed me, so I focused on the baby. He cried so much of the time. Many said that because I was so tense, I made my baby tense.

And every time I fed him, he would spit up all the breast milk. Then I would feed him again, and the cycle continued. The doctor said it was colic and that it would pass. I knew it was all my fault. My tension, my inability to manage as an adult, my bad breast milk. I was a terrible mother and I was hurting this little being I loved so much.

And the fear. The fear inside was endless. My insides trembled morning to night. I couldn't remain still. I had to move and I paced for hours with my baby, trying to soothe him. I couldn't turn the TV on as it terrified me, but the silence was worse. I felt afraid all of the time—a nameless, groundless fear, all-consuming, internal, and constant. There was never a reprieve.

Shortly after our move, my husband found a local hockey team to play with in the evenings, and I didn't blame him. I was awful to be around. I begged him not to join. I begged him to stay with me in the evenings. I barely managed the days alone; I couldn't manage the evenings as well. I told him how afraid I was, how scared I felt all the time, and he told me I had nothing to be afraid of which was, of course, true.

As I became more needy, more whiny, more miserable, bouncing from crying to yelling to pleading, I became harder and harder to be around, and the more difficult I was, the more my husband was away. And who could blame him? Two nights a week became three then four. He would come home from work, grab a quick bite, and head out to the game. Then he would join the team for drinks after. And how could I fault him? I wouldn't want to be around me either.

As the winter wore on, my husband was becoming more and more frustrated with me. I was frustrated with myself. I was failing him, failing our son, failing at life. We decided I should visit my parents for a week and try to get myself together. When I arrived with my constantly crying baby, my parents also became frustrated with me. I was irritating enough with my constant phone calls to them day and night, crying, anxious, and fearful. But now in their home, acting as I did, was just too much. I was too much for everyone. They told me I needed to grow up and "cut the umbilical cord." They told me I was an adult and a wife and mother, and it was time to behave like one. They told me to get my shit together and take care of their grandson properly. They told me he was crying all the time because I was a mess and I needed to fix it and fix it now. They told me to stop acting like an over-sensitive child and to start functioning like a grown human. They reminded me I had made my bed and it was time to sleep in it. I had chosen to become a wife and mother. No one made me do any of this. And I knew they were correct. I knew as they were telling me this that I needed to hear it. I knew they were right and that I had to get my life together and care properly for my baby.

I left and drove back home five hours away, feeling worse than I had before but knowing I had to do something. Anything. I knew my parents were right. I had a child now and I had to stop being such a loser. It was time to grow up. I knew I had to do it. I just didn't know how.

I searched my mind for where to begin. Then a thought came to me: The La Leche League. They helped me with my newborn and through my mastitis in my hometown, and I reasoned there must be a local group or something similar I could track down in my new location. That could be my first step toward growing up. I thought it could be a good way to meet people, maybe find friends, take some pressure off my husband and have something to fill the time. But most importantly, maybe they could help me figure out why my child struggled so much keeping my breast milk down.

I was able to find a local chapter and registered to attend the next meeting. I was so nervous. Would they be able to see what a mess I was inside? How I struggled to take care of my baby? I prayed I would be able to behave properly and even practiced what I would say over and over before the meeting day arrived.

With my seven-month-old son, I walked into a room filled with other moms and children. The furniture and floors were filled with big and small people, many nursing, and all seemed happy. Joy and laughter filled the space. I noticed many older children nursing. Children who could walk and speak. I was a bit taken aback. I thought I would never be able to do that.

I was welcomed warmly. The meeting was informal, and at one point, I was asked if I wanted to speak. I found my voice and my practiced words. I introduced myself and my son and told them I was worried my milk was bad for my baby. I told them he cried much of the time and spit up most of his feeds. They assured me that my milk was not bad and suggested I cut onion, garlic, and other spices out of my diet. And they recommended a doctor that was supportive, whatever that meant.

In the time I sat with those women, the fear subsided. I felt better. Getting out of my head and interacting with others helped. I committed to attending weekly and immediately booked an appointment with the doctor they recommended.

He was quite busy and it took a few weeks to get to see him. I hadn't told the League about what a horrible mother I was; I was too ashamed. But I did tell the doctor. I told him how my tension was making my son sick all the time, and how I made him cry with my inability to function. I begged him to help me.

He asked about my diet. I told him what I had eliminated, as per the League's advice, and reiterated my son wasn't any better. I explained again that it was me causing the issue. He said he didn't agree and suggested I eliminate all dairy. I didn't really like dairy, didn't think I ate dairy but upon examination of my diet, it turned out many items I ate regularly had dairy somewhere within. I cut out every bit of it. Within a week, my baby seemed happier. He was spitting up less, and he started to sleep up to an hour at a time. He was happy when he was awake. He felt better.

I felt relieved and horrible at the same time. Relieved he was better, horrible that I had been making him sick all those months.

My choices, what I ate, had caused him pain, and I hated myself for doing that to this precious little being. He had suffered for months because of me. I tried to put it behind me but the guilt held tight.

Spring was approaching and with days getting warmer, we started spending more time outside. Along with my weekly meetings, I started taking long walks with my son in the beautiful warming air, and I had started to feel better. Maybe I was finally growing up. Maybe things would be better. Maybe the darkness had passed. My husband was happier. My child was happier, and with the new hope and lightness in our tiny family, we decided to have another child. Soon I was pregnant again.

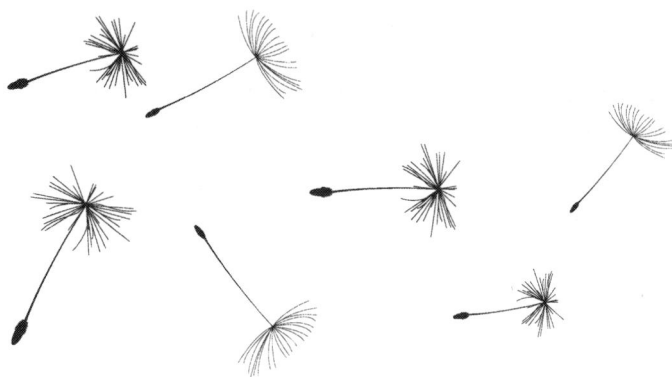

11.

DURING ONE OF OUR WALKS, I met a neighbour. She had a little girl the same age as my son. We discovered our homes were back-to-back and started having coffee together one or two mornings a week. We enjoyed each other's company and our children liked playing together. Soon she was also carrying her second child. We had much in common. We met at either's home and enjoyed our summer as our bellies grew and our children played.

Fall was soon upon us, and our time sitting on decks and watching our children play outside passed. Our visits were becoming less frequent, and I was getting ready for my second baby as fall drifted into winter. My husband started playing hockey again, and I felt the darkness once again creeping in. The fear was returning, not as bad, but it was there, looming. I felt it around the edges of my life, waiting to creep in and take over again. It was like a paper burning from the outside in, the black edges slowly furling as the flame got closer and closer to consuming the entire page. The darkness and fear slowly creeping in from all edges, much more slowly than the burning paper, but the same feeling, until at some point I would be consumed.

I felt the contractions start one morning. I was pretty sure these were real, but after the last experience, who knew? They continued through the day. My son, aged one and a half, was troubled and clingy. I knew he was feeling my mood, my tension, and my anxiety around what may or may not be happening.

My husband came home after work and I told him what was happening. He asked if I needed to go to the hospital right away. I said I didn't think so as it wasn't as bad as when we went in with our first child. He slapped together a sandwich, grabbed his hockey bag, and told me to call the rink if I needed him. I chased after him and told him he needed to stay with me, help me with our oldest as the contractions progressed. He waved over his shoulder as he walked to the car. Was he dismissing me? He shoved the sandwich into his mouth to hold as he threw his gear into the trunk. Approaching the driver's side, he took the sandwich from his mouth and yelled again as he slid behind the wheel, "Call the rink if you have to. They will find me." And backed out and left.

I ran to the toilet and vomited. My toddler was clinging to the back of my legs as I heaved, scared and crying. The evening wore on, and I continued to vomit and contract at regular intervals, and my son continued to cry. I was able to hold my nausea at one point long enough to rock him to sleep. Gagging and swallowing hard throughout, I was finally able to transfer him to his crib, and I bolted for the bathroom to purge my stomach once more. I continued to pace, contract, and retch, my stomach long since emptied, until my husband returned later.

He asked if I felt we should go to the hospital, but remembering the intensity of the contractions from my firstborn, I again said I didn't feel it was time. We tried to lie down and get some rest. I drifted in and out of sleep, being awakened every few minutes with contractions.

At 4:00 a.m., the bed was flooded; my water had broken.

My husband called my neighbour and friend, as pre-planned, to tell them we were bringing our son over and then heading to the hospital. We had promised to watch each other's children when our respective babies came.

Soon we were in a tiny room in the small hospital. It was unlike where my first son was delivered. There was no maternity ward; all patients were housed together. The contractions weren't as bad as when my water broke with my first child. I told the nurse this, and she said because I still had lots of water behind the baby, who was well-wedged into my pelvis. I remembered the words "dry labour," and I guessed that's what that was about.

I paced and contracted. I even joined my husband for a cigarette. I didn't smoke at all during my pregnancies, but for some reason, I felt the desire. Stupid idea. I puked nothing once again. Soon it was time to push and the nurse called the doctor.

The doctor arrived, a mirror was positioned, and I was once again in stirrups. At this time, watching your baby be born in a mirror was the thing to do. I only pushed for half an hour and my baby was born. The doctor hit the mirror somehow and I couldn't see anything after his tiny head emerged. "Stop," my doctor said calmly, "No pushing." He grabbed scissors. I held my breath and willed my body not to push. A short time later, he told me to push hard. And there was my second boy. The doctor put him directly on my belly and I was able to touch him. He wasn't whisked away as my firstborn had been. I reached for him and lifted him to my chest. He was very bluish. The nurse was suctioning him as I held him and kept giving the doctor strange looks. Certainly disapproving, bordering on hostile.

The doctor said the cord had been around my baby's neck when he was born and that he just needed a little time to perk up. He let me hold my new baby for a few more seconds and said he would just pop him over to the incubator for a bit while he cleaned me up. He sutured away, chatting happily, no concerns at all. He hadn't had time to gown when he arrived and showed me his new Christmas sweater with way more red on it than originally designed.

I was worried about my baby, but the doctor's endless chatter was somewhat of a distraction. Then he sat back and announced he was done. I immediately asked when I could see my baby.

"Now, if you like," he said, "You had a baby. You didn't break your leg. You can walk." He chuckled to himself, "He's right over there." He pointed across the hall. I was surprised. Last delivery, I wasn't allowed to walk until the next day, and with the nurse by my side.

I didn't need to be told twice now. I popped off the delivery table and rushed across the hall. The nurse followed me, cursing the doctor and bitching about the mess I was making. I overheard her mumble some four-letter words along with "these new-age doctors." She was displeased but I didn't care. I needed to see my baby. And there he was, in the middle of the room in an incubator and as pink and pretty as could be. I stood just looking at him, marvelling, feeling so blessed.

The nurse was able to peel me away and drag me back to the tiny delivery room to "clean the completely unnecessary mess up." The doctor giggled and told me he would be back later to see us both.

My baby was born at exactly 7:30 a.m. By nine, I was settled into my room, had eaten a bit of breakfast, and was anxious to see him again. I waddled down to the nursery to look at him through the window.

A tiny, wizened, old woman stood gazing into the nursery. At my four feet eleven inches, I towered over her.

"That's a new one today," she said, pointing to my newborn. I smiled with pride.

She turned her rheumy eyes to me and scanned my body.

"When is yours coming?" she asked.

"That one is mine," I said. "Only an hour and a half old."

She grunted and replied, "You'll lose all that fat in no time," and she turned and shuffled away. I was stunned. There was a unique boldness that only old ladies seemed to possess, and I laughed heartily at her comment.

My baby was severely jaundiced and needed to be under ultraviolet lights for a few days, so it was almost a week before I was able to go home. My husband continued to work, but my dad had come to take care of our little one at home.

It was time to set up the tree and get ready for Christmas. I had shopping to do, baking to do, so much to do, and I had a newborn and a toddler. But I was going to do it. I had finally grown up. I was able to do it all; I made myself do it all, but I grew increasingly more exhausted. My toddler was still getting up several times a night, even more so with the new baby in the home. And of course, the baby fed every two hours. But this time, I didn't risk any dairy, and this baby didn't cry as much as my older child had.

We made it through the Christmas season, had travelled to both of our families, and stayed for a few nights in each place. I was so relieved to get home. Trying to care for a newborn and a toddler in someone else's home, trying to keep them quiet, was incredibly stressful. My husband, on the other hand, loved going to visit his family. He got to relax, laugh, have a few drinks and play cards. He seemed to relish these times.

The first six weeks of my newborn's life had been a blur of activity and chaos, so I hadn't noticed the darkness creeping closer and closer. Those burning edges had crept in unmonitored, and then suddenly, there were only charred remains of my life. The familiar numbness punctuated with bouts of consuming terror was back. The darkness once again consumed all. How had I allowed this? I tried to think, what I did to make it go away before? It was so hard to form thoughts. I tried to focus my mind, but it would drift, and soon I lost grip on the thought at hand. I moved numbly through days and nights, caring for my children and occasionally remembering to think about how to get better.

One day, nursing my baby with my toddler wedged in beside

me, my mind drifted to the La Leche League. My friend. People. "Get out of the house. Don't think. Yes." I remembered. I was finally able to maintain a thought long enough to catch the solution.

But it was once again a miserable, frigid northern winter. It was hard to safely bundle up two children and take them out. Somewhere. Anywhere. And I felt so exhausted all the time that just the thought of trying to get everything together to leave the house was too much. But I knew I had to do something. I needed to behave like a grown-up.

The most I could manage was bundling the kids, putting them in our tiny sleigh, and pulling it across the alley to see my friend who was soon to have her second child. As the world crowded in and the fear rose, I would call and ask if she could come for coffee to my home or I could go to hers.

After a time, I sensed that something had shifted—something in her voice. I knew the sound. I couldn't quite grasp it but it was familiar.

And then it became clear. I was frustrating her. She was too polite to say it but I knew it. Just as I had frustrated my husband and my family, I had now frustrated her. I heard the shortness. I heard the sighs. I heard her say many times she was too busy, and she would try to call later in the week, or maybe next week. But I hadn't listened, and the next time the fear grew large, I would dial her number. I heard her need to get off the phone and my need to keep on it. Needy Nikki was back and irritating the world.

I put a note beside my phone to remind me not to phone her every day, and I tried my best to stick to it. My husband could not understand my obsession with my neighbour. He couldn't understand why I had to remind myself not to phone or see a person every day. It made no sense to him. But, mostly, he couldn't understand how a mother could not be alone with her children all day. Every other mother he knew functioned. Why couldn't his wife?

He knew I resented him for leaving to play hockey at night, but he couldn't understand why. No one else's wife was so demanding. He didn't understand my ridiculous fears and my unreasonable neediness. I didn't tell him that this had been my whole life. I didn't tell him how I felt shortly after our marriage in the first small town we lived in. Back then I was able to hide my flaws, but now things were crumbling, and it was harder and harder to keep my weakness a secret.

My neighbour had her second child, and we watched her daughter while she was in the hospital. After she came home, she was far too busy to see me, even occasionally. She said it was the new baby and having two kids, and I knew that was some of it. But I also knew the truth. I was just too much, again.

12.

ONCE AGAIN, MY HUSBAND WAS promoted and we were moving, this time to a large city only an hour's drive away from my parents. This had to make things easier, right? But I needed to remember, I was a mother of two and a wife. I was expected to be and act like an adult. Not to run to my parents afraid all the time. So even if they were closer, I needed to be vigilant and not slip back into my childish, needy patterns.

My husband had to begin work six weeks before we could move. That time alone with the boys, all day and all night, counting the hours until the weekend, was extremely difficult. I was working so hard to do everything correctly. I tried to focus on what needed to be done. Packing. Sorting. Cleaning. The weather began to warm and we could spend some time outside again. But the fear. The terror. I felt imprisoned by it so much of the time. I was frantic to keep my boys safe. I cared obsessively for them. I watched them as they slept. I couldn't let them be alone. I don't know what I thought would happen, but I was terrified of something, an unknown horror.

My husband would arrive home late Friday nights, and I would make sure my hair and makeup were done, a lovely romantic dinner was ready, the house clean, the children bathed and asleep. I didn't want him to be aware of the train wreck I was during the week. I wanted him to only see goodness and perfection. I had caused him so much disappointment and I vowed to make that stop. This move was to be the beginning of the new me. The perfect me. I would become the perfect wife and mother I needed to be. Starting with these weekends. When I was alone all those hours and days, I had crafted an image, a mask, and that was to be me from now on. I didn't need to feel safe; I just needed to act it. I promised my two little boys as they slept each night and I sat on guard in their room that was exactly what I would do.

Soon, we moved into our new home. It was spring again, and I made it my goal to meet my neighbours. But this time, I knew how to behave correctly. This time, I had my mask. My character. Perfect Nikki. Fun, engaging, humorous, kind, helpful, available, but never needy. I knew if I behaved correctly, kept my mask firmly in place, I had the opportunity to not feel so dreadfully alone and terrified all the time. I had been gifted a new chance and I was not going to mess this one up. And for the most part, I nailed it. My mask rarely slipped. I was managing. I had finally grown up. I was twenty-four years old.

Most of the women living in our neighbourhood worked full time. I carefully managed my days so I could be outside when they got home from work, playing with my two little boys, so I could meet them. I managed to meet a few, and I was able to space my visits out among them all so as to not be Needy Nikki. It was a careful balancing act. I was doing very well and actually enjoying my new friendships. I was finally enjoying my life for the most part. My kids had playmates, and I felt better than I had in quite a long time. Make no mistake, though; the darkness and fear still lingered, stuffed under the mask. It wasn't gone. It never would be. It waited for a break, a crack, an opening. It watched me as I watched it. I could see it, feel it, touch it at any time, and knew I needed to remain vigilant. I was never allowed to relax, just be.

Dark, fearful Nikki was right there, waiting to take over. And I couldn't risk that.

Ivy, a single mom with two grown daughters, lived right next to me. She was a lovely lady and once or twice a week we would have coffee after she got home from work. We had gotten to know each other fairly well, but I didn't relax. I didn't allow her to see Dark Nikki, ever.

One summer day, we were on her front step, drinking cool lemonade as my two little boys played on her front lawn. By then, I was also well into my third pregnancy. We were chatting about the normal things we chatted about when, out of the blue, she told me she had psychic ability and knew things. Then she said to me that I had psychic ability as well, and that's why I had the terror running through me all the time.

I became very still. I pretended I hadn't heard her. I spoke as if she hadn't said anything about Dark Nikki.

But she didn't stop. She continued speaking. "You need to accept your gift. Learn to use your gift and you will feel better. Hiding and burying your ability is what is causing your pain."

I sat paralyzed. My eyes focused straight ahead.

"I can help you," she said. "I can read your thoughts and I can guide you so you feel better."

I was terrified. But a tiny part of me heard her. What if this was the answer? I knew it couldn't be. It was crazy! There was no such thing as psychic ability. But how did she know? I must have let my guard down. I must have let my mask slip. I wasn't careful enough. I had blown it again.

"I know about the demon that lived in your apartment," she said softly.

I was suddenly unable to breathe. I think I dropped my glass. I heard something shatter from far away, but I couldn't be sure. My vision blurred, and I saw a million dots swimming in front of my eyes. My chest was folding in on itself. My lungs were constricting.

I couldn't get air into me. I heard voices far away. I think someone touched me. I was standing but my legs were so wobbly. I was moving, as if through quicksand, toward my house. I wasn't able to speak but I motioned for the boys to follow me. Thank God they listened. As soon as I got myself and my boys inside, I crumpled, gasping, trying to get air into my constricted chest. My heart was racing. Someone could see. Dark Nikki. Real Damaged Nikki. This changed everything. This was bad.

My husband found me a few moments later, sitting on the three steps that led to our living area, just inside the door of our home, panting.

"Is it the baby?" he asked, filled with concern.

I shook my head, trying to find my words.

"Just the heat." I was able to mumble.

Ivy had followed me, asking him if I was OK.

He answered as I had, "She says it's just the heat," I glanced up and saw her face. I knew she didn't believe either of us but she left us to manage.

Later that evening after the children were in bed, I casually brought up the conversation Ivy and I had shared before I was "overwhelmed by the heat." I told him she said she was psychic and could read my thoughts. He said that was the most ridiculous thing he had ever heard. I didn't tell him she said I was psychic too. I didn't believe it. I couldn't allow myself to entertain such nonsense. It was unthinkable. Although, that one weird moment years prior when I had seen my aunt dead niggled in the back of my mind. But that was the demon. Not psychic ability.

I decided to put the conversation with Ivy, and in fact that whole day, out of my mind. Clearly, the heat had gotten to me. Soon, I had convinced myself that was the case.

A few weeks later, on a weekend, I was sitting on our back deck as my husband barbecued our lunch. Our boys were playing in their sandbox and I was due in a few days. I was enormous and swollen and miserable. It was the end of June and unbearably hot, and the doctor had indicated concern over the excessive swelling in my legs and ankles. I was advised, and in turn advised the child within, that if the baby wasn't born soon, I would have to have a C-section as my swelling and corresponding high blood pressure were becoming an issue. I sat in one lawn chair with my massive legs resting on a second to elevate them as much as possible.

My husband looked up from the grill and said, "Test her." I had no clue what he was talking about.

I was irritable and snapped, "Who? What?"

"Ivy. Test her."

"What do you mean? What are you talking about," I barked as I wiped my face with a damp cloth.

"She's out at the lake this weekend. Send her a 'message.'" He put air quotes around the last word. "Say you need her."

"I don't know. That doesn't seem right ..." I mumbled as I wiped the sweat off my neck. I didn't believe she was psychic really. But she had known about the terror—and the demon. And if she actually was, it would ruin her weekend. She and her boyfriend had very little alone time, and they had finally managed to eke out that weekend for some quality time. They weren't due back until the next day. I hesitated.

"Come on," my husband pushed. "She's not psychic and you know it. What could it hurt?"

Of course she wasn't. What was I thinking? He was right. How could I even entertain such nonsense?

I closed my eyes and said in my head, "Ivy, I need you. Please come home right now."

I opened my eyes and told my husband, sharply and firmly, "OK, I called her. Now let's forget the whole stupid thing."

I felt uneasy and I wanted all of it out of my mind. Why on Earth would he bring it up today? I didn't want to talk about it any further and made that clear in my tone.

We had our lunch and forgot the whole event. The boys were hot and cranky. I was hot and cranky, and we all just wanted to cool down and find comfort. We set up our tiny pool in the backyard, and the boys played in it throughout the afternoon as I hosed myself down with the frigid water from the garden hose.

At 8:00 p.m., our front door burst open without any knock or warning. Ivy barged with her boyfriend right behind her.

"Is it the baby?" she demanded as she ran to me and put her arms around me.

"Um … Nothing. Everything is good," I stammered. I was filled with many mixed emotions. Shock followed quickly by guilt, wonder, and shame.

She released me, stepped back, and held my face in her hands, staring deeply into my eyes. Her brow furrowed. "You called me," she said so softly I wasn't sure if my husband could even hear her. Then her face hardened. "You were testing me," she stated a little louder.

"Um …" I felt like a piece of shit.

She turned and left the house. Not another word was uttered.

I met my husband's eyes and we just stared at each other. After a few moments, he turned back to the TV and I understood we were to continue as if nothing happened. There would be no discussion or mention of it. And it remained that way, at least until these words were penned.

Ivy and I didn't socialize again. Shortly after this event, she sold her house and we never spoke again.

13.

M Y THIRD SON WAS BORN and it was a very difficult birth. At the time, there were still no epidurals available. The baby had gotten wedged, his shoulders unable to pass through, and excessive damage was incurred. They were finally able to free him, and he was well and healthy, but something was wrong with me. I was shaking so hard I almost fell off the hospital table. I was unable to hold my newborn because of this involuntary, violent movement. They kept piling warm blankets on me as they tried to stitch me up, but I wasn't cold. I just couldn't stop the intense jumping and vibrating of my body, which made it very difficult for them to repair the damage. It took over three hours until I was finally finished and able to go to a maternity room and see my newborn.

The nightmares started shortly after I got home.

My newborn son was in a carrier strapped to my body. I was carrying him on my front and I was in a boat. I had my life jacket on. The boat would capsize as soon as I closed my eyes, and I would fall into the water. My life jacket kept me afloat but I couldn't get my baby's head above the water. I would feel his tiny newborn body panic and struggle and I would panic and struggle to get his head up. I would claw at the carrier and it wouldn't loosen and allow me to get my son out of it. I felt his tiny body struggle to live and then slowly stop moving. I knew he had died. I would jolt awake sobbing and struggling, still trying to rip off the carrier and save my baby. Every single time I closed my eyes for the next eight months, it was vivid. Real. Sleep became impossible.

I was completely exhausted. Days blurred. Weeks blurred. Time lost meaning again. I had three children under the age of four and was just getting by. My priority was the children but I had to be a good wife too. I needed to feel worthy and had to do all the things a good wife did. I made all my children's clothing and most of my own. I made large, balanced, homemade meals. I made favourite desserts; pies, cakes, and cookies were always available for snacking. I made all our bread. I purchased nothing processed. I had to earn my right to be alive, and every day, I worked as hard as I could to do this.

I recall driving to get groceries one day. I saw a large truck stopped at the light in front of me. A thought came to me: I could just speed up, rear-end that truck as hard as I could and this could be over. My three little boys were safely strapped into their car seats in the back seat, and I knew they would be OK. If I hit that truck, I could rest.

A tiny voice, my second son aged three, spoke from the back seat, "Mommy, don't hit the truck."

I froze. I hadn't spoken aloud. I had only been thinking.

His little voice, fear evident, snapped me back to reality and I knew immediately how selfish my thinking had been. I made these little people; I needed to care for them. I needed to stop being so weak. Mothers had done this for years. I needed to toughen up and I promised myself I would.

14.

M Y HUSBAND CAME FROM A large family, with ten children, and he was the eighth. Almost every weekend, he would invite a brother or sister or sometimes a few families at once to come and stay with us. I made myself entertain to the best of my ability. I would shop for each person's favourite food and drink. I would make large meals for breakfast, lunch, and supper and always had beautiful desserts freshly prepared. I would have the house spotless and make sure all bedding and fresh towels were available. I made sure my mask was firmly in place, so they never saw how broken I was, how poorly their brother had chosen when selecting a mate and mother to his children. I learned to make drinks and made sure that everyone had a good time. I didn't drink as I was constantly pregnant or nursing a baby, but that was OK as it kept me more on my toes and more in tune with my guests' needs. I laughed and joked and played cards and games when I wasn't attending to my children. It was a tight balancing act and I had to divide my time carefully. I worked extra hard on those weekends to make sure everything was in order. As time passed, this became increasingly harder and harder.

One Thursday, I was standing at the sink washing dishes. I was well into my fourth pregnancy and it was a tough one. I had gestational diabetes and had to give myself two shots of insulin a day. My blood sugar was out of control and the doctors speculated that I likely had gestational diabetes with my other three pregnancies, but the testing hadn't been done at the time. Now it was a standard test and I had failed it miserably. Each morning, I had to test my blood sugar, immediately call my endocrinologist with the reading, and he would tell me how much insulin to take that day. I had to eat very specific food every three hours and exercise for thirty minutes after I ate. My husband put an exercise bike in our living room, so I could tend to the children while I exercised to keep my pregnancy safe. I was supposed to do this every time I ate, but I just couldn't make myself get out of bed and ride that bike at night. I did, however, set my alarm for every three hours to eat the prescribed snack set beside my bed. On top of it all, my baby was breech, so every day, I had to do specific exercises to try to get my baby to turn. Add the worst morning sickness I had ever had, vomiting up to ten times per day and night, and I wasn't having an easy go at life.

As I stood at the sink that Thursday evening, my pregnant belly pressing into the counter, my husband shared that three of his siblings and their families were coming in for the weekend. Thirteen people in total, arriving tomorrow.

I heard a smash and realized that I had thrown my husband's favourite cup at the backsplash behind the sink. Shards of glass filled the dishwater. I thought I should be careful of the shards, but it was a neutral thought with no feeling attached. I felt removed, as though I was watching it all happen from outside. I saw the hand that had thrown the cup lift above the sink. I watched as it closed into a fist and slammed down on the faucet. I felt no physical sensation of pain. I saw the faucet snap and water shoot straight up. I was vaguely aware I was getting wet. I watched the water with mild interest.

My husband ran to the sink and had to physically push me aside. He was livid and his yelling brought me back to reality.

"How the hell am I supposed to fix this with company coming?" he screamed.

I became aware I had really fucked up. I had done something very, very wrong and had no idea why I had done so. I couldn't explain it to my husband. I couldn't explain it to myself. And now I created a horrible mess and extra work for him for no reason whatsoever. He was so angry and I couldn't blame him. I was causing problems again.

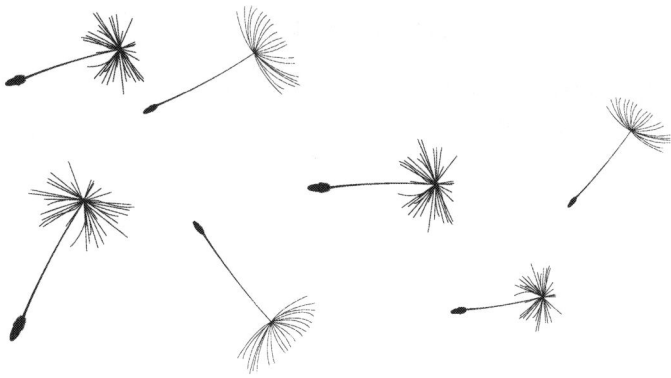

15.

A BABY GIRL! BORN FIVE DAYS before my oldest boy's sixth birthday. She had turned when I was in labour, so no longer breech, and I was able to give birth to her naturally. And she was fine! She needed to go to the neonatal intensive care unit for a day because of my gestational diabetes, but her sugars stabilized quickly and she was perfect. My blood sugars took longer to stabilize but I didn't care; she was well. All my children were well and that was all that mattered to me. Now, I had to get home to host my son's birthday party. I strived to give each child a big, themed birthday party every year. Even though my husband was a hard worker and a great provider, we didn't have any extra money, so I had to be very creative with the parties my children had. I made everything, created games, found cost-saving ways to make things memorable and special for each child. It was important that each of them knew how much they were loved and cherished, and this was one way I was able to show them.

I had to stay an extra day in hospital due to my sugar readings and only had one day to finalize all the party plans when I got home. But a good wife and mother makes sure these things are done, and I did them.

I didn't have the nightmares again after this baby, thank God. I knew I wouldn't be able to manage that. What I did have was fat. I was thirty pounds overweight and that was unacceptable. That did not fit with my ideation of being perfect. I needed to fix that and started trying to dance and exercise in my home whenever I could, in between breastfeeding, childcare, making clothing, keeping the house, and making all our food from scratch.

Everything started to slide. The mask was slipping more and more, and I was having enormous trouble keeping things in order. I struggled to do the simplest of things, like getting groceries. I would go into the store with all my children and rush up and down the aisles. My heart would race, my vision would blur, I would have trouble focusing on my list or the items on the shelf. I struggled to breathe. Sometimes, I had to leave my cart and bolt with my four children in tow, get to my car, buckle them safely in and try to breathe before I could even turn on the ignition. The children would cry, scared. I was making them scared. I was a horrible mother and a terrible person.

Other times, I would manage to get out of the store, somehow load my children into the car, but forget things I had purchased in the cart.

My husband was becoming more and more frustrated. I spent what little money we had on things that were still in a parking lot somewhere or came home with no groceries bought at all. I was starting to have trouble focusing while cooking. I would accidentally pour boiling water over my hand or slice open a finger when chopping vegetables. Taking the kids to preschool or activities was an enormous ordeal. I was always sure I had forgotten something and always carried a feeling that something awful was about to happen. I had to be always vigilant but was so scattered and unable to concentrate that I couldn't. Everything was becoming a problem.

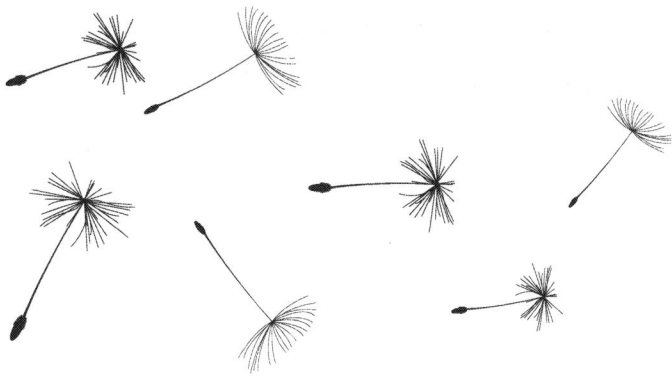

16.

MY PARENTS HAD A SMALL camper and my husband enjoyed camping. I liked the idea of camping, but packing everything we needed for the kids into a car and camper for a three-day excursion exhausted me. And now, for an unknown reason, leaving my house created a deep terror in me. But the children loved camping, so over the years, we had done an excursion a few weekends every summer.

The first time I struggled was when my firstborn was six weeks old. Packing everything needed for a newborn and trying to take care of him while my husband fished and golfed and swam felt so nearly impossible. It only grew more and more difficult with each child. I knew this was my problem as I had neighbours with children who would go camping for weekends or a week at a time and managed just fine. They even loved it. But somehow, for me, this was just getting harder and harder.

One weekend when my fourth baby was just over a year old, we were camping in a beautifully heavy-wooded area. We had a lovely day at the beach, a nice supper in our camp stall, and all the children were showered and tucked into bed. My husband was enjoying a beer by the fire. My baby girl was still nursing, so I enjoyed tea. It was a pleasant and relaxing evening. Soon we turned in and I fell asleep immediately.

Then I was running and I had no idea where I was. My feet hurt. I looked down and saw I was barefoot and wearing only my nightgown. I was out of breath as though I had been running hard. My heart was racing, and I knew it was not just from the running but from complete terror. I was frightened to my core. I was drenched in sweat and shivered in the night air. I couldn't focus. I was in danger. I tried to gulp air into my lungs and struggled. I was shaking from the chill, but more so from the fear. My eyes darted, trying to find the source of the danger. But where were my children? I was aware I was in the campground. I was running on the gravel path with campsites on either side. I spun in a circle looking for my campsite but I couldn't see it. I panicked. There was a terrible, unseen danger and I couldn't find my children. I ran wildly, searching. My fear was intense and I had trouble breathing. I had to find my children! Where was my family? Where was our camper? The terror filled me and I heard myself sobbing as I ran. After what felt like an eternity, I found our stall, rows away from where I found myself initially. All was quiet. Was everyone OK? My breath caught. My eyes blurred. I made myself go toward the camper. I forced myself inside, so sure I would find the worst.

Everyone was as they had been when they had gone to sleep. Everyone was fine, breathing, tucked in. Nothing was amiss. I backed out of the camper and went to the picnic table, sat down, and sobbed. My body ached with fear. My chest burned and still felt tightly constricted. My feet were bleeding. I couldn't process what had happened. I must have had a nightmare that scared me so deeply I was running in my sleep. I struggled to calm myself, to breathe. My body burned. Every muscle felt pulled and ripped. I felt the heat of adrenaline pulse through me.

I don't know how much time had passed when I realized I was very cold and went back into the camper. I crawled in next to my husband and absorbed his warmth. I focused on his breathing, counting his breaths, trying to calm myself though tears still flowed softly as I drifted off to sleep.

This was the first time I found myself wide awake in a place I hadn't fallen asleep, but not the last. I was never outside again; I was always somewhere in our home when I awoke. But the complete fear that engulfed me was always the same. I became afraid to go to sleep.

One night, I was propped against our headboard reading. I needed to sit up or I would go to sleep, and I hated the waking terror that would ensue. I always did drift off eventually and sometimes went through a night without the terror. But the panic in the night came often enough that I tried every night to avoid sleep. This particular evening, I was reading as my husband softly snored beside me. I heard the snarling first. I looked up from my book and in the doorway to our bedroom was a large dog, teeth bared, a low ominous growl filling the bedroom. An instant later, my second child screamed out. I jumped out of the bed and ran to my son. He was sobbing out of control, terrified. "The dog, Mommy. The dog." My husband came running into the room; and I told him about the large, wild dog in our home. He had to find it! He had to get rid of it! My son and I had both seen it!

My husband searched the house from top to bottom. He found no dog. The doors were both locked and all the windows were intact. He assured me that there was no way a large dog was able to get into our home. But I knew what my child and I both saw. I made him search again as I held my four-year-old close to my chest, gently rocking him in my arms. My husband searched the house as my son dozed off.

I laid him down, tucked him in, and found my husband in the kitchen.

"There was no dog. You must have been dreaming," he said.

I knew I was awake. And how could he explain our son crying out about the dog? As I argued with him and told him what had happened in detail, I realized the dog was standing in the doorway of our room when my son cried, when I jumped out of bed and ran to his room. I would have run right into it, but I didn't. And I didn't notice a dog running down the hall before me as I raced to my son's side. But I knew I had seen a dog. And I also realized it was impossible. But what about my child? What was happening?

I didn't sleep that night.

PART TWO
DIAGNOSIS
THE PATH

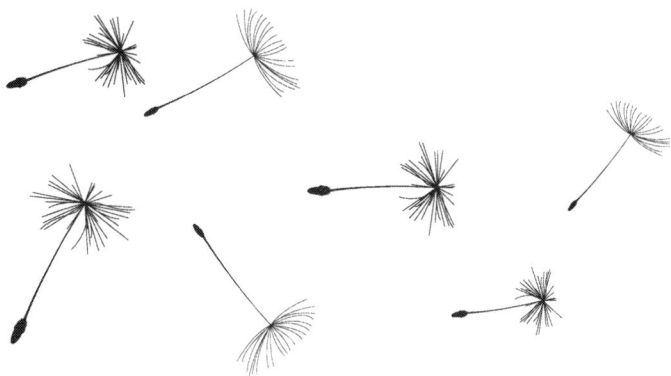

17.

A FRIEND I HADN'T SEEN IN years came to visit. She was the maid of honour at our wedding eleven years prior, and we had connected maybe once or twice a year over the past five years. She had two children around the same ages as my middle two boys. We were close throughout high school and our friendship consisted of dark humour, survival, and hysterical laughter. Every time we connected, we would laugh until our bellies hurt and tears ran down our faces.

Today we were chatting and drinking tea as our children played together. My friend kept looking at me strangely and there were odd pauses in the conversation, something we had never experienced before. I wondered what was wrong. I knew she was a very neat, organized, and meticulous housekeeper and I was not, and I wondered if she was perhaps disgusted with my home. Thoughts swirled in my head as we drank our tea and listened to our children.

I was looking out the window, over the shoulder of my friend, when I became aware she was speaking my name.

I dragged my eyes back to her face and saw her furrowed brow. I had missed something.

"Let me boil the kettle for more tea," I said as I started to get up.

"No!" Not yelled but firmly spoken.

I sat back down, uncertain.

"You are not OK, Nikki." Same firmness.

"Of course I am," I responded lightly. It came out sounding brittle to my ears.

"No, you aren't. You need help. You have had tears rolling down your face since I got here, and you've been staring into space for the last five minutes. You. Need. Help."

What the hell was she talking about? I was not crying. I was not staring. We were having tea, a lovely chat, and spending time with our children. I reached my hand to my cheek to show her how wrong she was and found it damp.

I went to the washroom, saw my swollen red eyes, and watched tears slowly dripping down my face. I felt so detached from the image in the mirror yet knew it was me and knew my friend was right. I needed help.

I came back to the table and sat down heavily, defeated. The mask was gone. I didn't know when or where I lost it, but it was gone. And I was a mess.

"What do I do?" I said softly.

She had my phone book out and had a phone number ready for me to call. Mental Health.

I was resistant. Mental Health? I couldn't. I wouldn't. I just needed a good night's sleep. I needed a cup of coffee. I needed ... I didn't know. But it wasn't a mental health clinic!

I don't remember much of that afternoon except the bits I've shared. I don't know if we kept talking or how long I resisted. I don't know what my friend went through trying to help me. Did she need to be loving and firm? Harsh or soft? Did she need to use my children to convince me? If I was staring into space with her, I must have been doing the same with my children, not caring for them, neglecting them. Did she need to play that card to convince me I needed mental health support? I know I am stubborn, so I don't imagine it was an easy day for her. But I do believe a part of me was relieved that I didn't have to pretend anymore.

I remembered being on the phone and heard myself say, "I need help." The phone was slippery and wet. I must have still been crying.

"Are you going to harm yourself?" the voice on the other end of the line said.

"I don't think so," I answered.

"Are you going to harm someone else?"

"I don't think so." My voice sounded flat, foreign, dead.

"OK, here is your appointment." I wrote it down and hung up the phone. I walked back to my seat. I felt as if I was moving through molasses. I was completely exhausted.

My friend looked at the date I had written down. "FUCK THAT!" she yelled when she saw it was six months away.

"Get up! Get over here! Phone them back! Tell them you need to see someone. NOW!"

"No, no … It's fine." I could hear the exhaustion, the defeat in my voice.

"GET! UP! NOW!" she screamed at me.

I got up. The phone had been dialled and handed to me. The same voice answered.

"I changed my mind; I may hurt someone or may hurt me," I said softly. I knew I wouldn't as I was too exhausted to do anything, including fight my friend.

My appointment was for the next day.

18.

I SAT NERVOUSLY IN THE CROWDED Mental Health Clinic office, looking around, waiting for my turn. I couldn't control my body temperature. I was hot, then cold. Sweating and shivering. Eventually, I was called, and I followed a nurse down a long hall to a large office at the end. A man, probably in his fifties, glanced up from a pad of paper and gestured for me to sit in the chair in front of his desk.

I sat and waited as he wrote. He finally looked up.

"What brings you here?"

"Um … my friend … I stare and may not be caring for my children. I cried," I stumbled over my words. I didn't really have an answer.

He once again was focused on his paper. He didn't look up again as he asked me more questions I had no answers for.

I remembered only a few things from my childhood and recalled little from my teens, but I shared what I knew. Things were patchy, disconnected, and I couldn't understand why he was asking me about these times. I needed to stop crying and staring into space and instead care for my children, not talk about obscure, unrelated things from my past.

He asked about my day-to-day life and I told him all I could.

He asked about my family history, and I shared that my grandfather had a few bouts of shock treatments. He asked about that; I shared that it seemed to happen in the fall when harvest was underway. I was aware my dad had extra work at those times because sometimes grandpa got sick. I told the doctor it was for diabetes. He had what we were told was "brittle diabetes" in that his blood sugars were difficult to control day-to-day. I had never been told this directly but overheard conversations. I also told the doctor I remember grandpa had medicine that could make him forgetful.

We saw my grandpa and grandma at least once per week, if not more, but one day stood out. My mom and dad explained to me that my grandpa might not know who I was because of his medicine. I was five years old, and it was true, he didn't remember me. But later that day, a very strange thing happened. My grandpa was in the bedroom with my twin siblings. They were babies and lying in their cribs. I heard a strange sound, like a giggle, but I knew it wasn't the babies. It was a weird sound, disturbing, and I peeked into the room to see what was happening. It was my grandpa making that sound. He had a smile on his face and was chuckling as he looked into the cribs. I remember being completely shocked. I had never seen my grandpa smile. I had never heard him laugh. It was unnerving and unsettled me as it was so out of the ordinary. But I did think, with my young reasoning, that the medicine must be good if he could smile and laugh, even though it made him forget.

For some reason, this all seemed important to this doctor.

After what seemed like an eternity, he told me he thought I had chronic depression and severe anxiety disorder and recommended counselling and medication.

I agreed to the counselling, but not the medication. That would mean I was crazy. What would people say? What sort of a failure needed medication to live their life? I saw other mothers with young children function. Many of them even worked outside of the home, which had to be way harder than what I did. I just couldn't agree to this. And what would my husband say? He would be so disappointed. A wife who was so weak she couldn't even take care of his children and a home without pills.

I shared all this through my tears as I begged the doctor to help me be better but not take pills. He was the doctor, after all; there must be another way.

He sat back in his chair, removed his glasses, looked directly at me, and spoke softly. He explained to me about brain chemistry, my heredity, my grandpa's shock treatments not being for diabetes. He explained in terms I could understand that mental illness was illness first. Just like the flu, diabetes, heart disease, cancer, it's just something some people have. He explained it wasn't something I had or had not done.

He told me I was in a hole, a deep black hole, like a well. And outside of the well was counselling and help. He said I needed to be able to peek my head out of well, over the edge, to see and use that help effectively. The medication he wanted me to try was like a ladder dropped into the well. It would help me climb up so I could peek out of the hole, and once I could see out and use the help, we would speak more about the medicine.

I recall staring into his eyes, examining, probing. He didn't look away. He met my eyes steadily. Could I trust this man? Should I trust this man? I felt a tiny ray of hope, barely discernible. Did this man have the key to help? The help I owed to my children and my husband? I decided I needed to risk it.

I agreed to take medication for six weeks. He said, by that time, I would know if this was something that would help me.

I stood, took the prescription for fluoxetine, and went to the front desk to set up my first counselling session with the clinic.

19.

THE PSYCHOLOGIST ASKED SO MANY questions, many more than the psychiatrist had. She seemed to find insignificant things so important to probe into. My childhood—I could only remember a few things. My teens—the same. My marriage—it was perfect. I was married to an incredibly patient man who tolerated my nonsense. We were solid. Yet she probed. My friendships. I had a few and had more or less learned how to manage them. My relationship with my children, my extended family, my husband's extended family, my eating, my drinking, my exercise, my sleep, my intimacy. It was endless.

After what felt like an hour of her asking questions and noting answers, she looked up from her paper and stated, "I think your marriage is a problem, among other things."

I was struck dumb. This woman was a complete and utter fool! She was supposed to help me? I felt the red-hot anger slipping through the mask. How dare she! I explained loudly and in detail how wrong she was and then questioned her ability to help me. I told her I was the problem, not my husband, and in fact, he had been more than supportive of me. I explained how hard it was for anyone to live with the Dark Nikki, and how she was completely out of line maligning the man who gave me everything, my children, my home, my life. If she meant I was a problem in my marriage, I would discuss it, but I would not entertain any insinuation that my husband was anything less than impeccable.

She said she understood, stated we would not discuss my marriage except for my role in the union, and we continued with our session.

I need to step out of my first psychologist appointment for a second and share some insights with you, dear reader. The journey you are walking with me, my life, with no exaggeration or literary license taken, seems dark. I share the darkness as that is the illness that was, and is, part of the very thread of me and the impetus for this work. These dark, unsettling events occurred just as I am stating, again from my perspective. But this wasn't my entire life. Often for weeks and occasionally months on end, the mask would stay in place and life was joyful. As with the crust of our Earth, we can live long periods without shifts that cause disasters; the same was true of my mask and me.

When I kept the mask in place, I had fun, laughter, and joy in my life. Underneath the surface, bubbling like lava ready to erupt through the mask at any moment, was the constant darkness. But I would be remiss and misleading if I didn't share that there were many joyful times as well. The children were fun and lively, creative, and mischievous, and brought tremendous joy to my heart. My husband and I had a loving, rich, intimate life when I was functioning well, and we shared similar life goals and interests. I loved humour and often used it as a crutch to manage the darkness, and the underlying core of most of my relationships was humour. My husband and I spent time with both our extended families and laughter was abundant. And I did laugh heartily many times through the years. But I was also always aware, even during the laughter, that the blackness inside existed.

As the weeks passed with counselling sessions every second week and daily medication, I noticed slight changes but nothing significant. A better statement would be that I became aware of just how bad things were. I saw how my mask, my brave front, my perfect wife and mother act were all perceptions of mine that didn't really exist. In the early years, I was able to play the role most of the time with only a few slips. As the years wore on and my family grew, I was able to play the role less and less effectively, and eventually not at all. I became aware that I was constantly crying or yelling at someone, mostly my husband, or completely zombie-like. I wasn't perfect and had never been. It was all in my mind, a fantasy I had created. In reality, I was unable to complete even simple functions like grocery shopping. I couldn't sleep. I was terrified of something, nothing, everything, all the time.

I became aware that my husband and I had fought off and on for years, those arguments growing worse after the birth of each child. I would wear my mask, believe and behave as I thought I should, and then the fury buried beneath the mask would erupt like molten lava, damaging everything in its path. I would scream horrible things. I would cry, yell, beg. And then drift back to nothingness, exhausted, knowing I was a horrible person. I would promise not to let that mask slip again.

I resented my husband for spending so much time playing sports and being away from us. I resented him for having a life outside of the home when I had none. I found out by accident at his staff Christmas party one year that he had been carpooling with a female co-worker for months. Someone commented at our table that night that he and Michelle had gotten a parking spot in the lot, apparently a huge accomplishment in this crowd, as they had been carpooling together so long. He walked to the bus stop every day, three blocks from our home, and she picked him up there instead of at our house. Because of me. He didn't tell me because I was so out of control, yelling and screaming all the time, and he knew I would lose my mind over this. And he was correct. Everything was either a damaging, unpredictable moment of explosive, vile fury …

or nothing. And there was no predicting what each moment would be. It was like living in a minefield. And he didn't deserve it, nor did my children.

The awareness was painful. The more I knew, the more I needed to fix and correct. And the harder I tried.

I continued to cook big meals and still made all our bread. I hadn't been able to make clothing for myself and my children for quite a while, and they were outgrowing what we had. I hadn't kept up with cookies and pies and snacks. The house was always a disaster and I never had the laundry done. I forced myself to get the groceries. Even if it took me five trips to the store to get all I needed, I did it. And I still took the children to every event and outing as required, even with my knuckles white as I gripped the steering wheel, trying to keep the fear at bay.

In hindsight, I was hanging by a thread.

The counsellor kept trying to bring up my marriage, but I continued to not talk about it. I was firm in my stance that we had an excellent marriage, marred only by my illness that I was now fixing, and that this subject was off the table.

20.

ONE DAY AROUND THE SIX-WEEK mark of the medication and treatment, I had to get groceries again. This was one of the worst parts of my week. I did the best I could to mentally prepare for the event, the nightmare it always was. I loaded all four children into the car and drove to the store, focusing on keeping my breathing even. I unloaded the children and headed to the entrance, knowing the overwhelming fear would hit me as soon as I heard the whoosh of the automatic doors opening.

The doors opened and we crossed the threshold. I felt mild fear, but not the heat filling and spreading through my body as usually happened. I found a cart and put the two younger children into the cart and had the older two hang onto the side and walk along with me. Normally, I would have been having trouble breathing evenly at this point. I pulled out my list and could read, even focus on it. I decided to get as much as I could before I had to bolt back to the car.

The children and I were chatting as we walked slowly up and down each aisle. For some reason, I noticed there was a cow tongue packaged and ready for sale. I picked it up and showed it to the kids. We all stuck our tongues out and compared the bumps on our tongues with those on the cow's and had an in-depth discussion about who would eat such a thing. One of the children asked why there were so many cartons of eggs, and we set about exploring all the different sizes, comparing them, and talking about comparative chicken discomfort while laying them. We had a philosophical discussion, as much as one can have with a one, three, five, and seven-year-old, about why the good cereals were on the low shelves and the yucky ones were on high shelves. This discussion included a demand for an explanation as to why we bought the yucky cereals when they could obviously reach the good ones.

We had a lively debate about the best apples, with one child demanding that pears defeated all apples. There was a strong marketing pitch made toward the purchase of treats and, full disclosure, the children won. In my defence, unquestionable logic peppered with statistics was included in the request.

The children helped load the groceries on the conveyor belt, and together, we went through the check-out, chatting with the clerk, each child explaining the reasoning behind the treat they had chosen as it was being bagged.

The older two children latched themselves to a part of the cart as we travelled the parking lot. The sun was shining, and it was a beautiful warm day. The two eldest children helped put things into the trunk and my seven-year-old taught his baby sister and youngest brother how to throw things into the trunk from their cart prison. Eventually, everything was packed away, and we all piled into the vehicle and I buckled everyone securely into their seats. We revisited the cow tongue discussion all the way home.

At home, we all got out of the car and each child carried an item, manageable according to their size, into the house. The groceries were out of the bags and strewn all over the kitchen floor. The car trunk was empty, everyone was inside, and the kids were off playing as I surveyed an entire grocery order for a family of six spread all over the kitchen.

Suddenly, I was overwhelmed with a feeling. Not anger, the only feeling I had experienced in a long time, but a different feeling. I couldn't even describe it. It felt foreign and a bit unnerving. It filled me with warmth and I became very emotional. I leaned against the wall and slowly slid down to the floor. I felt tears well in my eyes and then slowly trail down my face.

Is this how people live? Is this what normal feels like? Are people able to get their groceries without having to abandon the cart and rush out of the store because they couldn't breathe? Are people able to take their time and get all the things they need without constantly focusing on making sure they focus and breathe? Are people able to make sure they have all the things off the cart as they load their car without obsessing about just getting the kids safely buckled in? Are people able to bring the groceries in as soon as they get home and not rush the children and themselves in, breathe and wait until they stop shaking enough to go out and get the groceries, sometimes hours later? Are people able to have fun getting groceries? Fun with their children? Fun at the check-out? Fun?

I realized, as I silently wept on the floor, that I was sick. I had a mental illness. But I also realized I was getting better. I was doing something about it. The darkness wasn't in control any longer. I knew my life would never be the same again. And that brought hope.

21.

I FELT LIKE A NEWBORN IN many ways, learning how to live again. Or maybe learning how to live for the first time ever. Things looked differently. Things seemed different. My counsellor wanted me to reflect on my past, my childhood, my marriage, but I wasn't interested in any of that. I only wanted to move forward and experience life through this new lens.

She also recommended I pursue some interests outside of husband and children, something for myself. I tried to explain that taking care of my children and husband was for me. They were my life and my entire existence. I explained how much better I was at taking care of my family. I told her of all the new projects and activities the children and I did during the day. I wanted her to know how much better my thinking and focus were and how much better I was able to engage in reality. I explained I created bowls of dry ingredients and wet ingredients to make muffins. I knew exactly how many tablespoons of each were needed to create one muffin, and I had an array of "extras" available to add to the basics. Chocolate chips, blueberries, coconut, raisins ... Anything I had in the house now that I could actually shop. The kids made several signature muffins. That was a new activity for me, I told her, and showed my ability to concentrate and create—all the things she wanted me to do.

I explained to her that I started making my children's clothing again, but this time, I took them to the store with me to choose fabrics and appliques. I shared how I couldn't do that before because I was always too anxious, but now I was doing that for myself and having fun with my children. I told her how the children would help me plan meals and desserts and shop to pick the correct things.

I shared how my children were all fussy eaters, and how each meal had been a struggle and caused me so much stress in the past. But now, I was able to make a plan that eliminated the problem. I told her, in detail, how I had gathered stacks of magazines and some bristle board, and how we had cut out different foods and glued them to the bristle board in different areas labelled in accordance with the food guide. I told her we stuck it to the fridge and every meal when one of the children didn't like something served, they had to go to the board, find something in the same category, and replace the item they wouldn't eat. Meat was often replaced with peanut butter. Milk was replaced with yogurt or cheese. The system worked well and none of this would have been accomplished without my medication and her help. I explained to her that this was for me! This was solely for me as it made my life easier. But that didn't satisfy her. I didn't know how she couldn't understand all the changes I had made for myself and how much better my life was—for me!

After weeks of back and forth, I finally agreed to one thing for myself that seemed to meet her criteria. I agreed to try an exercise class that I would attend alone. The only reason I agreed to this was that she convinced me it would help my healing journey as chemicals released during exercise would make me feel better. And I also knew that I was a solid thirty pounds over my pre-baby weight and needed to do something about it. I always struggled with weight, and I also knew my husband didn't find heavy women attractive, so this seemed like the best option for everyone, and it finally got her off my case about doing something "just for me."

22.

I WAS ABLE TO FIND A community class that I could attend, but it meant I would have to leave all four children for an hour per week in the evening. My husband and I agreed that a class after the children were in bed would be best if we could find it. I found a twelve-week session, starting at 8:30 p.m. one evening per week. All the children wouldn't always be in bed, but some would, and that would have to be good enough. It was through the local community association at a school gym a block from my home, and it was affordable, a win-win.

I was very nervous for the first class. I hadn't gone to anything alone in so long and I was in brutal physical condition. I was fearful I wouldn't be able to keep up and would look ridiculous.

When I entered the gymnasium, I was somewhat relieved to find everyone looked like me, nervous and uncertain. The instructor was a wisp of a thing that looked like she could run mountains without losing her breath. I had exhausted myself putting on my running shoes.

We all lined up and waited for the torture to begin. Shockingly, I lived through the class and actually had fun. I was moving to music, something I had always enjoyed, and I grew to look forward to the classes each week. The attendees started chatting a bit before and after class, mostly about what hurt most after the session the week prior, but nevertheless, interacting. By the end of the twelve weeks, I had made two friends, both of whom I still communicate with today and one who was to become my closest and best friend.

As the twelve weeks wound down, I was excited to enroll in the next session with my new friends. Unfortunately, the session interfered with my husband's hockey schedule. When I shared this with my new friends, they were disappointed and suggested we look for other options together. I was shocked! They wanted to stay connected with me? Wow! They were enjoying our time together. I was incredibly bolstered by this. We decided to ask the instructor where else she taught to follow her. She shared she was under contract to a city facility that had several different classes running throughout the day and evenings and offered babysitting during the daytime classes. It sounded like a win for us all.

I did have one issue though: the cost.

Our funds were incredibly tight living on one income with four children, and we didn't have any extra to spend. If I wanted to do this, I would need to find a way to bring in the money to cover the extra expense. As I got stronger and stronger and better and better, I had started to take in sewing projects to help make ends meet. I was doing basic mending, hemming, and simple alterations. I decided to expand my small enterprise and was soon making dresses for wedding parties, wind suits for teams, and other large projects. With the extra bit of income, along with babysitting neighbourhood kids occasionally, I was able to cover the extra cost of my membership to this city-run facility. My husband was very supportive of my desire to keep it up. He had seen a change and growth in me and encouraged me to continue.

Joining this fitness centre changed the trajectory of my life.

I was attending exercise classes every morning of the week. My body was getting fit and I was starting to feel good. I made friends with the regulars and started having coffee with a group after class every morning in the cafeteria in the centre. The kids made friends in the babysitting room and were enjoying their fun time as well. I could still feel the darkness inside myself, but I was in control now. Life was starting to feel fun, not all days, but some days. I enjoyed the laughter and comradery of my new friends.

Soon, I caught the eye of one of the instructors. No, not one of the instructors, the instructor. The best instructor! One day after class, he approached me and asked me to consider becoming a fitness instructor. I guess my old dance training had surfaced in that I was able to follow choreography fairly easily, and as I got more and more fit and more and more toned, he felt I was strong enough to lead classes. I was flattered but dismissed the thought immediately. I was far too nervous to consider such a thing.

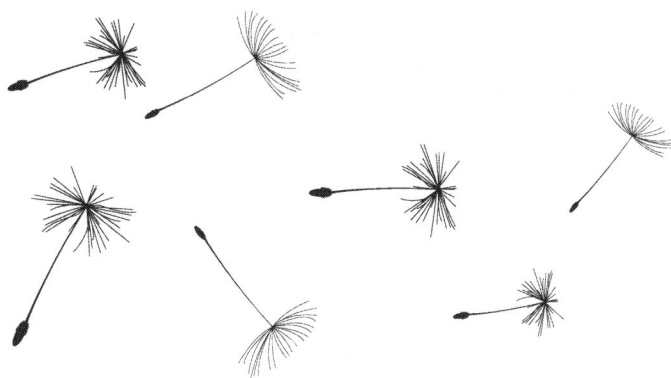

23.

A S WINTER APPROACHED, THE DARKNESS crept forward again. For several years, my husband and I had visited one of his siblings' homes for a New Year's celebration, and at the beginning of December that year, my husband shared that it was our turn to host. I felt that was fair. Then he told me that most of the family was coming. Forty-two guests for three to five days. My heart started to race, my vision blurred, my legs felt wobbly. The familiar panic was back. I said nothing to him, though. It was our turn. But it had never been everyone before; usually, it was just a few families. This time, it was everyone. In the early hours of the next morning, I found myself in our newly refinished basement running. I had once again woken in panic outside of my bed, outside of my room. I wasn't better after all. Slowly, over the next month, my symptoms returned. I became focused on how I was going to host all these people. How was I going to cook? Where was I going to put them all? Did I have towels and bedding? What was I going to do?

At my next regular appointment with my psychiatrist, I told him my symptoms were back, how I was once again having trouble breathing, focusing, going out of my house, and attending my exercise classes. He asked what had happened and I told him,

"Nothing, it just happened." He stated he suspected seasonal affective disorder and increased my medication.

I shared the same with my counsellor, and sometime during the session, we got around to how I was feeling stressed about hosting all these people over New Year's. She said I had to tell my husband that he was asking too much of me. To me, however, that was not helpful at all! She was supposed to give me tips, support on how to manage the coming guests. Not backing out when it was clearly our turn! Why was I even doing any of this if it wasn't to be a better wife and mother? She didn't get it. I was so frustrated with her. I decided I would simply take the increased medication and somehow make it all work. I skipped my next few appointments with her.

The holidays were a blur. I remember running to the store with some or all my children in tow to buy groceries and toilet paper so many times while my husband's family laughed, drank, and played games. I remember forgetting a box of mandarin oranges on the bottom of my cart and being so angry with myself, having to run out again in the cold to buy more for our visitors. I was washing towels twice a day, carefully timing wash cycles between my guests' showers, and often just staying up late at night to make sure everything was done. I was trying to make huge, varied, balanced, tasty meals for everyone. I was making sure, as best able, that delicious desserts and treats were available for snacking. I made sure chip bowls were always full, liquor was stocked, everyone had a drink in hand, and games and tables to play on were available and accessible, all the while trying my best to be a happy, gracious host.

One evening, amid the chaos, the phone rang. My new and dear friend from my exercise classes was on the other end. Her husband had been in a terrible car accident and she needed me. I found my husband in the crowd of people. "I have to go to the hospital. My friend needs me," I said to him. I told him where our children were and reminded him he needed to put them to bed.

He'd had a few drinks already but one of his sisters heard me and told me she would make sure they were taken care of.

I rushed to the hospital. I found my friend in the waiting room. Her husband was in surgery. The doctors said he had broken his neck and they didn't know if he would walk or even survive surgery. She was ghostly white and terrified and I was terrified for her. Her three children were small like mine. She worked full-time evenings while her husband worked days. And now her husband was hurt. I wanted to take all her pain.

Her mother- and father-in-law arrived and asked what happened just as the doctor approached to update us on their son's condition.

"His neck is broken and we were able to do what we could. We don't know his prognosis at this time but he made it through the surgery." My friend started to softly cry as I held her. I had no words, didn't know what to say to her. I didn't know how I would manage this news were it me on the receiving end.

We sat in silence, trying to process our own thoughts when we were startled by a sudden howl from across the room. All I remember is bright red lips wailing and crying out, "At least he didn't really break his neck." My friend's mother-in-law. We looked across the room at this dramatic outburst and then looked at each other, confused. I immediately wondered, is this how I am? Is this how I act? Not hearing words just said to me, believing what I wanted to believe. Was this woman as ill as I was and just rewrote life to fit her needs? Is that what I did?

Something in that moment, after that odd wailing statement was uttered, changed everything in that room. A shift, not seen, but felt. My friend's energy and demeanour changed as those bright red lips continued to cry out across the room. She dabbed her eyes, squared her shoulders, and with strength and determination I will always remember, looked at me and said, "OK." One simple word that conveyed such character I will never forget. As if she knew at that moment that everything rested on her shoulders and she would manage somehow. I envied her strength. This is how a real wife and mother reacts to stressors, not like I did. I held her hand and we sat like that for a long time until she could go and see him. At that point, I left her and returned to my home with the understanding that if she needed anything, I would be there.

I walked into a full-blown party at my house. Singing, drinking, dancing, streamers, noisemakers ... so different from the seriousness at the hospital. My friend was going through a horrible time, and I knew, in my heart, she would somehow manage it, but I was coming undone by having people in my home for a celebration. I was having trouble processing the two vastly different situations and making sense of things. I needed to find my children.

I found all four in our bedroom, curled into our bed sleeping. I crawled in with them, grateful that they were safe as I was feeling the fragility of life, feeling the pain my friend was going through, worrying what her future would be like, and wondering how I could become as strong as she. I was also fully aware that my arrival home had gone unnoticed.

24.

WINTER MOVED INTO SUMMER, AND my friend's husband slowly recovered. He was able to walk, slowly healed, and eventually returned to work.

I continued with my medication and my counsellor continued hounding me, but now only once a month, thank God! She felt it would be a positive step for me to take the fitness instructor training. My friend said the same, though frankly, I put more weight on my friend's opinion than my counsellor's.

I finally decided to speak to my husband about it. I told him how my favourite instructor continued to approach me to consider certification and how my counsellor thought it was a good idea.

His first thought was that this instructor was perhaps being inappropriate and hitting on me. I laughed so hard. First, the instructor was not interested in women, and secondly, literally no one would ever be interested in me. I was a mother of four children!

Then he told me how he felt my counsellor was just trying to cause more problems. I shared openly every conversation we had in session, and he felt she had been against him for months. I couldn't disagree.

And then there was the money issue. The training cost two hundred dollars, which was a huge amount for us.

After much discussion back and forth, we decided that I would likely make back the two hundred dollars if I worked as an instructor, and soon my husband was supportive of my taking the training. It was possible employment while the children were cared for, and that would go a long way to help us out. When the time came to go, I wanted to back out, but my husband gave me the strength to step forward when I had to. I'm not sure I would have gone ahead with the training if he hadn't given me the final push when it was needed.

I spent several full weekends training and taking exams in all different modules to become a certified instructor of all types of land and water fitness. My husband was wonderful, taking full care of our children while I pursued my studies, and even took me out to a nice dinner, just us two, when I passed the final certification.

Soon, way too soon, just two days after I was certified, I was put to the test. THE instructor asked me to lead a section of his class. I was petrified!

Somehow, I forced myself to put on that microphone and lead part of a class. Many members of the class were my friends that I had shared morning coffee with, and they were wonderfully supportive of me. After the class, I felt on top of the world. I had accomplished something. I was a fitness instructor!

At the end of that class, as I was still flying high from leading the warm-up portion, I was approached by the management of the facility and offered a job. They had evaluated me during the brief time I led the class. I was honoured and terrified. Thank God I hadn't known they were watching! I told them I had to discuss this with my husband and would get back to them the next day.

A job! My first job in ten years. My first job since I'd had children. My husband was excited for me. The childcare was in-house and I could help with family finances. This was fantastic. Life was beginning to look up. The darkness was put away, hopefully forever. But life would not be that easy.

25.

I BEGAN TEACHING FITNESS CLASSES REGULARLY, four to five classes per week. Some were in the evenings and my husband would be on childcare duties. I started to go out after class Friday evening for a drink, or two, or more with the other instructors and regular attendees. I was not behaving as a wife and mother should when I did these things, and my life began to unravel.

My husband was becoming extremely frustrated with the more outgoing, friendly person I was becoming and was very suspicious of my new friendships. He bought me a book called *Potatoes, Not Prozac* and asked me to read it and consider what I was doing to our family. He told me my counsellor was causing us problems and encouraging the breakdown of our marriage. He gave me articles on the damage my behaviour was doing to our children. He reminded me I was a wife and mother first and I had decided to "get well" for the children, not to abandon them to go out drinking with my friends. I would argue back, ask how it was different from him going for drinks after each hockey game. The fighting became constant and dirty. He was right, of course. The more I took my medication, the more I saw my counsellor, and the more I worked and socialized, the more we fought and the more trouble we had.

I started drinking at home with him as well and this too was an issue. While I was pregnant or nursing, I had never consumed alcohol. My husband had been a social drinker all through our marriage and would often have a beer or two at home while watching the game or working in the yard. Now, no longer pregnant or nursing, I started to drink with him, but I wasn't as hardy or good at it, and the more I drank, the more I ran my mouth about how pissed off or frustrated I was about something. And the fight was on, again.

We decided to buy a new home in hopes that a change would help us. With my contribution to our income, we could afford a slightly bigger home, just in time as our children were growing and needed more space.

We argued the whole time we were packing and moving. I recall one particularly intense screaming match that involved a man, Frank, who attended my classes and had been hanging around for some time. Frank was friends with both my husband and I, and he was effusively supportive of my newfound mental wellness while my husband seemed to be the complete opposite. I remember screaming that Frank seemed interested in me, listened to me, seemed to care about and support me. I recall taking that too far and yelling that I was feeling closer to Frank than I was to my own husband. I watched my husband's face crumple as he cried. I felt sick. I hated myself instantly for uttering those words, and even to this day, I feel sick remembering. I had only seen my husband cry once before when his father died. I thought it would make him support me, be by my side. If he was jealous, maybe he would work with me, and we could get better. It was childish, ridiculous, manipulative, mean. And it couldn't be unsaid. I was disgusted with myself. What a fool I had become.

Weeks after these horrible words were uttered, my husband and I were in our new home, hosting a housewarming dinner party. Frank, and Michelle, the woman my husband had carpooled with for several years, were among the guests, and with both being single, we were hoping they may connect romantically. Michelle left shortly after we finished eating. I guess she found no connection. The other guests slowly left as the evening wore on, but Frank stayed on. Then, out of the blue, my husband got up and said he was leaving to play hockey. I was completely shocked. I had shared that Frank might have an interest in me, had foolishly shared that I felt close to him, and even though I had retracted that, my husband was prepared to leave me alone with this man to go play hockey? I decided at that moment that my husband preferred hockey over me, a fight that had become commonplace in our home for years. I felt something in me break. The fight was never really about hockey, but rather, how I wasn't feeling valued.

I knew that day was the end. We were too broken and needed a break. Shortly afterward, we separated. The new house hadn't fixed out issues.

And then I found myself alone—the thing I could not do. The weekends I was without my children, I fell apart completely. If the children were with me, I was OK, kept my head above water, and was able to function. But when my ex-husband picked them up for his weekend and I watched the car, with everything my life consisted of, back out of the driveway Friday evenings, I dissolved. The first time this happened, I immediately ran to the washroom and vomited. The aloneness was worse than it had ever been before. I was terrified, unable to focus, pacing, unable to leave the house, and purging my stomach regularly for the entire weekend while they were gone. I would get a warning as my vision would blur, my chest would constrict, my body would vibrate. I would hear myself sobbing and then the bile would rise. I was unable to keep food down when I was alone. I didn't know how I could do this. I was on my own and it was my fault. Nothing was better, and everything was, in fact, worse than ever. I felt I would die.

26.

FRANK DECIDED HE WAS GOING to save me from my aloneness. He made himself available and easy and I was too messed up to deal with the reality of my life. Escape became my go-to. Frank was a heavy drinker, and soon, I was spending those lonely weekends with him, drinking the days away until my children came home. I was still taking my medication and still teaching fitness classes regularly but had stopped seeing my counsellor and my psychiatrist had long ago stated my meds were balanced and had referred me to my family doctor for maintenance.

Over the next few months, life once again became a blur. I had upped my teaching to three to four classes per day to provide the needed income. My body was wearing out, I wasn't eating, I was drinking away every other weekend, I had started smoking again, and I needed to take in more sewing projects to make ends meet. My life felt out of control. I felt out of control. I realized how good my life had been before and how ungrateful I had been. I needed my old life back.

I realized my ex-husband had been correct. I should never have taken the medication. I hadn't listened and I had screwed up our lives, and more importantly, the lives of my children. He had said I was behaving selfishly and he was right. We had been happy and then the counselling, medication, working, new friends, and how I was behaving had destroyed everything.

I met Frank as per usual on Friday evening, and instead of spending the weekend with him, I told him I couldn't see him any longer. I explained that my life was out of control and I needed to fix things. I said I had made a mistake. This man who had so convinced me that I was doing the right thing all along—stated how much he loved me and needed me, told me how my husband never had, told me how much he understood me, and promised me safety and a life together—didn't bat an eye. He stated he had been seeing someone else the same time as he was seeing me and would never have considered a permanent relationship with someone with four children.

I was a fool—a complete and utter fool—and I had destroyed everything being a fool. I knew I would never forgive myself. A grown woman, a mother of four ... I couldn't even look at myself in the mirror. I was disgusted with myself.

I returned to my home, ready to face the aloneness, the misery I deserved for what I had done to my family. I stopped my medication immediately. I picked up some classes over the weekend to fill the time. I remember sobbing in the break room, gathering myself, then putting on the mic and teaching a class only to return to the break room to sob again. I know the other staff were looking at me, watching me, but I didn't care. Someone asked if I wanted to go to lunch with them, but I said "no" since seeing my friends had been part of the problem.

When my ex-husband brought the children back Sunday after supper, I told him everything. How stupid I had been, how I had stopped my medication, how I wanted everything as it was before I had ruined it all. I begged him to give me another chance. He said we needed to give it time. He said he wasn't ready to come home, that we both needed to see if that was what was best for all of us.

I knew he was correct but I didn't want to give it time. I wanted things better immediately. I wanted my life back!

I taught my classes through the next few weeks, didn't stay after for coffee, worked on my sewing projects, and didn't see any of my friends so I could prove to my ex-husband that I was still the woman he married. I needed to show him I had stopped behaving like an out-of-control teenager and instead became the wife and mother I was supposed to be.

I had been pacing throughout Friday night, unable to sleep, running over everything in my head, creating a foolproof plan to get my ex-husband to come home and get my life back together. My children were with me, and he had gone to see his brother and their family for the weekend. I had been off my medication for three weeks. That was more than enough time to show him how I had changed. He'd said we needed time; I had given him time. In an instant, it became clear to me that I had to speak to him immediately. I had no choice. I had to talk to him that moment for everything to work out. It was time for him to come home. I tried to reason with myself. He was staying at his brother's home and it was 4:00 a.m. I tried to tell myself not to call, that it was rude to wake people, that surely, I could wait until the morning to bother them. But I knew that wasn't true. This was life and death. I had to call now, immediately. If I didn't make this call, speak to him, terrible things would happen. I didn't know what, but I knew they would. I found his brother's phone number and called.

No answer. I called again and someone answered groggily. I demanded to speak to my ex-husband. After what seemed to be an eternity, he was on the line.

"Is it the children?" he asked, concerned.

A woman's voice. "What is it? What's going on, honey?"

I heard myself screaming at him, "Who is with you?"

A woman he had been seeing for a while, he answered. I knew nothing of this. But why would I? And why shouldn't he be seeing someone? I had been doing the same. But my brain wouldn't process this. I heard a voice that sounded far away screaming shrilly. My voice. Then the phone went dead. I dialled again. Someone picked up and I heard that screaming again, my screaming. Click. I dialled again. Busy signal. I dialled over and over for hours. I don't know how long. At some point, I remembered I had a client's wedding dress fitting later that day, so I wandered into the dining room, which was also my sewing room, and began to work.

Hours later, the children were up and fed and playing outside when my customer came for her fitting. As I pinned, she kept asking me questions that made no sense. Where was the children's father, "fucking a whore." Did I have a babysitter, "yes, does this feel right?" Where was her number, "in the phone, do you want this longer or shorter?" Could she use my phone, "fine but take this off and I'll alter it while you make your call."

She left, came back, and I continued to work on her dress. Sometime later, my usual babysitter and her mother were at my door. I noticed but didn't think it odd. I was too busy working on the dress.

Then I was in a car, my customer's car. I had never been in her car; I didn't even know her.

The hospital. I was aware but detached. Why was I here? Had I cut myself? I checked my hands for wounds. My customer sat with me. I asked her what was going on. She said we were waiting on a doctor.

The doctor came. Before my customer left, she held my face in her hands, looked into my eyes, and said, "Someone did this for me once. I'm doing it for you." I will never forget those words.

I only have bits of memory from this time. Outpatient. Beds full. Medication. Supports available. I have no idea how long I was in the hospital that day. I can only vaguely remember a hard, ugly, beige, plastic chair. I don't remember people or conversations. There are big spaces of nothing. As I reflect, I can't recall events up to that day, only spotty instances I have shared here. Sobbing in the break room before putting a smile on and doing my job. Standing at my sink, unable to eat, but making sure the children ate. Sitting on my deck smoking, watching the children as they played, terrified to take my eyes off them. And the phone calls early that morning, the out-of-control phone calls.

Then I was home on my deck, and so many people were there. My parents, my ex-husband, my babysitter and her mother, the children, a friend. And tons of Chinese food. I laughed and said, "Are we having a Nikki is crazy party?" I thought it was a joke. It wasn't. We were indeed having a Nikki is crazy party.

Everyone ate as I watched, numb yet marvelling at what I was seeing. Everyone was chatting, being friendly, catching up on news, as if this was just any other day. No one mentioned the elephant in the room, or rather, on the deck. After the food was eaten and the garbage gathered, my ex-husband loaded the kids into his car. I told him to wait. It was my weekend; what was he doing? I didn't understand. My mom was packing up all the leftover food and giving it to him. None of this made sense.

My mom took me aside and said I was going to stay with them for a few days. Then I was loaded into my parents' car and was taken to their home, an hour away from the city I lived in, where I was to be treated as an outpatient for three weeks.

I remember running every day and doing whatever work was required of me. I was back on medication. I missed my children terribly but knew I needed to get well for them. I'd had a breakdown and should have been hospitalized, but there were no beds available for me and I was considered unsafe to be on my own. I don't know what my customer saw that day; I don't know what the group at the "crazy party" saw that day. My memories are too blurred and patchy.

I never saw that customer again and have no idea what happened to her unfinished wedding dress. But if she ever reads this, thank you for seeing what you did and helping me.

The path back was long and hard. I knew I had to keep taking the medication. I shudder to think of what I might have done to myself or my children if that dear woman hadn't helped me. I would never have hurt my children intentionally, I know that, but would I have neglected them? Thank goodness it hadn't gotten that far. I was told by their father that they never suffered and I believe him. I, however, suffered badly and had a long road ahead of me. One step at a time.

27.

P ART OF MY FOLLOW-UP TREATMENT was a three-week intensive
workshop on cognitive behavioural therapy. I attended every
session and did every assignment. I learned how my thoughts
precede my feelings and how my thoughts created the feelings I
was experiencing. I learned that even if I felt the feeling first, it was
preceded by a thought, and I needed to pause and break down that
thought to halt the feeling of anxiety or sadness or guilt or whatever
it was. It made perfect sense on paper, and I worked hard as I really
wanted to feel well. I desperately wanted to experience, once again,
the feeling I had the day I got all my groceries. I needed that feeling
once more. And if I had it once, I must be able to find it again.

In our classes, we would study the thought from back to front,
break it down, examine what about it was true or untrue. If there
was truth in the thought, which was rare, did it warrant that level
of reaction that we were providing? The process was exhausting. In
one session, I shared with the instructor that I had at least a million
thoughts per minute. My mind always raced and to break down
each of those thoughts was time-consuming and overwhelming. She
stated that I was to choose the reoccurring thoughts. I tried that
but there were so many of those! While I worked my way through
what I could, the memory of that well feeling motivated me. My

mind argued with itself every moment of every day. I tried to address and interrupt every negative feeling. They had to be argued, debated, and defeated. My brain became a constant battleground. I was completely exhausted by this work but I committed to it. The instructor promised, with practice, it would become natural and easier. But for me, it never did, which of course, meant I wasn't strong enough, which created a long argument in my head about how I was strong. Listing points to prove it as another part of my mind debated those points would go on for hours. I felt crazier than I had before cognitive behavioural therapy.

For the next several months, I focused exclusively on my work, my children, and my wellness. Every evening and on the weekends that I was alone, I would spend hours journaling the endless arguments in my dysfunctional brain.

28.

M Y CHILDREN CONTINUED TO SEE their friends from our old neighbourhood as well as made new ones in our new surroundings. They seemed to be adjusting well. My oldest son was very close friends with a boy from our prior location, and they would go back and forth to each other's homes for sleepovers about once a month. Susan and I, the moms, did the exchanges, and although we weren't friends and had little in common, we would spend a few moments chatting at every drop-off and pick-up.

After one such sleepover, Josh, the little boy's father, came to get him instead of his mother. I hadn't seen this man in at least two years, maybe more, and to be honest, Susan was such a strong presence in the neighbourhood I am not sure I really noticed or spent time with Josh at all. He was pretty much a stranger to me, and on this occasion, a stranger that looked like hell. His clothes seemed big on him, so I assumed he had lost weight. He hadn't shaved in a while, and frankly, looked ill. I asked what was wrong, and he stated that he and his wife had split up and that she had already moved on with his best friend. He was completely devastated. Having walked that path a couple of years earlier and knowing how it felt, I offered a coffee and an ear. We chatted for over an hour as he smoked and drank coffee at my table. This was a very broken man and my heart went out to him.

Soon he was often visiting for a coffee and a chat. I had quit smoking as part of my back to wellness plan, but as we coffee'ed together and shared our lives, I would smoke one or two of his cigarettes. The visits were always quite quick, and he usually would pop in over his lunch hour or after work before he picked his children up from school or daycare.

We had been having coffee for several months when Josh asked me out to dinner. I was very hesitant at first. I was doing quite well and wasn't sure I wanted to enter a relationship, but I had been on my own for a while and was often lonely. Josh and I had so much in common and had become very good friends, so I decided it couldn't hurt. We decided to go to dinner one Friday evening when my ex-husband had my children and Josh's ex had his.

We had an amazing evening together. Josh had an incredible sense of humour and we laughed heartily together. It felt so good to laugh again. We talked well into the night and spent time holding each other, feeling warmth and companionship that I hadn't realized how much I missed. I shared how I had been through a lot, as he had, and told him to be sure he was ready to step into this. I told him I didn't want to risk being hurt again, and if he wasn't ready, that was OK since I wasn't planning on going anywhere. I asked him to please not play with my heart. He stated he had been thinking of me for a long time, wanted a relationship with me, and was more than ready. He swore he wouldn't hurt me.

We spent the night together and I felt a warmth and happiness I had long forgotten existed.

He drove me home with a promise that he would stop by for a hug and a kiss later in the day as he "never wanted to go one day without that from now on." I felt good, happy, warm, and cared for. I had worked hard on my wellness and I felt ready for this next step.

Within minutes of entering my home, my phone rang, and

I knew it was Josh telling me he missed me already. I lifted the receiver with a smile on my face and before I could even say hello, I heard screaming and yelling. From the other end of the line came a shrill, profane, accusatory monologue, and it took me a few minutes to realize that this was not a wrong number. This was Susan. She didn't identify herself, but I was able to piece together who it was as I interpreted the words between the profanity. Basically, Susan saw Josh driving me home, knew we had spent the night together, and proceeded to question my moral fibre using an expansive vocabulary of four letters words. She also informed me, continuing to use an impressive selection of profanity, that Josh belonged to her, and I would no longer be spending time with him.

I was dumbfounded. Josh had told me a completely different story. At a few points in her rant, I tried to interject, to tell her I didn't realize they were still working on their relationship or whatever was happening, but she wasn't in the frame of mind to hear me and hung up on me instead. I was too shocked to even be pissed off. I immediately tried to call Josh on his cell. No answer. I tried several more times. No answer. Then I got angry, but that was soon overshadowed with worry.

I had shared with Josh how I had been played for a fool by Frank and never wanted that to happen again. I shared that my body, my person, was sacred to me. I wasn't a person capable of spending casual evenings with people. I had two partners in my life, before Josh, and I thought he understood that being with him was a huge step for me, a step of trust based on our months of friendship and understanding we were working toward something concrete and meaningful.

I tried to calm myself and, as my therapy had taught me, not assume things or create scenarios I didn't know to be true. I reminded myself that Josh had told me last night all about how his wife and his best friend were heavily involved and talking about moving in together. I reminded myself that just because she had told me something didn't make it true. I worked through my cognitive behavioural therapy training, journaling every step so I could continue to refer to it when my mind started racing again. I tried to turn my attention to a sewing project but spent much of that day re-reading my journaling to reinforce what I knew and didn't know and to keep my reactions in check.

At three o'clock, Josh arrived at my home just as promised. "See!" I told myself. "All the things you convinced yourself of, again, not true." I breathed a sigh of relief, ran out of the house, and threw my arms around him. I tried to kiss him but he turned his head.

All my alarm bells went off.

He came in, sat down at my table, and lit a cigarette. I poured him a coffee and sat across from him. I grabbed one of his cigarettes. I just knew I was going to need it.

He didn't speak, so I did. I told him Susan had called and basically lost her mind on me the second I walked through the door in the morning.

He was staring at the floor.

"Yeah, about that ..." Josh started, never lifting his eyes from the floor. "She says she wants to get back together and so I can't see you anymore."

"What the fuck?" I yelled. "You promised you wouldn't do this to me!"

"I know," he said softly. "I had no idea. She said she didn't realize how much she loved me until she saw us together, and she wants to put our family back together for the sake of our children." He paused. "I have to try."

I felt the tears roll down my face. Sadly, horribly, on some level, I understood. And I hated myself for understanding. I wanted to hit him and yell at him for bringing me into his mess. But I knew he wasn't a vindictive man. He was a kind man who loved his kids and wanted his life back. Hadn't I been there once?

He stood to leave. He reached for his cigarettes and I grabbed them before he could touch them. The fucker owed me that. He finally met my eyes and I saw tears in his.

"I'm sorry," he said softly and left.

I looked down at the cigarettes I held. I guess Susan was right. I was a whore, my services paid for with a half pack of cigarettes. I started to cry. How could I have judged this situation so badly?

I tried to work through my feelings with my therapy practices. I tried to go back to where I was before the whole stupid Josh situation. I tried to forget it ever happened but that didn't work. And on top of that, I missed my friend. His popping over in the middle of the day made my day, and now that was gone too. I was sadder and lonelier than I had been before, and it sucked.

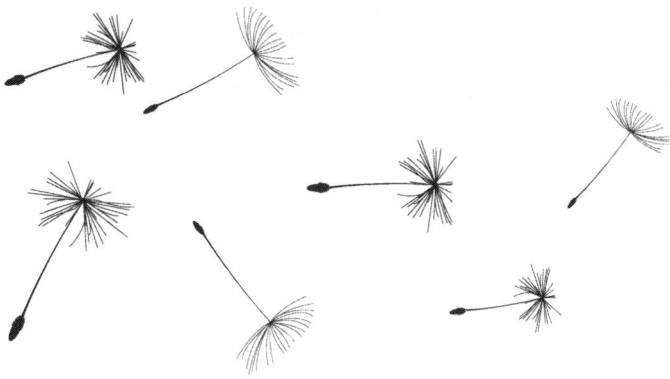

29.

A FEW MONTHS LATER, I WAS in a car accident. I was rear-ended and suffered a back and hip injury. Insurance made me go for an injury assessment, and it was determined I was not able to teach fitness classes for a time. I tried to reason with them. I needed the money from teaching those classes. I had four children who relied on me; I needed to provide. When I refused to quit teaching fitness classes, the physiotherapy clinic called my employer and informed them I was not cleared to work. My employer had no choice and terminated my contract. I was unemployed.

I was never truly free from depression or anxiety, even though I was medicated and doing what I was supposed to do. I always felt like I was walking a tightrope, and anything could tip me right back into the darkness. The medication certainly helped, but I was never completely free of symptoms and knew I never would be. I had struggled after the Josh situation and was just getting my feet back under me when the after-effects of the car accident knocked me flat. The darkness was always present, lingering, waiting for a chance to make itself known once more, and this was its window. I tried to use all my cognitive behavioural training, but I couldn't seem to get rid of the negative feelings and I slowly slid into depression. I was in pain, in physical therapy, had no job, had no partner, and felt worthless. I had fought so hard for a semblance of wellness and here I was again. I had done all the things the professionals told me to do but I wasn't better. I had moments of stability but I wasn't well. Would I ever be? Why couldn't I handle life? Would I ever be able to? Would I always be on the edge of falling apart such that any little thing would push me over? Is that what my life was all about? Was this my future? Moments of stability punctuated by illness brought on by things every other person seemed to manage?

As I slid deeper, I put the familiar outfit of depression back on. It was comfortable. I knew this life, and I lived it once again. More functional than before as I was still able to go to therapy, get groceries, take care of my children, have friends. But underneath it all was the sick little girl, watching and waiting for everything to fall apart. Racing thoughts, sleepless nights, waking up running through my house, excessive fatigue … It was so normal and so easy to fall back into. And I knew then that wellness was the illusion, the sickness was real, and that was my life.

I became numb, complacent, not caring as I slipped back into the familiar darkness and was comfortable to remain there. This was the perfect shade of grey, somewhere between that brief moment of happiness all those years ago and needing to go to the hospital. I could maintain this shade, care for my children, and when they were grown and didn't need me anymore, I could just fade away.

My psychiatrist had long since discharged me into the hands of my family doctor, who continued to prescribe my monthly fluoxetine. The emergency room psychiatrist who treated me during my break had agreed with that treatment plan. I had long finished my counselling sessions. Many others were waiting in the cue for both types of interventions and my time was completed. Our health care system had few affordable supports for my illness, and I was now deemed functional enough to move on in my care. Others needed those supports now.

I lived this way for a long time.

I continued my physiotherapy and took in as much sewing as I could. At some point throughout my therapy, it was determined that there was no assurance I would ever teach fitness again. It became clear that a job like mine wasn't suitable for a single mother who had to support people who relied on her income. It was too unstable, and as I was now experiencing, could vanish in a moment. I decided I needed to find something more permanent. Government insurance, after months of physiotherapy and several more assessments, told me they would pay the equivalent of two university or technical school classes per semester to retrain me since my previous career was no longer an option.

I felt exhausted and defeated but knew I had a responsibility to my children. I knew I was solely responsible for my situation, and I had no choice but to do something about it. I also recognized this insurance offer as a true gift, and I wasn't going to waste it. So I summoned what little energy I had and did what I needed to do.

I set appointments with career counsellors at my local university and technology school to see what my options were. After going through my counselling and my mental health diagnosis, I thought psychology was an area I would like to pursue, but I found out that the only way a person could earn a living in that area was to get their degree with Honours followed by a Masters. I knew I was nowhere near smart enough to do that and didn't have that amount of time to invest in that lengthy of an education, so that was off the table. I needed something that I could complete in a short amount of time and that would pay decently to achieve some sort of stability for my children. Those were the top criteria with interest falling much lower on that list. Then I had a brainwave. I went to those who managed the fitness facility I had been teaching at and asked what their education was. Kinesiology. Done. I spoke to my counsellor at the university. She was able to transfer some of my credits from my first university experience and soon I was starting classes. I began with three per semester since that was considered full-time and that was the only way I was eligible for student loans. I hoped I would be able to manage. I still needed to take in sewing and was looking for other part-time work I could do around parenting four children who were now ages five, seven, nine, and eleven.

Luckily, I knew I could still count on my ex-husband on two fronts. One, he was faultless in his child support payments to me. I still needed my insurance to pay for my two classes per semester, my sewing income, and my large student loans to barely get by, but without the child support for the children, it would have been impossible for me to return to school. Secondly, he always took the children every second weekend so I could pound out my classwork and work on my sewing.

As I became absorbed with my classwork and overwhelmingly busy, I forgot about the darkness temporarily. Sometimes, not always, but sometimes, if I was very distracted with something, I would be able to push it aside, corner it, make it recede. And this, thank God, was one of those times.

I enjoyed my psychology class the most, and my final assignment, worth forty percent of my grade, achieved a mark of a hundred percent and was shared among the faculty. I simply shared a portion of my life, how my husband and I co-parented during divorce, and I was asked if my assignment could be used in further teaching. I was honoured.

One thing my ex-husband and I have always had in common is that our children were and are the most important things in our lives. Even though we couldn't make it as partners, we worked together well as co-parents. Early in our separation, we realized that our children weren't receiving one-on-one time with us. When we were together, this was easier, unplanned, and just happened naturally. But living separately, we now needed to create this valuable time. We set up a system of special days where every Wednesday, one of us had one child and the other had three. This was rotated between all children and both parents, so essentially, each child had one day a month with one parent all on their own. That day the child whose special day it was chose whatever they wanted to do with the parent they were alone with. The variety of things each child came up with was fascinating and exciting, and for me, really helped me get to know each child as an individual.

The psychology professors at the university felt this was "important for individual development" and gave several comments to that effect as they passed my paper around. For my children's father and myself, we simply enjoyed getting to know how very diverse our four children were, how special and wonderful each was as an individual, and both of us believe that this small system did help our children manage life with divorced parents.

30.

DURING MY FIRST SEMESTER AT university, thirteen years after my last trip through such an institution, I was also managing the finalities of my divorce. Divorce had never been an option for me, and I never in a million years believed I would be a divorced person. The guilt weighed heavily on me, and I took full responsibility for where we found ourselves.

My ex-husband was loved and deeply respected by my family, and they were terribly disappointed in me, my behaviour, and my choices. One of my aunts, the one who held the bible study so long ago, phoned me to tell me how disgusted she was with me and how she would only associate with my ex-husband from now on as I was a complete disgrace to the family. My parents weren't as vocal, but they were a couple who had stuck together through thick and thin and still remained committed. Although they didn't say so, I knew I had disappointed them. I was the only family member to ever divorce and I felt like a failure. I knew they loved me, they had taken me to their home during my break, but they didn't understand or even support my choices. And I couldn't disagree with any of them. I knew they were right and I felt sick, ruminating day and night, thinking about the damage I had done to my children, my ex-husband, my family, and myself. I didn't even understand my choices, so how could I expect anyone else to? I knew what I had done couldn't be undone and I had to live with it.

During that first semester, Josh started calling again. He apologized to me for his behaviour months prior. He said it had been too soon after his separation, and he wasn't thinking straight when we first tried dating. I could relate to that. He told me that his ex-wife had never left her boyfriend, and they had never gotten back together again. He said they were all just confused and filled with feelings and it was now completely over. As he spoke, I recalled my frantic, insane calls in the middle of the night to my ex-husband's brother's home, and I understood fully how one could do crazy things at these times. I still enjoyed Josh's company and we started slowly, safely dating. We didn't spend a lot of time together as I was in university, working, taking care of my children, and very busy with life. But we did make time every two weeks or so to go out and do something fun together. I remembered once again how he made me laugh and I enjoyed that laughter.

Late in the semester, I received my divorce settlement, and I thought it might be nice to take a short trip somewhere for a weekend when I completed all my exams. I had never done something like that and thought it might be a nice break for me. It was unfathomable that I could do this alone. I couldn't do anything alone. With medication, cognitive behavioural therapy, and all the treatment in the world, alone was still not an option for me. So I invited Josh to come with me, all expenses on me. We chose the West Edmonton Mall for our stay and decided to go all out and get a theme room in the attached hotel.

I checked with my ex-husband, and he was OK with taking the children earlier than usual for the weekend, so Josh and I flew out right after my last exam my first semester. I felt happy. It was a strange feeling, but a nice one. We spent the weekend exploring all the activities the mall had to offer, and there were many. I can recall a very specific moment very clearly to this day. I was standing in front of a kiosk that sold cinnamon buns, holding Josh's hand, and a feeling of complete peace descended over me. It was real, palpable, and something I had never felt before in my entire life. I was completely free from the darkness. It wasn't lurking, it was gone. There was not one negative thought in my head. It was brief and momentous. It was overwhelming and filled me with warmth. I felt tears well in my eyes. I felt whole. Maybe this is what life could be? Maybe the therapy was finally working? Maybe it had finally become more natural to wrestle my mind as the cognitive behavioural therapy people promised it would. Or maybe it was Josh. Something about Josh brought me peace. I think I had fallen in love. I knew I must keep this feeling and savour it.

We had so much fun that weekend, both of us enjoying each other and saying over and over how nice it was. As we packed to go home, I was excited to see my children but also hopeful for the future. Maybe the listless sadness and sickness were finally at bay. Maybe Medicated Nikki just needed the right person and I believed I had found him.

We left our bags at the front desk and checked out. We had time before we needed to leave for the airport and decided to wander the mall a bit and grab a quick breakfast. We decided on the cinnamon bun place in the food court, the place where I had experienced my magical moment. It felt like the perfect ending to the perfect weekend.

As we sat with our coffee and treats, I was chatty and happy, but Josh seemed more serious than usual. I paused my joyful monologue and asked if he was OK. He said no.

"I have been thinking all weekend about Susan."

I was stunned, completely speechless.

He went on to say that he, Susan, and their family had visited this mall a few years prior, and all he could think about all weekend were the happy times they had shared. Everything reminded him of Susan, he said, and he needed to try to put his family back together. He told me he realized how much he loved her, and the entire weekend had shown him what he needed to do. He said as soon as we got home, he was going to ask her to give their marriage another chance.

My vision blurred. He disappeared. I couldn't see anything. I was shaking violently and I wasn't able to breathe. I was sure I was having a heart attack. My body went tingly then numb. I couldn't think. "Get away! Get away! Get away!" I heard a voice screaming. My voice. Inside, not aloud. Screaming. I was running. I stumbled. "GET AWAY!" I tried to get up but my legs were numb. These weren't conscious thoughts. These were "knowings." I couldn't see, I couldn't breathe, I had to get away. My legs didn't seem to be working. My thoughts had stopped. I felt only terror. Terror from inside and out. And I knew I was dying.

Then I was in the lobby, sitting on a soft chair with my bag in front of me. I had no feeling. I was aware I was exhausted. I noticed the hotel front desk. Faces looking at me. Worried. Judging. But I felt nothing. It was like watching TV. I was removed. I noticed but didn't care. Nothing was entering me. I was dead.

Then someone was taking me to the ladies' room. I looked in the mirror. The face that I knew was mine was swollen and blotchy. It didn't impact me. I just noticed it. That face had been crying. I used the facilities as instructed and returned to my chair in the lobby.

Soon we were in a cab. Then the airport. Then on the plane. After lift-off, I heard someone speaking my name. The receptionist from my doctor's office was speaking to me. I was confused. How was she here? I felt I awoke and realized I was on an airplane heading home, and she was telling me she had just visited her grandchildren in Edmonton. I tried to respond normally, now fully aware that I looked like shit.

After this brief chat that dragged me out of my internal self, my thoughts returned. What Josh said came rushing back to me. I felt the tears slowly rolling down my face. I was destroyed. I couldn't imagine how this had happened. Hadn't I seen and felt what he had? Weren't we having the same weekend, the same experience? I watched him smile and laugh and hold my hand and hug me. We were a happy couple. Clerks had commented on what a cute couple we were. I had felt peace and safety with him. Could I have been this wrong? We were intimate, loving, and tender with each other. We talked about the future. Or did we? My mind was racing. What was real? What was sickness? What shade on the continuum was this? Was he the biggest fucking asshole on Earth? That wasn't my experience with him up to that point. So was I the biggest fucking idiot on Earth? My mind was out of control. My thoughts were racing. I tried my cognitive behavioural therapy but nothing made sense. In every scenario, I was wrong and I was the idiot. Either I misjudged a human terribly, or I was so needy for companionship that I made something out of nothing, or, and the worst option by far, I had no concept of reality and what was really going on. That's what happened when I had my break; was it happening again?

We landed and took separate cabs to our individual homes. Later that night, Josh called to see how I was doing, which led me to believe that my latter two analyses of the situation were likely the correct choices. Either I had broken from reality completely again or I had made something out of nothing in my head and created a whole thing inside that wasn't real. I had done this with the demon in the apartment in the first small town my husband and I lived in. I had found this out in therapy that I had the ability to create huge imaginings in my head and fully believe them to be true. So, essentially, I was once again level crazy and delusional on the continuum. Shade—completely insane. Would life ever be easy? I thought not.

I called my family doctor and booked an appointment. I explained what had happened and she upped my medication.

I increased the dose as required and was able to celebrate Christmas with my family and keep a smile on my face throughout. I knew I would never be well. I knew I would never know what was real or imagined. I knew I would never have a normal life. But I also recognized that with the increased medication, I could fake it more easily.

31.

BY JANUARY, THE NEW LEVEL of medication was in full effect. It took six weeks of misery every time I upped my medication to be free from the side effects, and I was once again feeling better. I had left Josh in the past and was now attending five full-time classes that semester. I had achieved an over eighty-five percent average in the three classes from last semester, ninety-eight percent in the psychology class alone. My physiotherapy from the car accident was also completed, freeing up some time each week. It was a heavy load with my part-time work, but I felt well and strong once again and was ready for the challenge.

At the end of January, Josh called. He asked how I was doing and I shared I was doing quite well. Out of politeness, I asked how he was doing. He told me that when he called Susan after our trip, she had told him that she would get back together with him if her new boyfriend did not propose to her at Christmas. Ridiculous, I thought. Who would let themselves be played like that? Oh right ... That was something I would do.

Apparently, shockingly, Susan's boyfriend, Josh's best friend, had not proposed to her. She had used Josh's wanting her back as a leverage tool and it had backfired. She never had any intention of working things out with Josh and they never did reunite. I'm not proud of it, but it made me happy that he got played. Join the club, Josh! But I was still the winner of the Loser Club since I had provided an all-expenses-paid trip while I was being played.

We didn't communicate for a month or so after that. The next contact was initiated by me. I was working through an assignment on Baby/Child Development and markers, and we were asked, if able, to find a child between newborn and four years of age to work with as part of a lab assignment. My children were all over that age, but Josh had a daughter who was three. I called and asked if he would communicate with Susan to get permission for me to meet with either of them and their daughter and work through the lab questions. He spoke with Susan, and they agreed he could bring their daughter and I completed the lab.

I completed that semester again on the Dean's Honour Roll with an average of over ninety percent in all my class and lab work. I immediately enrolled in summer classes, needing to attain my degree as soon as I possibly could.

I must share with you, my reader, I am not a brilliant human. I am a stubborn human and an exceedingly cheap human, especially when barely making ends meet. I was feeding my children what I could on a very limited budget and often didn't eat myself to just be able to get food into their mouths. In fact, I recall not so long before this writing, my daughter at the age of thirty years, asking, "You were hungry when we went to the restaurant weren't you, Mom?" I took my kids once a month to their favourite fast-food place to try to give them something fun and to normalize their lives in keeping with their classmates and friends, and I never ate as I just didn't have the money. They would ask and I would always answer that I just wasn't hungry, even though my stomach rumbled. Tears sprung to my eyes; she didn't know then but she knew now, being a mother herself, what I was going through. I could only nod that, yes, I had been hungry. The point being, dear reader, my mindset was that when I paid four hundred and fifty dollars a class,

I was determined to get four hundred and fifty-one dollars worth of information. I was able to get scholarships and bursaries with good marks, and that helped very much and was desperately needed.

And Josh was also calling more and more frequently to chat after I opened that door again.

Part of me could understand what he had gone through, having those memories in Edmonton with Susan and their children. I also learned, seeing the doctor when we got home, that I was not on the correct dosage of medication at the time, therefore, I couldn't trust my interpretation of the events. I wasn't on the well end of the continuum, so how could my assessment of the weekend be trusted? What if I was indeed imagining all the joy and happiness? It seemed I had been, and I judged him based on my perspective. I had come to understand my perspective was not trustworthy.

32.

I N THE FALL OF THAT year, as I began my full-time classes once
again, I was approached by a newer professor to be his Teaching
Assistant. I was elated! I admired his work very much, had taken a
few classes from him prior, and I was being asked to be a Teaching
Assistant at the University! I was blown away. I took a moment to
reflect on how far I had come since that apartment in that small
town when I was certain a demon hounded me. I now understood
that was my illness. I still struggled to determine what was illness
and what wasn't. Where did things in life fit on the continuum?
What shade were things? That demon had seemed real to me and
yet it wasn't. Josh and I falling in love seemed real to me and yet it
wasn't. I was constantly trying to navigate where things and events
in my life fell: what was the shade of well; what was the shade of
sick? When I was ill, I never questioned it; everything was real.
Now that I was getting well, everything was questioned. What was
real? What was illness?

I continued with my heavy class load, at one point getting
special permission from the Dean to take more classes than were
allowed per semester. I was driven to graduate, find a job, and
provide for my children. I made the choice to be a single mother. I
robbed them of stability, and the sooner I could begin working and

provide better food and a better life for them, the sooner I would feel better about myself.

And I was once again dating Josh.

I worked hard over the remaining years at university, taking on as many classes as a teaching assistant as I could and continuing with sewing. I completed my classwork in December, a full semester ahead of schedule, and secured employment as a Recreation Therapist, beginning the job the Monday after I wrote my last exam. It was an exciting time, a time of accomplishment and gratitude. I was grateful I had been able to get student loans. I was grateful my ex-husband had supported me by taking the children every second weekend and Wednesdays for special days. I felt accomplished. I had completed something and I was feeling good. The darkness, the sadness, lived inside of me still and I could easily see it, but I was able, for the most part, to keep it at bay, during the day at least. The night was different. It would always come out in my sleep and I still often found myself running when I woke. I never left my home during these nightmares; at least, I don't think I did. When I woke, I was always in my home, thank goodness. Sleep was a luxury I didn't get to have most of the time. But I lived on coffee and cigarettes and I had graduated!

In May, I convocated as the top graduate in my faculty and was nominated for the University President's Medal. I had worked so hard for this day! My parents attended the ceremony as did Josh and we had a celebratory dinner at an amazing restaurant afterward. My job was going well, the darkness was staying at bay during the day, I was taking my medication as instructed, and felt I had turned a corner.

A week after my convocation, Josh and I were chatting on the phone as we did almost every night. Our schedules were so busy we only were able to see each other every second week or so, but we did chat as often as we could. This time, Josh sounded odd, strained on the phone. I asked if he was struggling at work? With the kids? What was up?

Well, three times is the charm. He told me, once again, he was having conflicted feelings and wanted to step back and reassess his feelings for Susan. He stated that he loved me and was pretty sure that he wanted to move on with me but had to be sure he closed all doors on that part of his life, so he wanted to talk with Susan one last time to see if they could make it work and resurrect his family. I hung up the phone. I was done. I had enough strength now with my medication at an appropriate level to know that a man who dated a person for years and then wanted to get back together with his ex-wife was not a man ready for a relationship. This time, I didn't doubt myself or my wellness. I felt sure my decision to hang up that phone and not to answer the endless ensuing calls from him was a decision from the wellness end of the continuum.

Still, I was sad. I cried lots, paced, slept poorly, and had endless arguments with myself in my head as to how I could have been so stupid over and over with this man. He had literally dumped me three times for the same woman. It was outrageous! But what if it was me who was wrong? Could I be sure that he was the villain? What if I saw only what I wanted to see, heard only what I wanted to hear? But what kind of asshole does this? What kind of spineless woman tolerates it? Every thought like this, I argued internally, employing the cognitive behavioural therapy techniques I had learned.

Every single thought solicited an extensive argument. It was an exhausting time for me. My mind worked over and over, hours and hours, with hundreds of thoughts a day needing attention. Add into this mess endless phone messages from Josh and me coming home from work often to find bouquets of flowers or gifts in my home (he had a key from when we dated). I read none of the cards and deleted all the phone messages without listening. I didn't want to add further confusion to my brain, it was difficult enough as it was.

During this whole time, I continued to parent my children well and work hard at my new job, but I was brutally exhausted all the time. Trying to stay well was the hardest thing I had ever done. Should it be this hard all the time? Every bump? Often, I thought it would just be easier to go to sleep for a long, long time and not have to argue with my mind day in and day out. I wanted to rest and not have to wake every day and fight to feel well. But this was my life and I needed to remember I was better than I had been prior. So every single day, I put one foot in front of the other … One day at a time … Sometimes one minute, one thought at a time. Wellness was exhausting work. I felt very little joy in wellness which seemed completely at odds with the entire goal.

33.

OUT OF THE BLUE, FRANK walked through the door. Literally. I hadn't seen him in years and there he was, on my doorstep. He knocked and walked right in as if no time had passed.

"Want to go for ice cream?" he said.

That day, I had deleted four phone messages from Josh and torn up two cards without reading them. It was Friday evening and the kids were at their father's. I had worked a full day and was exhausted, but frankly, also terribly lonely. So, something in me grabbed my purse without a word and followed him out my door. I wasn't even thinking. I was so done with thinking.

Over the next months, it became clear that he wanted another chance at our relationship. He had an explanation for his past behaviour: he was desperately in love with me but didn't think he could manage four children. He'd had unfinished business with a past lover and had needed to work that out. What the fuck was with this seemingly global obsession with exes? He said it was fear, but he had addressed those fears and had come to terms with them, and now wanted me and my children in his life. I listened, considered, and said I would ponder his request. All the while, relentless Josh was still providing the yearly income for some local florist.

One of the things my counsellor from years ago had advised me to do was journal my thoughts and feelings and see if that helped in my wellness journey. Off and on since then, I had done so, and for the most part, I found I just puked a lot of anger on the page and I just wasn't comfortable with that. I preferred to keep my anger tightly wrapped within and keep it well-hidden. With the medication, I was often able to quell that angry feeling as it arose. Not always, but for the most part, I could swallow it and behave in a way I still believed to be correct. Medication hadn't changed my belief system; it had just allowed me to live it more easily.

This was one of the times in my life that I decided to journal. And as I wrote, I noticed I was developing strong feelings for Frank, and I was enjoying his company very much apart from any discussion about parenting. We disagreed completely on how to raise and discipline children. My favourite past move was to ignore the things that didn't align with my beliefs and walk deeper and deeper into the relationship. But this time, I was writing everything down, including the things I didn't agree with like how he would discipline a child this way or that way for certain behaviours. How he would use corporal punishment on all children when he decided it was needed, the complete opposite of my views. Often, when I shared what one child had done and how I had handled it, he would say, "That was the wrong thing to do, you should have done this," inserting whatever the punishment he believed was warranted instead of the discussion method I had used.

It nagged at me. It unsettled me. I was more jaded than I had been in the past and I didn't place my rose-coloured love glasses on as quickly as I once would have.

One evening, when I was at Frank's home, we were barbecuing and chatting about nothing in particular when, for no reason whatsoever, I knew I had to leave immediately. My body was filled with tension and fear. It wasn't a panic attack, as I had come to learn. This was not the familiar out-of-control terror that took me over. This was anxiety with a reason. It had purpose. I didn't understand it but I absolutely had to get to my house. I had to leave that instant; there was no question. Something was terribly wrong.

Frank tried to reason with me to just stay for supper since the steaks were about to come off the grill. I couldn't. I grabbed my keys and left. I had to get home immediately. I had no choice.

I drove as fast as I safely could. I burst into my home. No one was there. I knew the kids were with their father, so I immediately called him to make sure everything was OK. He stated everything was fine. But something wasn't fine and I knew it in my core.

The phone rang right after I hung up and I grabbed it, knowing something was wrong.

It was Josh.

I hadn't even checked the caller ID as I was so certain the call would be about my children.

"Don't hang up!" he begged. "Please, just listen to me. Just let me say what I need to. Please."

Was this important? Was this the reason I had to get home? I paused. I didn't hang up.

"What?" I said. I felt so rattled still, my mind racing, trying to figure out why I needed to leave Frank's in such a rush. My body had moved on its own; my mind had screamed at me to get home.

"I need to see you, it's very important, extremely! Can I come over?" His words were rushed. He sounded like I felt: anxious and terrified.

I wasn't able to think clearly, still feeling an unspoken need that had forced me to bolt from Frank's. I was having trouble breathing effectively. I was having trouble forming thoughts. I felt fear, but different from my other panic attacks. This was about something specific that I couldn't articulate, and that somehow made it worse, and I knew I had to figure it out.

"OK," I said, not really thinking, and hung up. I just wanted off the phone so I could try to process what was happening.

I couldn't sit. I paced, searched my entire house, tried to think.

Why? Why did I need to get here? As far as panic attacks went, this one was mild. I was able to drive, able to think. I hadn't lost vision and was aware of where I was at all times. But the purpose behind it? I needed to figure that out. It was somehow critical. That I knew for certain.

Josh arrived and I let him in. The first thing I did was ask for a cigarette. I had quit again after Josh, but for tonight I was done quitting. I lit the cigarette, grabbed a saucer to use as an ashtray, and walked to my living room. Josh followed. As I inhaled deeply, drawing the smoke into my lungs, I felt the anxiety begin to fade. I felt the remnants, the adrenaline in my body, dissipating. It seemed to align its departure with the lighting of the cigarette. "What a completely insane thing to think," I mentally chastised myself. But I pushed the thought aside. I was here, smoking, feeling calmer, and apparently, Josh had something to say. I would listen to him for as long as I had to, get him out of my house, and then journal about the situation and try to understand what the hell had actually happened.

He sat across from me and tried to take my hands but I wouldn't allow it.

He talked for several minutes straight, stumbling, trying to get words out. He cried.

The gist was that he apparently just wanted time to think and make certain that he was sure how he wanted to move on with his life. He apparently had never asked Susan to reunite. I called bullshit. He told me how he had been unable to get me out of his mind, how he missed me terribly, and how horrible he felt about hurting me. Then he asked me to marry him.

What the actual fuck? Marry him? Was I sick again? Did I need more medication? I behaved rashly at Frank's and now I was hearing complete nonsense. Nothing made sense, and that was usually an indicator that I had slid to the sick end of the continuum without being aware of it.

I lit another one of his cigarettes.

He went on to tell me how we could buy a really nice home together in a safer, upscale neighbourhood and raise our children together. How, together, we could give our children more. He reminded me that not many people would want to be with a woman with four young children or a man with three young children. He reminded me of how much our children liked each other and how my children liked him and his liked me.

I listened as long as I could, again took his pack of cigarettes, ushered him to the door, and stated I would think about his offer and chat with him soon. I mostly wanted him out of my home so I could think.

I locked the door and leaned against it heavily. Was I sick again? None of this evening made sense. I could never trust myself anymore. Often when I thought I was fine, so many times, I hadn't been. Was this one of those times? I hadn't behaved normally when I bolted from Frank's house, that much I knew. Sane people didn't act like that. Then this marriage insanity. Had I really heard that? Had that actually happened? I had experienced things I totally believed to be real before that had never happened. Had I slipped once again? Had Josh even really been here? My God, was I really losing it?

But I had Josh's cigarettes. Or did I? Had I lost track of time, not been fully aware, and stopped at a convenience store on the way home from Frank's? My mind was spinning out of control. Was I falling apart again?

I ran to the living room. I needed some sort of confirmation that I hadn't completely lost it again. I saw five cigarette butts in the saucer. I counted the cigarettes in the package. There were twelve left. I never smoked in my car, and I hadn't smoked twelve cigarettes since I bolted out of Frank's. I hadn't purchased these cigarettes in a random fugue. And I could still faintly smell Josh's cologne. OK. He had been here. I tried to focus on breathing and calm myself. He had been in the house and we had talked. I was sure of that much and needed to get a grip on myself. I used every tool I had to try to control my mind.

Being completely and wholly sick was easier sometimes. Before my diagnosis, I had never questioned myself. I believed completely that every experience I had was real. But that changed when I learned I had this illness. The path to wellness was always questioned. Everything in my life, every experience, every feeling, became suspect. Even with the medication and all the work I had done, I still had regular panic attacks. I still woke up many nights running. I still had bouts of depression and had times when things didn't make sense. Did normal people have these things as well? Was my life now a shade of normal and I just didn't recognize it? Or was it always going to be some shade of sick?

34.

I SAT UP LATE AND SMOKED and journaled. I couldn't make any sense of the evening and let my words flow as they wanted to.

As I wrote, I realized I needed to think more logically about my life and my future. What trajectory was I on? I had somehow fallen in love with Frank and wanted a future with him. But that was a future for me. And I was not just me. I was five people, and I knew that I would never be able to subject my children to a life with him and his parenting style. I knew it would be hell for them and that was not an option for me. I cried as I wrote, knowing that I would never be with Frank since my children were first; they always had been and always would be. Frank and my children would never work. Frank had to go.

And what about Josh? I wrote from the basis that the entire evening played out as I believed it had. I would confirm that later, but if my recollection was accurate, unbelievably, he had made some sense. Together, we could offer a better life for all our children. Somewhere in that night of smoking and journaling, I lost my belief in love and rainbows and butterflies and fairy tales. I actually started to consider his offer, if it had indeed occurred. Josh, in all his wandering pleas, had stumbled onto something that made sense. I was thirty-seven years old, had four children who I was responsible for, who I had cheated out of a stable home life, and maybe this was a chance to make things right for them.

Eventually, I wandered into my bedroom, dropped into bed, and soon fell into a deep sleep. Though I don't often remember my dreams, that night I had a dream so vivid it felt real.

I was with Josh on a dirt bike (a pastime of Frank's, not Josh's). Josh and I drove to Frank's home and Frank came out his front door and saw us. All my children were then somehow on the dirt bike with Josh and I, but it didn't feel crowded. Frank looked at all of us and tears started to flow down his face. He watched as we rode away and slowly turned and walked back into his home. I startled awake and felt physically sick. I knew I had to end things with Frank. I loved him but I could not be with him. The dream was telling me what I had to do. My heart ached. I couldn't go back to sleep. I tried to think of how I could make it work with Frank so we could all be together, but I knew that was impossible. My journaling had shown me, and the dream finalized it.

The next morning, lit cigarette in hand, I called Frank when I knew he would be out of his house. It was a chicken-shit move. I left a message telling him I wouldn't be seeing him again. I knew I loved him and knew he loved me. But I also knew he would be a horrible, even abusive stepfather, and I wasn't going to do that to my kids. I cried for a long time after I made that call. Frank called back after a time and I watched the phone ring. I didn't answer. He left a message. He didn't understand and was terribly hurt. He said he knew I had called when he was gone to avoid telling him directly. He asked me to please call him to discuss it. He said whatever it was, we could work it out. He ended his message stating if I didn't call, he'd know we were done. I never called.

Josh also called a few times and left messages, but I didn't respond. I needed time.

35.

EVENTUALLY, I DECIDED TO CALL Josh and agreed to meet him for lunch. I invited him to bring more cigarettes.

I didn't bring up anything that may or may not have been discussed. I still wasn't completely sure I was sane, so I waited for him to broach the subject. As we ate, he indeed brought up the topic of marriage. He spoke of love and how I made his life complete, how he needed me and wanted me, how wonderful our lives together would be. I cut him off. I wanted to know that he was done with Susan because, no matter what, I wasn't going to deal with that drama further. That was my line in the sand. If we got married, we were committed to each other as a couple who would build a life together. We would base it on friendship and respect and fun and companionship. I was over love. I stated I still wanted a happy marriage and believed I could have one but shared I was no longer in the place of gooey-eyed love like I had been in Edmonton. I'd had that with my first husband right through to the end and still had love for him in my own way. Most importantly, I told Josh that no matter the underlying feelings, I was going to be the number one woman in his life. It was not optional. He assured me I was and asked that I just give him time to prove it.

"We will see," I stated.

I strongly believed in faith, signs, synchronicities, prayer, and guidance, and so I asked God for all of those. This was a huge decision and I prayed fervently for guidance on what to do. Was this the best thing for my children? For me? I begged God for an answer, a sign. I was open and honest with Josh about my prayers and said very clearly that without a sign one way or the other, we were not getting married.

Josh suggested we list our homes and use that as a sign. Several years prior, soon after my divorce, I had tried to sell my home. It had a large mortgage and expenses were very tight. It was on the market for ten months without even a nibble.

"How so?" I asked Josh.

"We each use a realtor of our choice, and if both homes don't sell in a week, that is a sign that we shouldn't get married at this time."

That made a lot of sense to me. I knew my home would not sell in a week and I felt that would be a good test. If God wanted me to marry this man, he would make the impossible happen. I doubted Josh's home would sell in a week either, but his was much more affordable and had a way better chance than mine.

We listed our homes the same day and waited.

His sold twelve hours after listing, and mine sold the next day.

I guessed I had my sign.

36.

THE NEXT FEW MONTHS WERE a blur of activity. We found a beautiful home in a newer area of the city that would house our seven children and us. We were both incredibly busy and I was having fewer symptoms. This illness was so hit and miss. Sometimes, having too much to do helped me focus and pushed the darkness away. Other times, I was so overwhelmed I wanted to stay in bed and not do anything. At this point, the busyness pushed the symptoms aside and I was grateful for that. There was too much to do in a short time to be sick.

I didn't see much of Josh while we were both so busy packing up our respective homes. We had to make sure we set aside time to try to meet for a meal together at least once every second week. During those times, it was all discussing what we needed, planning the move, or shopping for household items.

One evening, when making our plans to meet up, Josh said we needed to fit in ring shopping. He wanted to buy me an engagement ring and "do it right," he told me. I hadn't thought about that as we had been so busy with everything else. I was terribly excited at the thought. This was way more fun than couch shopping. I couldn't wait!

We arranged to go ring shopping three weeks later, with lunch to follow. He asked me to think about what kinds of things I would like in a ring. With the sales of our respective homes and after the purchase of the needed items, we had a little money left and Josh was adamant we spend that on a ring. I barely slept the night before the big day. I was finally missing rest for a fun reason! I had been waiting excitedly for this day since we made the decision to make this purchase together. After all the work, this sounded like so much fun, and after the decision was made and "the sign" received, I had thrown myself wholeheartedly into getting married and moving on with our lives. We had agreed to settle in before the actual wedding day, but ring shopping brought the excitement back front and centre and I was ready.

"Ring shopping day," as it had become known to me, finally arrived. The stores didn't open until 10:00 a.m., so I had time to dawdle over my coffee and pour over a few bridal magazines I had allowed myself to splurge on. I searched for rings that I thought would suit me and be reasonably priced. We had five hundred dollars to spend, a virtual fortune in my mind.

We agreed I would pick Josh up and then head out. I arrived at his home promptly at 9:45 a.m. That was the very longest I could wait to begin this day. I was smiling so wide I felt my face would burst. I was literally vibrating with excitement!

I handed him my keys so he could drive and asked, "Where should we start? A mall? Or just a stand-alone store? What do you think? Oh, and I have some pictures to show you. Isn't this fun?"

He had just opened the driver's door and was standing prepared to get into the car when he turned to answer me.

"Oh, about that."

I was on my way to the passenger side of the car and stopped in my tracks in the middle of his driveway facing the front end of my car.

"Susan didn't get engaged for her birthday, so we won't be able to get engaged or married yet."

I felt heat fill my body. It felt like scorching lava flowing into me, starting at my feet and slowly filling my body from the bottom up. I felt it oozing and bubbling through my every nerve, vein, and artery. I felt every inch of my body on fire. I started to shake. I wasn't cold; I was burning. I wanted to scream, to cry, to run to him and beat him with my fists. But I remained exactly where I was, mute. I focused on the grill of my car. Everything vanished except for the grill. I stared at it intently as everything else faded and the heat boiled in my body. I don't know how long I stared at that grill. It felt like several minutes.

"So let's grab breakfast." I heard from far far away. I remained staring at the grill.

Everything slowly became visible again as it faded back into my reality. First, I saw the headlights of the car. Then the royal blue hood. Then the pavement on the driveway where the car sat. The hedge along the right and the house on the left faded in. I saw Josh sitting in the driver's seat. He was on his phone. I willed my legs to move. They felt like they weighed a hundred pounds each, but I lifted and moved each one toward the passenger side of the car. I got in, sat down, and buckled my seat belt. Then the thought came to me loud and clear.

I WAS FUCKED.

I had messed up again. Our houses were sold, we had bought a new one together, both our names were on it. I had once again acted like a stupid fool and it cost me. So fucking stupid! I couldn't get out of this and he would never be in this. I was trapped by my stupidity. Why couldn't I just be smart? Just for once? Why couldn't I just do one fucking thing right?

We went for breakfast, but I didn't eat. Ring shopping was firmly off the table. He drove himself home, got out, and I got into the driver's seat and drove myself home. Nothing was ever said about what happened. It was clearly nothing to him, which translated to me that clearly, I was nothing to him.

I called my realtor to see if I could undo everything, and he stated it was nearly impossible at this stage. We were two weeks before all the possession dates.

Susan was not out of Josh's life and now she was an even bigger part of mine.

Then the move was on us and everything was in chaos. Since the "no ring shopping day," my panic attacks started increasing. Moving was stressful enough but adding all the layers to this move made it more difficult. I felt trapped. Everything I owned was in the new house. My name was on the mortgage. I had lost trust in Josh. I felt all my reasons for making this move were ridiculous. How could I have fallen for such nonsense! And my sign? Selling my house? What was I? A moron? What sort of idiot would make a decision like marriage based on the real estate market? Oh, wait, what marriage? Turns out I decided on a fictional marriage based on the real estate market! What a complete disaster!

As my anxiety increased, so did my concern for my children. Would they be OK living in the new house? Was this the best thing for them? Would it be too much to share a home with three other kids? My mind raced constantly. Questioning. Arguing. Obsessing. Why had this ever seemed like a good idea? What had I done?

But here I was, and I couldn't get out of it. My kids had a huge adjustment to make, and they needed a mother who at least faked stability. I needed them to believe this was good for us all, that this would make our lives better. So I did all I could to make their transition as easy as possible, at least I hoped I did. I hid my hurt, my panic, my sadness. I often went for long walks to a nearby park and cried. I was so miserable. I felt betrayed, lied to, and hopeless. But I didn't want anyone to see it. This was supposed to be a happy time and I needed everyone around me to believe that it was. So I buried my misery once again. I was slipping back into old habits, slowly sliding backward on the continuum, inching toward a shade of darkness. But of course, I didn't see it at the time. I was doing what I thought was best for us as the insidious darkness that constantly haunted me was winding its way into the fabric of my being once again.

37.

SUSAN WAS A CONSTANT IN our lives.

One day, I came home from work to find my dining room set gone, replaced by Josh's from the basement.

"Where is my table?" I asked.

"Susan said it didn't look good in here. She said mine would look better, so I put yours in the rec room downstairs."

Another day, "Where are my pictures?"

"Susan said that they looked like a kindergarten collage, so I took them down."

It was endless.

He would ask me to leave the room when Susan called. Often, after such a call, he would walk out of the house, tell me Susan needed him, and he would be back when he could. I would feel so angry, so hurt, so valueless. I would smoke and pace and obsess, and when he returned, I would yell and cry and beg—but mostly ask him why he was treating me this way. Why wasn't I good enough? And every time, it was the same answer.

If he didn't do what she told him, she would take his kids away from him.

I would scream and argue and tell him to grow up, grow some balls, tell her to fuck off, and make me the primary woman in his life like he had promised. I would rage and cry. Then I would go numb and ignore him and try to ignore the situation. But every week or two, there was a new Susan drama, and it was wearing me out.

And then one day, journaling pages and pages of what a piece of shit Josh was, it all became clear to me. I finally got it. I knew that Susan wouldn't take the children from Josh because I knew she valued and enjoyed her private time with her boyfriend. But it didn't matter what I knew; it mattered what Josh believed. When I screamed and cried for Josh to put me first, I wasn't asking him to put me before Susan; he heard me asking to be put before his children. Something clicked in my brain and I was able to put myself in his shoes. How would I feel and act if I thought I would lose my children? If I thought they could be taken from my life? I had to admit I would act the same way. My children would always come first, no matter what, so why should he be different? The reason for this move, this whole situation, was because I thought being with Josh would improve my children's lives. So how was I any different from him?

I tried to swallow my pride, to bury my need to feel important to or valued by Josh. I reminded myself that I had made this choice for my children, so who was I to demand more? He had said he loved me, needed me, valued me, all those beautiful words that I had heard and wanted to believe. I pretended it didn't matter to me, but it did. I wanted all that. But when I thought back to all the conversations we had, when he was trying to convince me that this was something we should do together, he also said a lot of other things. He spoke many many times about buying a new home in an upscale, beautiful area. He had mentioned over and over how important and beneficial this would be for our children. Why couldn't that be enough for me? It would be more than enough for most people. Why was I so difficult to please?

I wish I could say that I withdrew my claws, folded up my

anger, and became a rational, calm person. But that would be a lie. I tried and I would manage for about two months at a time, and then I would explode and lose my mind over yet another of Susan's antics.

One instance that riled me was when Susan decided it was a good idea to yell at my oldest son. It was bad enough she was controlling Josh and messing with my life, but I would not tolerate her interference with my children. That was a hard no. She was furious with my son when he drove Josh's daughter to a movie. Instead of discussing the issue with Josh, who had given permission for the whole event, Susan decided to come into our home while I was at work and yell at my son. I told Josh that I was getting a restraining order and that she was not going to be allowed in my home ever again. He begged and pleaded with me not to do that. She would take his children away, he cried. We argued for days. Finally, I relented, but only under certain conditions. I told Josh he had to talk to his ex-wife and make sure she understood that he had given permission for my son to drive their daughter, and then she had to apologize to my son in my presence. And, finally, he had to tell her that she was never allowed in our home again. He promised and swore he would do everything I asked, but I knew all too well about Josh and his promises. She never yelled at or spoke to any of my children again, but she never apologized and was still in my house every time she decided to be.

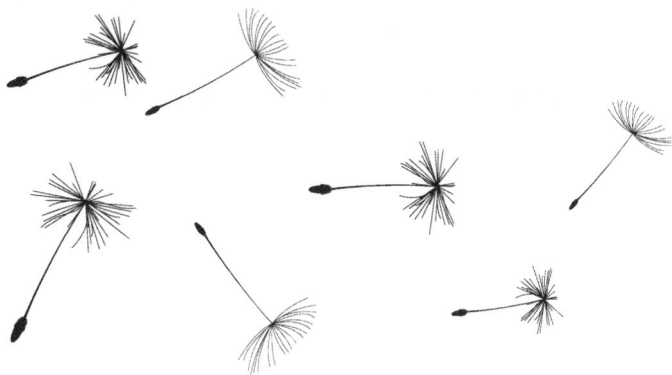

38.

As my children grew into teenagers, they started acting out. My parents said the problem was that they had no stability. I had promised to provide a stable situation for them and I had not done so. I wasn't married and my parents felt that was causing my children emotional harm. I needed to get married or leave since it was such an unhealthy environment, especially for children in their teens. My parents were the most stable people I knew, so I believed them.

I shared my concerns with Josh, shared how I believed my parents were correct, and we had to do something about our situation. By this time, Susan and her boyfriend had built a beautiful new home only blocks from ours and had been living together for a while, so I reasoned that shouldn't have been an issue. But I was wrong. It was an issue. Susan wasn't married so Josh couldn't be married.

I had to leave then, I said. My parents made perfect sense. They were right. If we didn't get married, leaving was my only option. I knew I would have to move my children to a poor, possibly dangerous neighbourhood as that was all I could afford, but if it helped them in the end, that was what I needed to do. I explained this all to Josh. We would have to sell the house and I had to leave.

It was black and white to me; it seemed completely logical and that was what I was going to do.

I think Josh could see I was not bending on the issue. When my parents spoke, it was law to me, and even though I was thirty-nine years old, I wouldn't consider questioning it.

A few weeks later, he took me ring shopping.

We purchased a lovely sapphire and diamond ring, and we shared the cost as per our original agreement. Then we set about planning our wedding. I thought it would be nice to get married on the anniversary of our first date. Seven years had passed, and a lot of shit had gone down in the interim, but I felt that would signify something. Full circle, leaving all the garbage behind, a new beginning, all those lovely sentiments. I told Josh the day I had chosen.

But then there was Susan. Fucking Susan.

The day I wanted to get married just so happened to be the very day that Susan was getting married.

Un-fucking-believable.

I was livid.

I asked Josh when he had learned that Susan was engaged and had set her wedding date. He couldn't remember. I asked if it was before we bought my ring? Possibly, he told me. His mind was foggy. Why did it matter, he asked? Everything was working out perfectly. We were getting married, we both were doing what we needed to do, what was the issue?

I felt the fury filling me. I knew I was going to completely lose control. I had to swallow it. He was right. What was the issue?

"EVERYTHING WAS THE ISSUE!"

I grabbed my keys and ran out of the house. I needed to get away. I jumped in my car and drove. I was sobbing and soon I couldn't see for the tears. I couldn't drive. So I stopped somewhere, nowhere. And I cried. I cried until my body ached. I cried until my cheeks burned. I cried until there were no more tears but my body continued to wretch and spasm. I have no idea how long I sat in the random parking lot I had pulled into. It was light when I left and it had gotten dark. I wasn't even really sure where I was. Eventually, my body stopped jerking and shaking and I was suddenly completely exhausted. I felt nothing except profound fatigue. I wasn't sure I would be able to even lift my arms to hold the wheel and find my way home. It took everything I had to start the car and try to figure out where I was. I drove around until I found a main street I recognized and then found my way home. I considered just sleeping in the car. Moving was so difficult. I made it as far as the deck and dropped to a lawn chair to rest. I didn't think I could go further. I woke up in the chair the next morning.

39.

I DECIDED IT DIDN'T MATTER WHEN we got married. I decided it didn't matter if Josh agreed to marry me after he knew Susan was getting married. Josh was right. Why did I care? We were getting married, my kids would be better, and that was all that I cared about. The sooner, the better. I just wanted to get it over with so life could get easier.

We decided we would fly to Las Vegas, get married, and honeymoon there. We told the children our plan and they were disappointed. They wanted to be at the wedding and that did make sense.

Even though I knew it shouldn't matter when Josh agreed to marry me, and even though I kept telling myself it didn't matter; deep down, it did. I felt listless and uninvolved, and I knew I had to pull myself out of my funk and at least try to make the day something, if for no other reason than for the children. They needed to see that marriage was important and a commitment of significance, and I had already set a bad example in that area. This was a chance to rectify that, so somehow, I needed to engage in the process. We agreed to get married in town and then fly to Vegas for the honeymoon.

I didn't want anything big, so we settled on immediate family only. I found a lovely little venue, and my dad, who stopped farming years prior and had returned to university to become an ordained Lutheran minister, performed the ceremony. He did a beautiful job and his words reminded us that we were responsible for seven people and needed to take that and our vows seriously. Our mothers were our witnesses and our seven offspring looked on.

After the ceremony, we blew bubbles, took pictures, and shared a cake. I had decided to make dresses for all the girls, my daughter and Josh's two, and even made my own dress. The girls all chose the colours for their dresses and mine was a simple, lovely, café au lait cocktail-length gown. We bought the boys new clothing and Josh, who lived in sweats, wore dress pants and a nice new shirt. The whole family looked so nice, and I was glad we had decided to get married this way. I knew I would treasure these pictures, and it was beautiful to have our children with us as we made this commitment. We left for Vegas the next day for our honeymoon.

When we returned home two weeks later, we developed all our pictures from the wedding to make our album.

I was shocked, literally speechless when I looked at our wedding pictures. I didn't recognize myself. I was enormous! I had an ugly, fuzzy perm, was as wide as I was tall, and covered in a beige sack. But worse than that, my expression looked blank. My eyes were dead.

As I tried to maneuver my life with Josh the two years prior to our wedding, as I tried to push down my feelings, as I tried to live as I thought I should, that sneaky, insidious, darkness had wound its way back in and slowly led me down the continuum toward ill. I didn't notice because I had stumbled on a tool to help manage: I ate. Eating somehow kept the darkness away, but only for a short time, so I had to keep eating to keep things in order. Without paying any attention, I managed to gain seventy-five pounds since we moved in together, and I really hadn't noticed. I was numb so much of the time that I assume I bought clothing in increasing sizes without consciously being aware. I made my wedding dress and wasn't even aware of my size then! I was a size two when I met Josh and was a size twenty-four the day we married.

The woman in the wedding pictures wasn't me. It wasn't a person I recognized. It was a miserable shell of a woman I once knew. The woman who had been raising her children on her own, gotten her degree, graduated top in her class, gotten a job right away, and worked hard every day was gone. The woman who had survived a breakdown, survived a car accident, and rose to become better and stronger was gone. And it was my responsibility to find her and bring her back. I hadn't really noticed the slow slide back toward the darkness, but seeing those pictures jolted me. I knew I needed to get medical attention. I knew I was ill again and I knew I was the only one who could fix this.

The doctor pointed out I had gained a lot of weight and said I wasn't taking enough medication because of all that extra weight. He upped my medication yet again and off I went with my new dosage, was miserable for several weeks again while I adjusted, and continued my life as a newlywed.

The kids did not get better after our wedding. In fact, they continued to get worse.

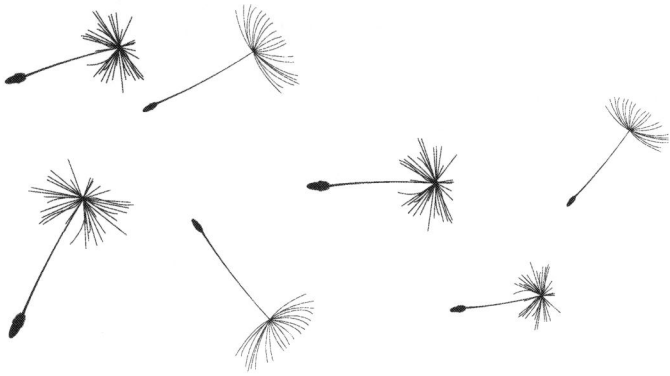

40.

JOSH DECIDED A COUPLE OF years after we were married to buy himself a dog. He brought home an adorable Alaskan Malamute Labrador Retriever cross. Correction. He did not bring the dog home; he brought the dog to my workplace to show me his gift to himself. All the residents in the home I worked in loved the dog. Who wouldn't? It was such an adorable little puppy. But Josh knew how upset I would be because he also knew my second son was terribly allergic to dogs. We had agreed when we moved in together no dogs unless they were hypoallergenic. He brought the dog to my work because he knew I wouldn't yell at him there. But that didn't stop me from unleashing my fury later.

That night after he introduced the new dog at work there was a particularly epic explosion. I asked how he could possibly be so selfish knowing that my child would get sick? As he usually did when I exploded, he ignored me. I felt so enraged and helpless. I wanted him to take the dog back. "No," he simply stated.

I begged.

"No."

I cried.

"No."

I screamed.

"No."

Once again, I felt completely helpless. I didn't know what to do. I hated always feeling so helpless, so out of control of my own life. And I was always so angry. I lived either furious or numb. And it was getting worse.

A week later, my son moved in with his father full-time. His allergies were out of control. He was sick that whole week trying to live with this new puppy. He was living on antihistamines, and why should he have to suffer because his mother was a weak-ass fool who couldn't protect him? I understood his decision completely but was still devastated.

A few months later, my oldest child moved in with his girlfriend's parents. I was losing everything. I needed to do something. I needed to leave. I realized that I made this stupid life-changing decision for the benefit of my children, and it was costing me. I needed to stop being a doormat and take care of myself and my children.

I started looking at possible apartments to rent. It didn't matter what I had invested in the house. It didn't matter that I probably didn't have the money to move. Nothing mattered except fixing the situation I had created.

I had finally had enough.

41.

I WAS IN THE MIDDLE OF an assessment of an elderly woman at work when I was called into the director's office. Two other managers were with her. They indicated a chair for me to sit in.

They slid a paper across the desk. I tried to read the words but I was unable to focus; everything about this situation felt wrong.

The director asked me if I understood. I shook my head no.

She stated that my position was gone. My job had been abolished to create a position for an in-scope care aide position. I didn't follow her words.

Another manager handed me a plastic grocery bag. I saw my degree sticking out of the top of the bag. It registered finally. This was my stuff. I was fired.

I can't remember much of what happened next. I know I was sobbing. I knew I was acting out, not taking this news professionally or correctly. I knew I was making it difficult for those trying to usher me out of the door. But I needed the job to get out of where I was, to get my kids to a place we could all be together again. And the job was gone.

I remember someone pulling my arm as they walked me to the front door. I told them my car was parked out behind the building and it was forty below. I asked them to please let me go through the building as it was a long walk all the way around the building in such frigid temperatures. They said no and pushed me out the front door.

The next thing I remember is being on my friend's doorstep. She let me in and I sobbed in her arms. It never occurred to me to call my husband.

I knew I had to go home and tell everyone I had been fired. I knew this halted any chance of finding a place for me and all my children to live. I was devastated.

I shared the news with the whole family over dinner that night. Josh said he had an idea and called a friend of his who was a lawyer and told him of the situation. We met with his friend the next day and he read the paper they had given me and told us there was nothing we could do. They had done everything correctly. I was simply no longer needed and I was fired. Laid off, they said. But they meant fired.

So I ate. Somehow, eating made me feel better. While I ate, I started applying for jobs.

A few weeks later, Josh's lawyer friend called me and asked me if I could type. I told him yes, I could type over fifty words a minute. He asked if I could help in his office for a couple of weeks. They had just terminated a legal secretary and needed a person to help until they filled the position. I agreed immediately to take on the work while also thinking in the back of my mind, "Terminated … a nice word for fired, like me."

I began work the next Monday and really enjoyed it, even more than the work I had been doing prior. I had zero legal knowledge and misspelled many of the foreign words when listening to the Dictaphone. The lawyers were kind and patient with me and taught me what I needed to know. The other administrative staff were nice to me and invited me on coffee breaks with them. I thought maybe this was work I could enjoy. It paid much less than what I had been making and was only for two weeks, but maybe, it was something

I could pursue. It wouldn't get me into an apartment but it was better than nothing.

Two weeks turned into a month, then two months. I know they were looking for a real legal secretary but also didn't seem so rushed to replace me. That felt nice.

One morning I went to the washroom at work and found things were not right. Something was out of place.

I had been seeing my doctor for several months, by this time, complaining that I didn't feel right. I felt tired. Something was wrong. With each visit he grew more and more frustrated with me. He told me I had to change my lifestyle if I wanted to feel better. He reminded me that I was on the highest dose of fluoxetine I could be, and he said he couldn't give me more medication. He told me I was too heavy. I needed to exercise, eat better, and reduce my stress. He had done blood work and a urine analysis three or four times and said I was physically fine and there was nothing more he could do for me. I could tell I was just a big pain in his ass. In fact, on my last, visit he told me if I came in one more time with the same complaints, he would have to stop seeing me as a patient.

Well, this time, I had a solid complaint and I was going to take it to him.

He examined me and stated that my uterus had prolapsed. Probably due to my excessive weight, he added. He quickly checked off boxes on a form, clearly wanting me out of his office, and sent me for an ultrasound to see if there was something internal that had caused the prolapse. He made sure to remark a second time that it was most likely solely caused by the massive amount of weight I had put on in a few short years but was still best to check.

I was now almost a hundred pounds over my weight from when I was teaching fitness classes. I was already ashamed of what I had done to myself, but to have caused myself injury because of it? I was sickened at my lack of control. I had let my life get completely out of hand. At one time, I had been able to hold on tightly and control things, but I had lost that ability, and with it, all illusion that I would ever get it back. I was simply a mess. A disgusting, mentally ill, obese mess now with a prolapsed uterus.

I had undergone so many ultrasounds in my life, more than I could count, so this was the same old same old for me. I had suffered with my reproductive centre for years, ever since the ovarian cyst had ruptured when I was fifteen years old. I had numerous surgeries and had several other cysts rupture throughout my life. I was in emergency at least twice a year with this issue. I was diagnosed with endometriosis at age fifteen, and then another doctor had told me I had polycystic ovarian disease sometime later. I was told at age seventeen that if I wanted to have a family, I had better do it sooner rather than later and always felt so blessed to have had my four children by the time I was twenty-seven. For years, I had wanted rid of the whole system, so maybe, this prolapsed uterus was my way out of the brutal monthly pain I had endured my whole life. Maybe they would remove it all and throw it in the garbage where I felt it now belonged. I certainly had no use for it any longer.

I put on the gown, got on the bed, and waited for the technician. She came in, asked me what brought me there, and I told her my uterus had prolapsed. She looked confused. She looked at the requisition again and stated that this was not a pelvic ultrasound, the standard I was used to, but an abdominal ultrasound. She showed me the paper from my doctor and the checkmark beside "abdominal." Odd, but OK.

She squirted the gel on my abdomen and then started sliding the wand around. I stared at the ceiling as was my usual during these assessments.

Suddenly, the ceiling tile I was staring at slid open and I was looking across a beautiful blue river. I closed my eyes. I was clearly hallucinating, although, it was the middle of the workday and I'd had nothing stronger than coffee and certainly no medication other than those prescribed to me. I opened my eyes and looked at the tech. Everything seemed normal. I looked up again. Everything was NOT normal. I looked at the tech again. I reached out and touched her arm. She smiled at me and then looked back to her screen. She was real. I looked up again and the beautiful scenery was still in the hole left by the ceiling tile.

I looked back and forth a few more times. Whatever it was, it was staying there. I was awake, lucid, and apparently losing my mind.

I examined the scene before me. I noticed a stone bridge with wooden railings, rough-looking, rustic, and spanning the river. The colours were extremely vibrant. More vibrant than I had ever seen. They exploded into my mind. The beauty brought tears to my eyes. I couldn't understand what was happening. I had a mental break once before but this was different, completely different. Could it be a different kind of mental break? I didn't feel fear. I only felt peace as I viewed the scene above. I felt I should be afraid that my mind was once more unravelling, but I felt only wonder and joy as I was drawn into the scene before me.

I saw people on the other side of the river engaging in all sorts of relaxing activities. Some were reading, some were walking, and some were lying on the lush grass. Everyone was smiling. There were animals around the people, animals that should have been wild and dangerous, but all seemed tame and at one with everything in their environment.

I noticed a woman close to the river's edge. She was painting with an easel, her back to me. I watched her work, focused on her brushstrokes as she created a beautiful work as vibrant as the scenery she stood in. After a time, she finished her work and stepped back to survey it. Then she turned and looked at me. She smiled and waved with the hand holding the brush. She was beautiful. Ageless. I couldn't tell if she was young or old. I knew her but I didn't know how or from where. But she was important to me. Then I realized! It was my grandmother! She looked well and vibrant and beautiful and very alive. I lifted my hand and waved back. She smiled and returned my wave and then turned back to her painting.

Suddenly the ceiling was tile again. Just poof, the scene was gone like it never existed. The technician was speaking. She was wiping my belly off and telling me the doctor would call me in a few days with the results. I wanted to ask her if she had noticed the change in the ceiling, but I knew she hadn't. I even wondered if I had. It was so vivid and so clear, and to this day, I can still see it clearly in my mind when I think of it. But obviously it hadn't happened. That was crazy … but then, so was I.

42.

I was working at my desk the next day when my phone rang. It was my doctor's office; they wanted to know if I could come in immediately. It was my forty-first birthday. I checked with my boss and she said I could go. I called Josh to tell him as well.

He said he was free and asked if I wanted to pick him up on the way so he could come with me. I agreed and we both arrived at my doctor's office a short time later.

I was ushered into the room and sat beside the doctor's desk while Josh sat across the small room. The doctor came in but didn't look at either of us. He was focused on the file in his hand. He sat down and seemed to read the file for a little longer than usual. He didn't have his usual impatient attitude with me, maybe because Josh was in the room with me.

After studying the file for what seemed an eternity, he lifted his head and met my eyes, "You have kidney cancer. It's a huge tumour. You should get your affairs in order."

I was stunned silent. I stared at him. I felt nothing. He returned his eyes to the page and pretended to be absorbed by it. I knew he was avoiding looking at me, but I continued to stare at him. I literally felt no emotion, no feeling, just nothing as I stared at his cheek. I was intensely focused on the hair follicles on his cheek. I could barely see his dark beard starting to show.

When I found my voice, I stated firmly, patiently, as if talking to a child.

"No. You have made a mistake. This is not how this goes. You are wrong." My voice rose slightly and I could hear a little vibration in it. "You say 'there is a chance,' 'we need to do more tests,' 'you might have something.'"

I took a deep breath. My body was now vibrating. I spoke again, very softly, my voice cracking, "You do not say I have cancer. You are not allowed to say it like that."

I was shaking all over.

His face softened. He looked completely different from the man who had been impatient with me, frustrated with me, rushing me out of his office every appointment for the past few months.

He spoke softly, kindly. "We are able to tell some cancers by ultrasound and kidney cancer is one of them. You have a large tumour on your left kidney and it is cancer. I'm going to refer you to a specialist immediately and he will tell you your options. I'll go make your appointment with him right away; I'll be right back." He touched my vibrating arm gently and stood to leave the office.

I was alone with Josh.

Josh looked at me and asked softly, "Are you OK?" He was white as a ghost.

I felt heat fill my body. I felt anger fill me. I felt my insides swell with red hot fury. I felt I was suddenly on fire.

"Of course I wasn't OK! This was all fucking wrong! None of it was correct! Somebody just told me I have cancer! You don't just tell a person they have cancer. It was fucking bullshit! And it was my birthday! YOU DO NOT TELL A PERSON THEY HAVE CANCER ON THEIR BIRTHDAY! How could this idiot doctor not know this? Had he even been to medical school? And what the actual fuck is wrong with you, Josh? Am I OK? Fuck no! I am not

OK! I'M FORTY-ONE AND HAVE CANCER AND NEED TO GET AFFAIRS IN ORDER!"

I wanted to scream all of this at him, but instead, I just looked at him and said, "I'm OK. Are you OK?"

"I don't know," he replied softly as the doctor entered.

I was handed a paper with my appointment with a nephrologist on it and stood and left. Josh followed. As I walked past the receptionist desk, walked past the waiting room I had just waited in, I thought, "Last time I walked here, last time I sat here, I was fine. Now I have cancer." I got in the car and thought, "Last time I was in this car, I was fine. Now I have cancer." Everything was to be that way from now on. Life when I was fine, then I had cancer.

We drove home silently.

I walked into the house and that's when the tears came. What would I tell my children? How would I tell my children? Was I dying? What had just happened? I had cancer. Cancer. No one in my family had ever had cancer. What a horrible word. Cancer. Cancer. I repeated it over and over in my mind.

Josh held me and together we cried and cried.

Work. It hit me. I had to call work and tell them. I had to get back to work.

Josh took care of that for me. He insisted he be the one to call and share the news. They gave me the rest of the day off.

43.

I NEEDED TO TELL MY CHILDREN. They were aged nineteen, eighteen, fifteen, and thirteen. Two didn't live with me any longer and I was not going to tell them over the phone. I set up a meeting for that evening to tell them all together. I did a significantly better job than that fool doctor had. I softened it, said I would likely need an operation or some treatment, but it would be OK. Said it wasn't a big deal, and they caught it early, and I was sure to recover quickly. Everyone offered me their kidney, and we even laughed together when my oldest son added that I may want someone else's as his had filtered quite a bit.

We tried to make light, but I knew they were upset, and I felt like such a shit for causing them worry and sorrow. I wondered if I shouldn't have said anything or waited till I knew more. I wished there was some sort of guide to parenting; I felt I never knew the right answer.

I saw a side of Josh that day that warmed. A supportive side. And there was no way I could leave now battling this illness. And maybe, just maybe, there was a shred of hope.

After all the children had left or gone to bed, Josh gave me my birthday present. It was an all-day spa treatment at a top-rated facility in our city. He said he knew I had been feeling tired, now we knew why, and he wanted to give me something that would take my mind off work, caring for a home and seven children, and life in general. Now, he hoped it could give me a few moments to take my mind off cancer. My heart softened. Somehow our problems seemed like nothing compared to the "c" word. And the gift couldn't have come at a better time. He told me the appointment was for the next day, a Saturday, and he would drop me off in the morning. As he turned to go to bed, I spoke, "Would you consider marriage counselling for us? To get us on track? To make things better?"

He turned to me and said, "Of course." I felt a tiny shred of light on this dark day. Maybe this horrible thing would bring us closer together, and we could find a way to make this union work.

Josh went to bed and I sat alone in the dark, unable to settle. I was trying to process everything that had happened during the day. The ultrasound popped into my mind. I had forgotten about the strange vision or whatever it was I'd had during the ultrasound. Was it my mind, my illness, my craziness playing tricks on me? Maybe. But somehow, even if all that were true, it didn't matter. A peace came over me in the dark and I knew I would be fine. My grandmother had sent me a message. I wasn't going to die. I was going to be fine. Gravelly voiced, tough as nails gramma was with me and I would make it through this. Crazy or not, I knew it. Cancer was not going to take me. Cancer was losing this battle.

The next morning Josh drove me to the spa. My full-day treatment started at 9:00 a.m. I vowed to put the day before in the back of my mind as best I was able and try to enjoy this day. I knew the next months would be busy and this may be the last relaxing few moments I had.

Josh left me in the care of the two lovely ladies who outlined my treatments for that day. I was to have a manicure, a pedicure, a facial, a body scrub, and a massage. Josh agreed to be back at 4:00 p.m. to pick me up.

I was taken into a beautiful room that smelled of fresh flowers from several arrangements that had been placed around the room. I settled into a deeply comfortable armchair that felt like it hugged me, with a cup of fresh-brewed herbal tea by my side. One of the ladies asked if I had any allergies. I said "no," and she disappeared and left me in this Zen space. I closed my eyes and sunk further into the chair, letting the soothing music wash over me. "Cancer, cancer, cancer," screamed in my brain and I tried to will it away.

The woman returned with a scone and fresh fruit artfully arranged on a beautiful plate and a clipboard with paperwork on it that I was asked to leisurely fill out as I enjoyed my tea and breakfast. I filled in all the basic information and turned the page. Did I have any illnesses? The question jumped out at me. Cancer. I had cancer. If I had come two days earlier, I would have said no. I never ever shared my mental illness on forms like this and never would. But cancer. I had cancer. One of the worst illnesses. I forced myself to write it down. Seeing it there in my own handwriting jolted me. I started to feel the dizziness, the inability to breathe, my chest constricting. What I now understood after so many years of this frustrating illness was that I was at the beginning of a panic attack. Why now, why today? Why not yesterday when I was told of this? Tips, clues, look around. What can I see? Who told me to do that? Touch the chair. Was that a thing? I felt for the soft covering of the chair and stroked it. Smell. Smell what? The flowers, smell the flowers. I closed my eyes and tried to breathe, inhaling the scent of the fresh bouquets. Listen. TO WHAT? Just listen … I strained my ears. I heard the music. I focused on it. I tried to discern what the sounds were. Birds? Rain? A flute? Was there a voice? "Taste the tea." I picked up the cup and took a sip. I felt it in my mouth. I tried to focus on it. The warmth, the earthiness.

Not today, mental illness. Not today, cancer. Nothing was taking this day from me. I needed this day.

I continued my sensory journey and tried to calm myself. My

brain was screaming, "Act OK, act OK, act OK. You don't need to be OK, just act OK."

The woman returned and sat across from me, reading my paperwork. Thank goodness she hadn't really looked at me when she came in, focusing on the clipboard I had handed her. Rub the chair, rub the chair; Smell the flowers, smell the flowers; listen to the music, listen to the music. The words rushed through my brain over and over.

Then I realized I was thinking. I was thinking thoughts. So I was managing. I was still OK! And I told myself, "You can think, so you are OK. Breathe, think. You are OK," I said it over and over in my brain, chanting it internally like a mantra.

The woman frowned as she read.

Then she looked up and said, "I see you have written you have cancer."

My eyes started to blur. "NO NO NO! STOP!" My brain screamed.

I heard my voice, thin, reedy, far away, "Yesterday. They told me yesterday."

She stood. The welcoming smile was gone and replaced with a frown. She said softly but firmly, "Well, I'm sorry but we can't work on you if you have cancer. It's against policy. We could cause damage or cause it to spread during massage or something. We just can't do your treatments today."

I heard myself again, I sounded small and far away, "Please," I heard the pleading in my voice. "A pedicure? My feet? Please?"

"No," she said firmly but not without compassion. "Come with me, you can use our phone to call your husband."

She took me to the front waiting area that now held a few other women waiting on their treatments and led me to the front desk. She dialled our home number and handed me the phone. Why was it wet? Oh. I realized I was crying. My tears were soaking the phone.

My husband wasn't home and he didn't have his cell phone with him. I left a message. I wasn't sure he would be able to understand it. I was crying hard by this time.

She indicated a chair for me to sit in near the other women.

"Can't I ... Private ... Please?" I heard myself say between hitches in the sobbing noises. My voice sounded so small and far away.

She didn't meet my eyes. She handed me a box of tissues and pointed to a chair.

"Please?" I heard begging from far away.

"We can't. We don't have a room," she said and turned and left.

I could see everyone in the waiting room stealing glances at me. I felt their eyes on me, and my chest started to tighten and my breathing became shallow. I felt crowded, watched, and soon the panic attack I had tried so hard to keep at bay had taken over. I was lost within it. Nothing outside of terror existed.

Then I was in the car, my husband driving.

"I'm so sorry," he kept saying. Something about having gone shopping, expecting me to be there till four. Had no idea this would happen. Apparently, I sat in that chair in full panic and sobbed for well over an hour. I worried how I looked to everyone coming and going but was not unaware of how grateful I was that I couldn't remember the time.

The next day, when I was able to process thought, I realized that the spa must have had a room available for me to wait privately. They had some room reserved for my treatments and certainly hadn't filled my appointments in the time they walked me to their front desk. They just didn't want me near them, in their rooms, as if I could give them cancer. I realized I now had a second disease that society would shun me for.

44.

I FOUND A HIGHLY RATED MARRIAGE counsellor and set up appointments for us. I was also attending many medical appointments and tests and continued working full time, running between work and appointments as needed. I only ever missed that one full day of work, my diagnosis day.

I saw the nephrologist two weeks after my terribly delivered diagnosis. If I was hoping for a more sympathetic bedside manner from this doctor, I was sorely mistaken. Josh attended with me, and the doctor did not once look at me throughout the appointment. He only spoke to my husband, telling him about my cancer and my options as if I wasn't in the room.

"We will do several levels of testing on your wife, and if we find her cancer has metastasized to her bones, we will not operate. We will simply treat her with chemotherapy and radiation to try to extend her life for a time. If we find the cancer isolated to the kidney, we will do surgery to remove the kidney and tumour."

I wanted to jump and scream, "I'm still here you asshole! I'm not dead yet. Look at me!" But I didn't. I sat mute, forcing myself to remain polite and respectful. I still tried to be a perfect person on occasion, even though I was usually a complete failure in that area. This guy was my only hope at wellness; therefore, he was the last guy I wanted to piss off.

I began a series of tests while my cancer continued to grow inside me. It bothered me, knowing this thing was growing in me, this thing that could kill me, but I tried not to think about it.

A month after my diagnosis, we started our weekly marriage counselling sessions.

In our third counselling session, we were focusing on my cancer. I had "passed" all my tests, and the cancer was limited to my kidney, so I was going to be scheduled for surgery. The therapist asked Josh what he was planning to do to support me through recovery after my surgery.

"Will you cook for her?" she asked.

"No, her kids can do that," he replied

"Will you do her laundry?"

"No, her kids can do that."

"Will you clean your home for her?"

"No, her kids can do that."

I was shocked. I couldn't believe I was hearing this. I was fighting for my life and he was acting like an asshole. A cold-hearted, unfeeling asshole.

The questions went on in this fashion. Finally, seeming exasperated, the counsellor asked, "What will you do for her?"

He paused for a long time. We waited. Finally, he answered, "Maybe I'll watch a movie with her."

The counsellor turned to me and said, "You need to leave this man. As soon as you are well, you need to leave this marriage."

As soon as we left, I was all over Josh, asking him why he had been such a jerk. He simply said, "I didn't like her."

I asked him if he really was only going to watch a movie with me? Was that the sum total of the care he was going to give me after I had a tumour and organ removed? He refused to answer.

I was never given another explanation, but I knew there was

truth in what she had said. How could anyone even act that coldly, that harshly to their partner, no matter how they felt about the person asking? I would have to revisit my plan to leave him, but I had bigger things on my plate. First, I needed to get well.

And now that I saw Josh for what he really was, I absolutely had to get my affairs in order. Knowing how little he cared, it became critical to me that Josh got nothing if I didn't survive my cancer or surgery. Anything I had must go to my kids.

I spoke to Josh's friend, the lawyer whose firm I was working in, and asked if he could draw up a will for me. He agreed to do so with no charge.

We met over lunch one day as my surgical date neared, and I explained what I wanted. I needed the will to say that if I died, Josh would sell our home and give my half of the profits to my children. The lawyer advised me that was highly unusual, something about homesteaders' rights, words, words, words. I said I didn't care. That's what I needed. He then spoke as Josh's friend and said it would be unfair to Josh to put him out of his home right after he lost his wife. But he didn't know what had been going on for years in our home. He didn't know "the Susan obsession;" he didn't know Josh only agreed to watch a movie with me. We kept our issues very well hidden. For me, I was too embarrassed to show the world I had made yet another stupid mistake. I was forty-one years old and still hadn't gotten my shit together and now was possibly dying. The least I could do was make sure my children were taken care of.

I insisted, and he relented but wanted me to know he was not in agreement with the parameters of my document. I further stated I wanted my ex-husband to be the executor. He and my father were the only two men I could trust, and I knew the father of my children would make sure their needs and interests were taken care of.

A few days later, I had my will in hand, signed and notarized, two weeks before my surgery. That evening I took my official will home and showed it to Josh. He was very upset. I had never really seen Josh angry. When I would rage, Josh would just shut down or leave. I yelled and ranted and he would remain quiet. But not this time.

"You can't take my house. I deserve this house. I worked my whole life for this house. This is my house and I will not sell it," he actually yelled at me.

"You have to sell the house if I die. It's in the will," I yelled back.

He picked up the phone and threw it across the room, screaming. No words, just screaming.

Then he faced me, his hands clenched tightly.

"I earned this house. I did everything to get this house. I WILL NOT LOSE THIS HOUSE!" Then he stormed out.

All of a sudden, it dawned on me. The whole thing became clear, like a veil was lifted. I was a stepping stone to a house. I remembered talking before we even sold our homes and moved in together. How the house had to be in a certain area, had to be a certain size, and had to be a certain age. I recalled him saying that he and Susan had a dream to live in that area, that they had a certain house they wanted. I wanted to live in a completely different area, closer to my children's father and their school, but somehow, his logic had made sense at the time, and I agreed we should buy where he wanted. I remember how he had taken Susan to the home before we even moved in. She was the first to see the home other than he and I, even before our children. I recalled the "let's get married" sales pitch and how prominent a new home was in that pitch.

Then, when Susan and her husband had built their home a few blocks from this house, Josh would endlessly compare the two. His home was better, more square feet, better yard, better bay, less traffic, closer to amenities. Better, better, better.

When I finally looked back with open eyes, I could finally see. It was never me, marriage to me, being with me. It was using me to get the house. The house that would beat Susan. She controlled so much of his life by constantly threatening to take his kids away. This was a way he could show her, put her in her place. This was a way he could feel some control in his own life, and he saw the way and jumped on it.

I hated him and pitied him. She did have control over him and through him; she had control over me and my life. How he must have hated being made to do her bidding all the time. How victorious he must have felt having a huge expensive home in the area they planned their future in. It was a brand-new area with a pretentious name, close to their children's school, a goal they both still wanted, even separately, and he had won the race. It was indeed all he had worked for. And I was threatening to take it. Not just threatening. If I died, I would.

45.

I WORKED EVERY DAY UP TO June 11 at the law firm, and knowing I wouldn't be back after my surgery because there were too many unknowns, the lawyers and administration staff all took me out to a beautiful lunch to say goodbye. My two-week position had turned into four and a half months and I had thoroughly enjoyed my time. My home life was in shambles, my health status was abysmal, but my work life had been a saviour. It had been fun and I had been treated well.

The next day, I arrived at the hospital at 6:00 a.m. for my surgery. To say I was nervous would be an understatement. Josh came in with me and waited with me while they did blood work, urine tests, started my IV, and got me all prepared.

The orderly came, I gave Josh a hug, and he turned to leave for the waiting area as the orderly and I walked to the operating suite. I had several surgeries prior and always hated this part the most. Walking or being wheeled into the room and seeing the table, feeling the cold, and knowing I was about to be anesthetized always terrified me. What if this was the time I didn't wake up? Or worse yet, what if I didn't really go to sleep, but was paralyzed and actually experienced my whole surgery? I tried to swallow the panic as I walked toward the operating table in the middle of the room.

There was a massive orangish-tan lump on the table. I had never seen anything like that before. As I crawled onto the table, I asked what it was and was told it was a massive sandbag that would enable them to position me best to be able to access my kidney. I watched the OR staff moving around the room as I laid there, shivering. Everyone was bustling, preparing to cut me open and remove this cancer from me. I felt tears silently being shed, pooling in my ears as I stared at the ceiling. I willed it to open, for my grandma to send me a message, some sign that I would be OK. But I knew that was ridiculous. I still didn't trust that I had, in fact, seen the "first message." It made no sense, yet I believed it and do to this day.

I held that vision in my mind as everyone moved close to the table. I pictured the beautiful scene and clung to the "knowing" I would be OK as the anesthetist injected something into my IV line. I had experienced this so many times, but each time I felt terror. I started to count backwards as I had always done and panic rose; I was not falling asleep.

I woke up in recovery. The pain was excruciating, as expected. My throat was raw, also as expected. But I was awake and it was over. I had made it through another surgery. I was groggy and in intense pain but was grateful that I was on the other side of the experience.

I overheard a nurse saying what sounded like, "We can't find her husband but her parents are here, so you can talk to them." There were many of us in recovery; it must have been about someone else.

I drifted in and out and soon found myself in a hospital room. My parents and my sister were there.

"The doctor is pretty sure he got it all, love!" my mother said softly. I could feel the caring and relief in her voice. I felt her warm hand holding mine. I felt safe, loved, with my momma by my side. "He said he removed your kidney and some adrenals and will send everything away for analysis, but he is pretty sure you won't need more treatment."

I tried to smile. I think I did.

I turned. My dad. My rock. I found out later that he had called the Minister of Health several times, advocating for me, rushing my surgery, making sure I was taken care of. I am so grateful to this day for his advocacy, his unwavering tenacity, and his strength of character. Would I be here today to write this had he not fought so hard for me?

I scanned the room. "Where is Josh?"

"Who the fuck knows!" my sister barked. My parents both gave her a dirty look. "What? Where the hell is he? Home watching TV! It's ridiculous!" She answered my parents' looks. I hadn't seen her yet, standing at the end of the bed. She was angry. Something was wrong.

"What?" I croaked.

My mother explained. Apparently, Josh had left the hospital while I was in surgery. He told the nurses that he was going home to shower and would come right back to the hospital. Then, apparently, he lost track of time while watching a basketball game. The doctor had wanted to talk to him after my surgery, but the nurses couldn't locate him in any of the waiting areas. They had paged him, assuming he might have gone to grab coffee or something, but he hadn't responded. My parents and sister were waiting and overheard the announcement paging Josh and approached a nurse identifying themselves. The doctor shared the update with them as my sister went to find a payphone to try to find Josh. She was the one who found him at home, watching basketball, not a care in the world. And she was pissed.

I was in too much pain and too drugged to process the magnitude of this at the time. I was just confused that he wasn't with me, and incredibly grateful my parents and sister were.

An hour later, Josh arrived. My sister and parents were none too pleased with him. Shortly after his arrival, they left us alone to visit.

I don't know how long Josh stayed as I was in and out all day.

I do remember being cold and asking Josh to please bring me a blanket from home. I told him the one I wanted and asked him to make sure he washed it before he brought it as I knew the dog loved to lie on it. He promised. When I awoke later that afternoon, I was snuggled warmly under my blanket.

A friend of mine came to visit the evening of my surgery. She gasped when she saw me. She was a special care aide at the care home I used to work in and was still in her scrubs, having just come from work. She grabbed the crocheted blanket from home and ripped it off me.

I was confused and still groggy.

"This blanket is filthy!" she exclaimed. "You have open wounds!" I looked down at the sheet covering me, the sheet that was under the blanket from home, and saw it was covered with dog hair and other things. She left the room and came back with a nurse, clean sheets, and warmed blankets. Together, they deftly remade my bed around me.

After I was all tucked and warm again, I looked at my friend and croaked, "He promised he'd wash it."

The next day, I was up walking. The surgery had been done laparoscopically, and I had five incisions and twenty staples. The next day was also my second son's graduation and I was so sad that I was going to miss it. He came to the hospital in his tuxedo and looked so handsome! Josh took our picture and I still look at the picture today with mixed feelings. I didn't have cancer anymore and was happy, but I was missing a very important day in my child's life.

Josh promised to attend the graduation activities in my stead and take many pictures. I spent the rest of that day and evening alone as everyone close to me was attending the festivities.

On the third day, the surgeon came in and told me he had gotten all the cancer, and I was considered cancer-free; no chemo or radiation was needed. I was good to go and the doctor discharged me. He told me to schedule an appointment at an outpatient centre in two weeks to have my staples removed and to see him in his office in six weeks. At least this time, he talked to me since Josh wasn't there. I was nervous to leave the hospital and told the nurse. She said I was discharged early as I had support at home, and they needed the bed. Josh already said he wouldn't support me, so I knew I was going to have to rely on my children.

Josh picked me up and took me home. I was in so much pain still and was moving very slowly. Three days after such an invasive surgery seemed so soon to leave the hospital. I was unable to do much on my own and was going to need help. I didn't want my children to help me go to the bathroom or have a shower. I hoped that Josh would minimally help with that.

On the way home, I asked him first how the graduation had gone. I had another question in the chamber for him but wanted the "good stuff" first.

He hadn't gone.

"Why? You promised me. What about the pictures you were going to take for me?"

"I think your family took lots," he answered and refused to explain why he didn't attend. I expect he felt uncomfortable without me being there. There would be lots of pictures, and in a way, I understood and decided I could forgive his discomfort. But then why had I sat alone all day?

"So why didn't you at least come and see me at the hospital then?" I demanded.

"I didn't think of it," he answered.

Now I was pissed off.

"And why didn't you wash the blanket?" My voice was raised and I started to cry. My pain increased substantially. The mere act of raising my voice crying increased the agony in my body.

"I didn't have time and didn't think it was that big of a deal."

I told him about my open wounds and how I could have gotten a serious infection. I wanted to know how he could be so thoughtless and put me in such danger. I wanted to yell at him further but the pain was too much.

He didn't respond.

I focused on recovery. My children were amazing and took care of me so well. They did cook for me, clean for me, do my laundry. Josh did help me in and out of the shower and I didn't have to force him, but my kids did almost everything else.

Soon my staples came out, my follow-up appointment was completed, and all that was left was recovery.

46.

I N September, I was cleared to go back to work, and I thought
it would be reasonably easy to find employment. I had my degree.
I had a strong work ethic. I had worked right up to my cancer
surgery and had great references from the law office. I had that
"termination" on my record, but as it was considered a layoff, I felt
that shouldn't cause me issues. I thought I would be OK, and most
importantly, I needed to get my feet back under me so I could leave
Josh. After the counsellor's statement and the issues through my
surgery and hospitalization, there was no doubt in my mind. I had
a goal and needed to start my path toward it.

I was hopeful as I started my job search. I had grown so bored
staying at home and was very excited to get out of the house and do
something again. I applied for everything I had any qualifications
for, from both my skills and education perspectives. I applied for
administrative positions using my experience from the law office,
as well as everything that required my formal education. After the
first month, with no response from any application, I started to feel
defeated. The second month I had three interviews but no success.
By the third month, I was applying for any and everything that I
felt I could even possibly do. I had applied for over three hundred
and fifty jobs. I had written over three hundred and fifty cover

letters. I had twenty-five interviews. A full four months later, I was finally offered a position with a non-profit agency that worked with people with disabilities.

I started part-time, and within a month, was full-time. "Three months," I kept saying to myself. Three months. I had to work full-time for three months, finish my probation, save money and then I would move.

The counsellor was correct; she told me to leave my marriage as soon as I was able, and I fully intended to do so.

47.

TEN MONTHS AFTER MY SURGERY, three months after I started working, I found a house to rent. I signed a one-year lease. I set up movers and started packing. And I told Josh.

He was surprised, which shocked me. He thought things were OK between us. I explained why there were not.

Mostly, he was just devastated he had to sell the house. He was unable to afford it on his own. He tried to talk me out of leaving. He tried to make me change my mind. He promised to change, be better, do all the things I had asked him to for years, fill promises I had heard over and over that had never come to fruition. I told him this day actually happened a year prior and just took this long to happen in reality. I explained that when he told our therapist that he would only consider watching a movie with me after my surgery, I knew we were done. He said he hadn't meant it. He said he didn't like our therapist, didn't want to keep seeing her, and instead of saying that, he was trying to purposely piss her off.

He had reasons for everything. Excuses and rationalizations. Nothing changed my mind.

On moving day, Josh made himself scarce.

In the new home, my children were all present to help me unpack and set up. My second son decided to come and live with

me again and I was excited. We worked throughout the day, and I
was exhausted and fell into bed, asleep almost before my head hit
the pillow.

I awoke kneeling on grass, unable to breathe, my heart racing,
my bare feet burning. The terror of my sleep rose further within me
as I realized I didn't know where I was. I scanned my surroundings,
having trouble focusing my eyes. My vision was blurring so badly
I was having trouble seeing. My heart was pounding. I was gasping
for air. I needed to get home. I needed to get to my kids.

My kids were old enough; they didn't need me to be home every
day for basic care, but I knew they would be worried if they woke
and found me gone. Thought. I had that thought. So I could bring
this back. As long as I could think, I could function. I felt the grass
with my hands. I closed my eyes and tried to breathe. I stayed like
that for a long time, pulling at the stiff grass, making myself feel
the coarseness.

I was shivering, both from the panic attack and from the cold.
I was in a light nightgown and the night was chilly. I saw the
faint pinks and purples peripherally as they began to fade into the
darkness. I noticed. I was processing thoughts. OK. I made myself
try to smell. Earth. I could smell woodiness, grass, and earth. I
made myself feel. Grass, stiff grass, poking my hands. And cold. I
was so cold.

Now vision. What could I see? I had been staring unseeingly at
the ground I was kneeling on. I raised my head and saw I was in an
empty field. The grass was hard, wiry, wild grass and it was poking
into my bare knees, shins, and palms. I saw a chain-link fence far
in front of me across the span of brownish grass. I turned my head
slowly to the left and right; expanses of the wild grass lay to either
side. I twisted to look behind me and saw houses. A street of houses
lined this expanse of wild grass. And then I saw my house. Yes. It
was on the corner of the street across from a large open area where
the kids could play frisbee and football. We talked about that as we
unpacked. Relief flooded me and I became aware of the adrenaline

still burning in me. My body hurt with hormones flowing through me, a physical, palpable pain.

I had run several yards and the house looked a long way away. I tried to stand up on wobbly legs and became aware that my left foot was wedged in a gopher hole. That must have been what stopped my run. Thank God for that hole. I was able to pull my foot free and noticed my ankle was swollen and discolouring. I didn't feel any pain; I just noted it somewhere in my racing mind.

I was able to hobble back to my house just as the sun peeked over the horizon. The door was standing open. Fear filled me again. Had I let someone into this house to harm my children? I hopped and hobbled through the house as quickly as I could, checking on each child. All were safe and sound to sleep. I scanned every room for an intruder. No one. I breathed relief.

I had started to cry. Or maybe I had been crying for a while and just noticed it. I plopped heavily onto my couch and wept. How long was this going to be my life? Every time I tried to move forward, my illness tried to push me backward. It was a constant fight, me against the darkness. Would I ever have peace? Would I ever feel stable? Safe?

I heard someone in my house and I stopped breathing. Had I checked everything well? Was someone in here and I missed it. I felt my heart pounding in my chest and I struggled to my feet.

My third son came down the stairs, rubbing the sleep from his eyes.

I quickly dried my tears. I didn't want him to see me crying. I was once again forcing them through an adjustment, and I needed to show some strength. I turned to hobble toward the kitchen to find some cereal for him and he immediately noticed my limp.

"What happened?" he asked.

Oh yes. My ankle. I became aware of the pain; I felt my heartbeat pounding in it. I flopped back onto the couch.

"I stumbled and fell down the stairs this morning," I lied. "Want to help me find a tensor bandage somewhere in these boxes?" I asked. Together we set out looking for the bandages I had used for a lab in university. After pawing through several boxes, we found them and wrapped my ankle. My son wandered into the kitchen and found himself some breakfast, and I put on a pot of coffee. I was able to use my sprain as the reason I was upset and had been crying, but inside I knew differently and was feeling emotionally drained and worried.

I poured myself a coffee, got a blanket, wrapped myself up, and hobbled to the front step. I sat sipping my coffee, tears silently coursing down my cheeks. I was exhausted. Emotionally, physically, mentally. What had I hoped for? Had I really believed that leaving Josh would suddenly make everything better? That had been the goal for so long. I had been so single-minded and had completely convinced myself that leaving Josh would fix my life. I would be better once I recovered from cancer, got a job, and left him. Everything would be better. But nothing was better. I had just experienced one of the worst nighttime attacks in a very long time. Was it an omen? Had I made a mistake leaving Josh? Maybe I hadn't tried hard enough to make things work. My anger, my illness, I had to get my medication adjusted so many times, mostly because I kept getting fatter and fatter. And who would want to be with someone who looked like me?

When we met, I was tiny and fit and now I was morbidly obese. And who wants to be with someone who can't even manage life? Someone who couldn't hold a job? Someone with cancer? Who could be expected to live with all that? It was hard on a person. He had the right to act out! And Susan did keep threatening to take the kids from him. What would I do in a situation like that? Was I the liability? Was I the problem in the marriage? I was so busy blaming him that I didn't look within. I was so busy finding a way to leave I never considered finding a way to stay. Had I once again overreacted, just as I had with my first husband? Was my illness ruining everything? Again? Still?

I never knew what was right, correct, how to behave. Would I ever learn? What was illness and what were healthy boundaries, a phrase my therapist loved to use when I saw her right after my diagnosis. How could I find that out? I had a massive self-help library, several works focused on boundaries as well as every other nuance of life that I was unable to manage correctly. Anger, depression, anxiety, co-dependence. You name it, I had it. I read everything I thought could help me. I participated in endless workshops; some were considered very new age and "hippie." I never got better. I had good times, times when I managed. Lots of laughter and joy at many points, but the darkness was always right there, waiting, watching for the slightest opening. And the panic. Was it trying to show me something? I desperately wanted to believe, needed to believe, that there was a reason for all I was going through, and all I had gone through. Was the panic sending me a message and I had never listened or understood? Should I try to understand this more? Was there a message that I constantly missed? A message that would make my life better and I just wasn't getting it? I was sure leaving Josh was the right decision. But was the panic showing me that maybe I was wrong? Could I have been? Would I ever live a life of peace?

I made yet another appointment with my doctor. I was now seeing a different doctor than the one who had diagnosed my cancer. She completed a full physical, further adjusted my medications, and recommended I seek counselling again. I had seen a few counsellors since my diagnosis and was very hesitant to go that route again. Always talking about childhood, my constant answer of I can't remember. My teen years, again, I just couldn't remember. Talking about my parents, my parents were great. Eyebrows raised. It was the same thing over and over and over again and it didn't help me. I became an expert in cognitive behavioural therapy, but it never became natural or became a way of life. It was a constant mental argument. I certainly had the ability to argue and reason with every thought, but why did I have to do it all the time? If this was life, who wanted it? It was such an exhausting existence.

She recommended a counsellor who was "different" and said her practice was a little unusual, but many liked her and were helped by her. I acquiesced and made an appointment.

48.

ALTHEA WAS DIFFERENT. FIRST, THERE was no huge waiting room with other people jammed into it. There was me and a small electric fountain bubbling away in the waiting room. There were a few very serene pictures, two soft chairs, a few throw pillows, and a water cooler.

She opened the door, met me with a warm smile, and led me into a larger office. Mismatched, stuffed, well-loved chairs were everywhere. There were ottomans and side tables, but the place was not crowded. It looked like a well-loved living room. A small desk was against the far wall with a phone and computer on it.

There were several bookshelves lining the walls. Then I started to notice weird stuff. There were a few drums, bells, feathers, dream catchers, what looked like several copper bowls, pieces of driftwood, rocks of all different shapes and sizes, and two larger rock formations that looked like tiny shining caves with tons of stones from the formation poking into the centre of the cave. I was later told these things were geodes and the rocks were crystals. There were candles lit strategically throughout the space and a warm woody smell that I found comforting. I found the source when I noted a thin plume of smoke rising from one of the tables.

Incense. Not overwhelming and perfumy, just nice. There was another fountain gurgling gently nearby.

She invited me to choose any chair that spoke to me.

Hmm ... OK then.

I walked past the window as I waited for some chair to speak up and noticed a crow sitting on top of a telephone pole outside the window. She followed my gaze.

"Friend crow speaks to us of transformation and change, from uncomfortable to useful, a good omen for our time." Then she looked out the window and slightly bowed her head, "Thank you, friend crow."

Oh shit. Well, I wanted something different. This was different. I gave a brief nod to "friend crow" and waited for a chair to call out.

As expected, the chairs did not speak but I did find one that looked comfortable and sat carefully on the edge, gripping the arms until Althea suggested I allow the chair to "welcome me into its depths." I became aware of my posture and sat back, loosening my grip.

She pushed a worn ottoman in front of me and I lifted my legs to it. The chair was insanely comfortable.

She asked a bit about myself, why I was here, a bit of history, and I made it very clear I did not want to talk about childhood, or parents, or anything like that. I was on as much medication as I could be on and wasn't better. I wanted solutions, not just endless babble. I didn't want to talk about my feelings. I wanted to be a productive human that wasn't terrified every second, waiting for the next panic attack. I wanted to know if my panic attacks were telling me something, and I wanted the darkness to go away. I wasn't going to take reams of paperwork home with me to fill in, and I wasn't going to have lengthy discussions about arguing with every thought I had. I was, in fact, quite a bitch with her. After my ranty intro, I thought she would probably have preferred to be sitting across from "friend crow."

She just smiled at me, that same warm smile, a genuine smile, not that fake therapist, "I know best you crazy fucked up thing and we will do what I say we do," condescending smile that I had seen so many times over.

Then she said, "Well, let's ask the last panic attack if it was telling you something."

This was a different take. In the past, it was always about managing my panic attacks, minimizing them, not acknowledging them, and just making them go away. I certainly never asked it in any way. This was the complete opposite approach of anything I had learned in the thirteen years since my diagnosis. And that alone had to make it better.

She asked me to sit back and close my eyes. She spoke softly, asking me to focus on my breathing. She asked me to scan my body, one section at a time. Her words carried me from my head to my feet. I released as much tension as I possibly could in that first session. I was still about as supple as a plank after the scan as my body was so used to being constantly rigid and tense. After the scan was completed, we talked to the panic attack. We talked for what felt like a long time, and my panic attack wasn't interested in answering. It was as mute as the chair. Lots of weird shit that was supposed to "speak" in this room didn't.

However, after the session, surprisingly, I did feel better. Not much, but a tiny bit. I could breathe a little more deeply. I remembered a few times a day to actively lower my shoulders. I didn't come out with paper and assignments and endless internal arguments, and that alone made this type of counselling better than any past rounds.

I continued to see Althea weekly. Every time, I sat in the same chair (it never did speak), and every time we did the full body scan while I breathed, and each time I felt a little better leaving. I felt rested leaving her office, lighter, like I'd had a great nap, or at least what I think a great nap would feel like as I don't think I had ever really rested in my entire life.

And I started to feel and know things. I can't explain how I knew but I did. Together, each session, after my body scan was completed, we would talk. But not talk, talk. I was getting better at letting the tension in my body go and becoming more and more aware of when my body was tense, even outside of sessions. I became aware that my muscles were always knotted, I always jiggled my foot when I sat, and everything was always on high alert as if I would need to run or pounce on something at a moment's notice. I shared once during a talk that as a child I had to thump my leg to go to sleep. Every night, when I was little, I would lay on my stomach and lift my right lower leg, bend the knee at a right angle, and let my foot fall to the bed, over and over until I went to sleep.

Now, when I say talk, it wasn't Althea and I having a conversation. It was Althea and "the flame" talking. After several sessions, I noticed a tiny flame inside that wasn't there but was. It was like a tiny candle that lived in my chest cavity, but of course, it didn't. But when I was with Althea, it was there. And the flame knew things. And I could communicate with it, or Althea could by asking it questions that it would answer, but I would say the words. I don't know who was talking to who, and I fully recognized that this sounds crazy, but we had already established my mental state years ago, so who was I to argue. I would leave feeling better and that had to count for something.

One of our sessions stood out to me in particular. I was pursuing wellness with everything in me and yet I experienced something memorable. Was I getting crazier? Or was this a reality of some sort? A memory or a wild imagining? I had done my body scan and somehow found myself in a basement with another little girl. Simultaneously, I was both a little girl in that place and an adult in the chair in Althea's office. I had completely forgotten this little girl; her family had been our neighbours on the farm when I was six or seven years old. My parents were friends with her parents, and we mostly played together when they visited, but this time,

I had been dropped off for a play date. My conscious mind had no memory of this event but sitting in Althea's office in the chair, was I remembering? Creating? Experiencing? It felt like a very real moment I had lived in the past but was also currently actively experiencing again as young me.

We were in her basement and I both saw and felt myself playing with her. It was a very dark and dingy basement and it had a dirt floor. I felt cold and was shivering slightly. We had found magazines and they were filled with naked women, and we were looking at them. I was very uncomfortable. Her father came down the stairs and caught us. I was so scared. I felt the fear firsthand and watched my tiny body react in fear as he stormed toward us.

Then a large grey wolf came out from the shadows of the basement and sat next to me, pressing itself into my tiny body on my right side. It sat very still, staring unblinkingly into the man's eyes. I felt its chest rise and fall as it breathed. I felt its rough fur against my bare arm. I felt its warmth seeping into my cold little body. I could feel its heartbeat against my shoulder.

And then I was fully back in Althea's office seated in my chair. I opened my eyes and inhaled deeply, trying to ground myself in reality. I had spoken throughout and shared every detail of what I had seen with Althea as I experienced it. I scanned the room and let my eyes focus on the drums, then the water fountain, over to the books, scanning the chairs, and slowly moved my head from left to right, focusing on everything as my eyes passed over it as I was instructed to after every session like this. It was part of grounding when we completed our sessions.

As I turned to my right, there was a large grey wolf. I jumped, startled. My breath caught. Was this the same grey wolf from my vision? Memory? Dream? Whatever had just happened. It was sitting on the right side of my chair, watching Althea with steely eyes.

Althea asked me what I had seen, why I had jumped.

I pointed to the right. "Can you see it?" I asked. "The wolf ... there."

She said no, but she could feel it and that it was my guardian. She said that it had always been with me. I looked at the wolf and looked away. I looked back and forth a few times to see if it stayed or vanished. It should vanish. Wolves don't belong in therapy rooms. But it didn't vanish; it stayed. I should be afraid, I thought. But I wasn't. It turned its head and its eyes met mine. I was drawn into those steely, almost white eyes. I saw only love. I felt a blanket of warmth and peace cover me. I felt whole and safe. I heard in my head only, "I have always been with you and always will be with you."

Althea spoke, "Would you like to ask his or her name?"

I hadn't taken my eyes off the wolf. My brain must have asked as I immediately heard the word "Oron."

"Orion?" my mind asked.

"No, Oron. O-R-O-N," she answered with her mind and I knew she was female.

"Oron," my brain said, and her strong head nodded slightly.

Then she slowly faded away. I watched as her form became gauzy and then was gone. But I could still sense her presence.

I knew this was crazy and I couldn't tell anyone what had happened. I knew it made no sense and couldn't have happened, but it felt so real. And it wasn't scary. I felt extremely calm and peaceful. Maybe I had finally just lost it? Maybe this was it and I had completely left reality? Or maybe this was a vision of some kind and was something that many share but never talk about.

When I got back to my desk after the session, I immediately searched the meaning of the word "Oron." I had never heard that word before and was pretty sure it would not mean anything; it was likely a word that didn't exist.

"Bringer of light" popped onto the screen before me.

I stared at those words for a long time.

"Oron: Bringer of light."

So I leave this story, as all of the others before and yet to come, in your lap, dear reader. What shade do you assign to this? When battling an illness such as mine, one never really knows what is real or not. I could never say what really happened and what didn't and when others scoffed, if I ever had the nerve to share some of my stories, I would agree with them. These things can't happen. Yet, for me, this was very real. I can still access Oron. Is this the product of a very sick mind, or something else, something we can't or don't want to explain in our world? When you mix illness in, everything is suspect, and I am just as suspicious as the rest of you. But, at the same time, sitting here typing, I can still feel my guardian wolf at my right.

49.

A s I worked with Althea over the months, I felt a shift within me. It was so subtle that it couldn't be tracked session to session but was clear from the beginning to end of our time spent together.

One of the things that concerned me for as long as I could remember was my fierce anger when it was unleashed. The fury would boil into me and leave me feeling out of control. When I threw my husband's cup into the sink, it was the type of fury that went from zero to red hot in seconds. It scared me and I wanted answers and help. I didn't trust myself and never knew when the anger would come. I needed to control it.

What I discovered with Althea's guidance was that depression was the suppression of all feelings, both the good and the bad. I had been so busy pressing down anger for so long that, in the end, I had managed to bury all feelings. She described depression as pushing all feelings away, and in my case, since I couldn't manage the bad one, it caused all feelings to suppress. It was apparently a package deal. I needed to somehow learn to deal with this feeling I so despised, this feeling that was bad, not appropriate, not good or kind or perfect, all the things I needed to be. This horrible feeling stood between me and what I needed to be, and it had to be eliminated. But how?

Althea explained that anger was normal, good in fact, and could serve us if used correctly. My mind screamed "bullshit," but I never uttered that aloud. I had seen anger and it was awful. Anger hurt. Anger wounded. Anger damaged. And I didn't want to have any part in that. My anger was the worst kind. My anger did all those things. My anger was explosive and unpredictable. My anger broke cups and faucets. It uprooted plants. My anger screamed horrible words that I knew cut to the soul. I felt helpless to stop it. On the rare occasion that my anger broke through the barrier I had painstakingly erected, it felt so right, so freeing, so entitled to what it said and did. It was power. Horrible, misused power that damaged. My anger wasn't physical with others, but it broke things, damaged things, which in turn damaged their owners.

I recall a couple of events that I will share with you, dear reader. I feel deep shame as I speak of these moments. As stated prior, my ex-husband often had one or several of his siblings with their families come and stay with us for weekends or even up to a week at a time. I did my best to do everything correctly and be a gracious, kind host. But as more responsibility was added to my life, my anger became harder and harder to suppress.

On one such occasion, preparing for a few families to arrive, I was yelling at my two oldest boys to clean their room. I needed to vacuum it. My oldest argued; he was around six or seven years old, and normal children sass their parents. For some reason, my sick, and at that time unmedicated, mind snapped. Not being listened to by my child was inconceivable. Anger tore through me like fire, and I picked up his most prized possession, a Lego ship that he had taken hours to build. Tears roll down my face, dear reader, as I write this, remembering, seeing my hands grasp each end of that ship and snap it in half. Lego pieces flying everywhere. Then the look on his little face. I saw the pain my anger caused, the shock, and then distrust. He could rebuild it, but the broken trust, the real damage, could never be rebuilt.

Another time, my ex-husband's brother and his family were visiting for a week. Again, pre-diagnosis and when my illness was about to peak. We decided to walk to a public swimming pool a few blocks away. I was running around trying to get the children ready to go. My husband was at work, and it was only me with our visiting family members. They were waiting at the door for me as I tried to gather all we needed. Their children were very impatient, and they finally said, "We will head over. Just meet us there."

The pressure felt intense. I was a horrible host and couldn't do the simplest things. I couldn't pack towels, snacks, juice, clothing, find hats, bathing suits, the stroller (how could a fucking stroller be lost?), sunscreen my kids, and get out the door. Every other human could do this without being unable to breathe and calm their heartbeat!

Finally, everything was ready and at the door. My second son had no shoes. I screamed horribly at this tiny, innocent boy, "Where are your shoes?"

"I don't know?" he said softly, clearly terrified of the lunatic towering over him. We ran through the house, searching for his shoes. They were nowhere. My anger was burning in me and I kept berating this little boy about losing his shoes. A normal human would have gotten another pair, but not this screaming inhuman beast that he was stuck with.

It took my oldest boy to bring another pair of shoes for it to even dawn on me that he could wear any other pair on his feet.

We left the house and walked as quickly as we could, at least twenty minutes behind our guests. The anger still boiled in me. I was no longer ranting but I couldn't make it go away. I was such a terrible person, not being able to do the simplest things. And how could his shoes be lost? I had seen them at the front door that morning. My mind raged.

When we finally got to the pool and all were in the water, the anger was still seething and now its friend, panic, was along for the ride. How could I have agreed to such a stupid thing? Taking four little children on my own to a large public swimming pool? I could barely get groceries and now I had four small people playing in deadly water, water that could take their lives at any moment. I had to be vigilant. I scanned the pool constantly, wildly, making sure everyone was safe as I struggled to breathe. In one of the sweeps of my gaze, my eyes froze, locked onto a tiny pair of shoes on the deck of the pool. My son's shoes. With my little niece's things. Immediately, I knew she had put his shoes on to walk to the pool. And I had screamed at my little boy. I had hurt his tiny heart, scared him. I, the one who was to love and keep him safe, damaged him.

That was what my anger did. And I wanted no part of it.

Althea and I worked on appropriate expressions of anger and I tried, I really did. But my anger wasn't the good, "empowering when correctly channelled" kind. Mine was evil. And I continued to try to keep it buried.

Other than that, many positive things did come from my time with Althea. A big one was the acceptance of my diagnosis. Prior to my time with her, I kept my diagnosis hidden. I felt shame—shame in my weakness, shame in having a mental illness, as if I had caused it by not being good enough. Althea helped me understand that my illness was the same as diabetes, cancer, heart disease, asthma, and any other disease people randomly get. She helped me understand I had not caused it. I became aware that acquiring mental illness was not something I had done or not done, but managing my mental illness was fully my responsibility.

I had also come to learn that taking medication wasn't enough for me to attain wellness. I learned that what I put into my body and how I moved my body impacted my wellness. I became aware that I wasn't eating nutritionally balanced food. I might have noticed that when I gained a hundred pounds, but it had apparently slipped under my radar. I became aware that I had stopped moving my body except when I had to, as in going to the freezer for ice cream. And I became aware of my surroundings.

My panic attacks never did speak to me, but they had reduced, and I hadn't found myself outdoors again in the middle of the night.

My home slowly filled with crystals, candles, incense, healthy recipe books, soothing music, soft lighting, and a bubbling electric fountain. In fact, my home began to mirror Althea' office. As few times a week, I would light my candles and incense and take myself through a body scan as I had so many times in Althea's office. One night, I recall my second son coming home from work and asking if we were planning a sacrifice of some sort. I looked around and laughed. It was very different from how I had lived prior. And it felt good.

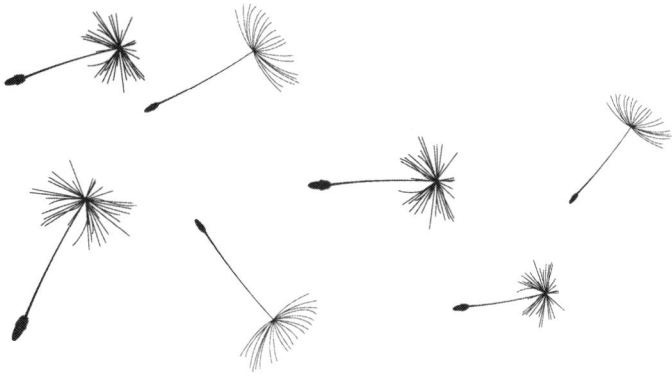

50.

JOSH AND I REMAINED IN contact after our separation. Josh had also gone into private counselling throughout the same time I was seeing Althea. We had been friends prior, so, after a time when we were both too angry and hurt to interact, we slowly wandered back into that friendship. We chatted about the things we learned in our respective therapy sessions. He was very clear with me that he wanted to try our marriage again with our newfound skills. I wasn't convinced.

I knew I was better, stronger, and he seemed different as well. Susan was no longer a daily influence on him. Our children were older now and they were able to decide and make their own choices, so Susan threatening to take them away was no longer an issue.

He openly shared with me how he felt he had messed up and took full responsibility for the issues he had caused. Of course, he wasn't fully responsible, I too had caused a big part of the unravelling and I took my own responsibility. I told him of my panic attack the night of my move and how that made me really investigate my part in the demise of our marriage. Now that I had accepted my mental illness, I said I understood how hard it must have been for him to live with that. My depression for all those years, and then my cancer, all while raising seven children, six of whom were teenagers at the same time. It was hard on both of us.

As time passed, Josh spoke of how in his therapy, he learned why the house had been so important and that it was no longer an issue. He spoke of how Susan was long gone from his life and living in another city an hour away. He said he hadn't realized it but had been dealing with a lot of childhood trauma that caused his behaviour and now he understood things much more clearly.

We once again laughed and had fun together as we had so many years ago, but to try our marriage again … I wasn't sure. I was doing so well on my own and was worried about my stability if we tried again. But I was also struggling financially. The home I rented took most of my paycheck and left very little for anything else, and I was going further and further into debt each month. My two older children had moved to other cities for their post-secondary education, and I knew I needed to move to a smaller home or apartment now that we had fewer people in the home. I needed to search out something more affordable, and Josh kept saying it would be just as easy to move back in with him. I was starting to wear down.

And then he did something that softened my heart. My daughter was a die-hard football fan and was obsessed with one particular player on our home team. Josh was able to get her an autographed football from the player. He showed up at my home one Saturday morning with the gift. My daughter was over the moon. Make my children happy? You got me.

I thought long and hard about Josh's relentless request, talked to my two remaining children at home, and after a long time, decided I would give it another try.

Josh was living in a modest home, surprisingly, in the area I had initially wanted to live in when we first decided to move in together. He still had his two youngest with him as well and his home didn't have room for all of us. Many discussions ensued, and we decided the best bet was to finish the basement in his home to create room for my children and myself to move in, as opposed to him selling and us buying something new together. He and his best friend, Susan's husband, were going to do all the work themselves to save money. We borrowed money for materials knowing that when I got my damage deposit back from the house I was living in, those funds would cover the costs.

I gave my notice and started packing. The construction took a couple of months, but the time flew by and soon we were within a few days of moving.

I decided to pop over to the house, drop a few things off, and see Josh, just a surprise visit for fun. I knocked and there was no answer. The door was open and I let myself in and followed the voices to the basement. I looked over the stair rail and there stood Susan in the middle of the work area directing traffic. She saw me and informed me that she had designed the whole layout of the basement and had attended to the build as many days as she was able to ensure all went according to plan.

I left before I even saw Josh. I'm not sure I even answered Susan. I just recall running up the stairs, bolting for the front door, jumping in my car, and getting home.

It felt just like "not ring shopping day" all over again. At home, I stood in my kitchen amid the boxes, gripping my counter, trying to calm my breathing. I was experiencing a mild version of my regular panic attacks. I was still able to process some thought and I was able to see, but my breathing was ragged and my heart was racing.

I tried to reason with myself. It wasn't the same as before. It wasn't the same thing at all. I was superimposing a memory on a present moment, something I often did. I spoke to my panic, trying to reason with it as I had been taught. This time, my panic was unreasonable, in the very literal sense of the word. I decided I needed to do something before it escalated. I had to change my focus. I grabbed some dishes and some newspaper and started wrapping dishes. I focused on putting them into a box and keeping my hands busy. I needed to calm myself to try to think rationally about what I had seen.

The tears flowed. This didn't feel right anymore. All my alarm bells were going off.

"Stop!" I yelled into my own head, yelling at my own brain. "Stop! What do you know for sure?"

I needed to think.

I knew Josh's best friend had been helping him work on his basement. I should have known Susan would be there. It was logical. But Josh had told me she was out of his life. No, out of his day-to-day life. That's what he said. And it did make sense she would travel with her husband on occasion. But designing the whole basement? Being there as often as she could be? Was he lying to me again? I could not be in another situation without trust. What if I was making another huge mistake? I did that over and over. Was I doing it again?

Wait. Stop. Did I know she was telling the truth? I didn't. Josh hadn't said anything about her being there. But would he? I needed to check with him. But would he tell me the truth? He had lied to me in the past. So was I already questioning him? Did that mean I didn't really trust him? And if I didn't trust him, why the hell was I moving in with him again? And was it that big of a deal that she was in the basement? It shouldn't be but it felt like it was.

Something nagged at me. I began obsessively thinking again. Was I making a mistake again? Was I being stupid again? Was I fucking up again? Was I sure I was doing the right thing? The semblance of peace I had attained when working with Althea was fading, replaced with racing thoughts and questions. I knew what was happening, and over the next few days, I did my best to push all these racing thoughts out of my mind and focus on the move. Focus on what I knew, not what I was perceiving. I needed to remember that my mind could not be trusted. It was ill. Focus on facts, reality, not skewed perceptions. I repeated that mantra over and over.

I never did ask Josh. I didn't want to start our new journey off without trust. It was too late to undo the whole deal, so I would try to go in with an open mind and leave my perceptions and assumptions at the door. I wouldn't let my illness and obsessions interfere with my life again. At least, that was the plan.

51.

SHORTLY AFTER WE SETTLED INTO his home together, Josh became very ill. I rushed him to emergency one night, and he was fully examined, declared to have an infection somewhere, prescribed antibiotics, and sent home. The next day, he was worse. We returned immediately to the hospital. Josh was listless, teetering on consciousness, vomiting, and had an extremely high fever. A nurse was getting Josh settled into his emergency room bed as I stood by watching, afraid.

The door burst open and I was roughly pushed aside. Susan barreled right up to his bed, displacing myself and the nurse roughly. I assumed her children had alerted her to the situation.

"I am his wife. What's happening?" she demanded.

The nurse turned to me questioningly.

"His ex-wife," I stated. I was too fearful to be pissed off. My focus was on Josh.

The nurse stated that Josh hadn't seen the doctor yet. Susan demanded to speak to the doctor immediately. The nurse left the room with promises that she would do her best and gave me a strange look as she left.

I approached Josh's bed from the other side, opposite Susan. She had his hand and was leaning over him, speaking gently, telling him she was here now, and it would all be alright. I heard Josh mutter her name.

I stood lamely holding his other hand, mute, fearful, and waiting.

The doctor came in and told both of us to step aside. Many tests were done as Susan and I waited.

Finally, hours later, the doctor came in with his diagnosis. He approached me to speak and Susan pushed in front of me. He tried to look around her at me, but she was begging him to tell her what was going on. I told him to go ahead and tell her. It didn't matter who he was talking to at that moment; all that mattered was Josh. Was he going to be OK?

Josh was diagnosed with a superbug. Susan was told, and I heard from behind her, that there was no guarantee he would survive. They had no idea what antibiotic to hit this superbug with. They said they had to do something, give him a strong dose of something, but if it was the wrong thing, it would kill him. But without anything, he would die.

Susan stated, "Give it to him."

The doctor stated, "That is his wife's decision and she has to sign for it."

Susan finally stepped aside, and I agreed with what she had said and signed the papers, praying I had done the right thing but knowing it was the only choice I had.

Josh was in the hospital for a week. I spent as much time as I was able to at his bedside. By day three, we were told the medication was working and Josh would survive. Four days after that, he was released and was very weak for a long time but did fully recover. And we moved on with our lives together as a couple.

52.

I WAS NOW THE MANAGER OF the non-profit I worked for. It was challenging work and I loved every minute of it. I shared my story, my personal journey with my disability, with all our clients. I told of my diagnosis, my work to get my degree, my termination, my cancer, my endless job search to find employment with the company I now worked for, and I did this so my clients knew I got it. I understood. And I was no different than they were. I wasn't special in any way. And that meant that they too could find their paths as I found mine.

In my role as manager, I focused on expansion, increasing the footprint in my region. I believed deeply in the work the company did, the need for it, and the rights of those with disabilities. I believed in our ability to help each client along their chosen, rather than prescribed, path. I believed in the mission and vision. As a person who was coming to terms with my disability, I believed we all deserved every opportunity we could find.

The work was demanding and stressful. Managing people was stressful and something I had never done. I took classes and workshops to try to figure out how to best create a solid environment of growth for staff and clients, but it wasn't always easy. I was growing slowly, mistake by mistake, success by success,

and spending many hours a week trying to be the best I could be …
trying once again to be perfect.

Over time, I became aware I was slipping again and, as per usual,
by the time I noticed, the darkness was becoming more prominent
in my life again. The obsessive thinking was back. Every night I
would replay the days' incidents, beating myself up for saying a
stupid thing or questioning a decision I had made. I would go over
and over emails I received, wondering about the deeper meanings
within them. I was so certain there was something deeper in most of
the emails I received, mainly that the sender was pointing out ways
I wasn't doing well, wasn't being a good manager, was dropping the
ball, and I would go over and over everything so I could pick out
that implied shortcoming and fix it before I got into trouble. And
once again, the panic attacks were getting out of control, especially
at night. I was withdrawing more and more, going into myself,
hiding. I didn't want people to see. I needed people to think I was
competent, able to do my work. I would overcompensate and be
too friendly or undercompensate and be cold. I was off balance and
I felt I was walking a tightrope and about to fall off.

One Sunday afternoon, Josh and I decided to go to a movie
with his youngest daughter. I didn't want to go but had no reason
not to. I again felt complete dread at leaving the house. Something
bad was going to happen. I was silently crying for no reason as we
walked into the cineplex. No one noticed. Josh didn't notice. His
daughter didn't notice. I began to wonder if I was really there. Was
I invisible? Did anyone see me? I felt numb, removed from myself.
I didn't feel present. I don't recall any of the movie we saw. I only
remember the feeling or lack thereof. I was either filled with dread
or nothingness. And I knew. I was definitely sick again. Even with
the medication, the exercise, the nutritional food, and all the work
I had done over and over again, I was sick. And I was desolate. It
felt like no matter what, I would never be well.

So back to the doctor I went.

I had a new family doctor once again. I told her what was happening. I told her that I was taking as much medication as I was allowed, that I was walking and going to the gym. I told her I was eating better than I had in the past and did body scans when I was able to. I realized as I was talking to her that after moving back in with Josh, I had reverted to my old lifestyle. As I spoke aloud, I heard my words but realized that I wasn't really eating well. I was eating what we had always eaten prior. And I had gotten busy with work and life and wasn't exercising as much. I didn't have my crystals, incense, or candles all around me. They were in the shed as there was no room for my belongings in the house. I didn't really do my body scans because I couldn't find quiet bits of time to do so. The TV was always on, and I was either watching it with the other members of the family or at the kitchen table trying to work.

I had been on the same medication, fluoxetine, for over eighteen years and had been at the highest dose allowed for almost seven. The doctor felt that I was simply no longer responding to it and recommended I stop taking it, let it all leave my body, and then start a new medication called escitalopram. She said it was new and had good reviews. She cautioned me that withdrawal was going to be hard. She told me I may have suicidal thoughts and to call the mobile crisis unit immediately if I did so. She told me to completely stop taking my fluoxetine for six weeks and then come and see her and we would start the new one.

I remember sitting across from her wondering why withdrawal would be hard if it wasn't working anyway. I shouldn't really notice, should I? Withdrawing from something doing nothing didn't seem to be a thing.

Was I wrong! It was a thing. A horrible nightmare of a thing.

First, I noticed the debilitating headaches. Then the bugs, crawling, deep under my skin, along my bones, as if my skeleton were their roadways and they travelled those roads day and night. I couldn't sit or lie still. I had to pace all the time to distract myself from the bugs inside me, everywhere, moving, crawling. It drove me crazy. Well ... crazier! The headaches made me dizzy. The bugs made me angry. I was pissed off, irritated, furious. I did my best to hide it, and I managed for the most part at work, but outside of work, I was a bitch.

And then the darkness came. And it was worse than I had ever felt before. I simply and desperately wanted out. I wanted to stop living. I saw no reason to continue to suffer. I realized my life had been too hard and too long. I saw no light, saw no reason to continue the struggle. My kids were almost grown and I knew I would never be well. No medication would ever help me. No eating, exercising, or meditating would ever help me. I was broken. And life would always be a fight. Every day I opened my eyes and felt worse. There was no point. I just wanted it to stop. I started to think of the best way to make it stop. Pills? I would puke them up and likely not die and then the whole world would know. So that wasn't an option. And I didn't want to do something where my children would find me. That was too horrible. And I didn't want to make a mess that someone had to clean up. I wanted it quick and as painless as possible. And assured. I didn't want to fuck this up too.

I didn't call the mobile crisis as I had promised my doctor I would. I didn't tell anyone. I went to work every day, did my best, and planned. Soon I wouldn't have to open my eyes ever again. Soon I would finally rest. Soon it would all stop hurting. Soon.

And then it was six weeks and I hadn't developed or executed the perfect plan. The doctor asked how I was doing. I told her about the headaches, the dizziness, the bugs, the irritability, but I did not mention the plan. I wasn't finished with the plan yet; it was a secret.

I started my escitalopram that day but continued with the plan. I had thrown around thousands of options and every plan had a flaw. I had decided that the best way would be for it to look like an accident. That way, I wouldn't purposely hurt my kids. But how to create a believable accident?

A couple more weeks passed. One day, I was thinking about my plan and a thought slammed into my head.

"What the fuck is wrong with you? You didn't survive cancer to kill yourself!"

I was stunned. The thought seemed to come from outside of me but I knew it was me. It was definitely me, talking to me, giving me shit. And I felt like I had just woken up from a nightmare. It was likely much more gradual than that, but to me, it felt like a lightning bolt, and in an instant, I wasn't suicidal anymore. In fact, I was shocked, fearful, and anxious about how close I had come. And even worse, how logical it had seemed. It hadn't seemed a bad thing; it was a necessary thing, an unquestionable thing, the next obvious step that needed to be taken. The biggest issue was simply the logistics.

When you go to an eye doctor, if you have poor vision, they make you look through these archaic-looking heavy things that have all these tiny lenses attached. The optometrist flicks those lenses up and down, changing the clarity of the view, asking which is better. That is what my life felt like, as though someone had clicked the right lens in front of my eye and what was blurry or invisible was now clear. With my new medication clicked into place, I saw. And I saw a lot.

53.

MY MARRIAGE WAS IN THE toilet. Things hadn't changed. My knowledge of what was happening had changed. I was so busy, so self-involved, so sick, I was out of the loop. Everything was as it had been the last time we were together. Actually, that's not fair. Things had gotten better in some areas, but Susan was still in charge for the most part and ran our home along with hers. I found out Josh had been lying to me for quite a while about big things and little things, about completely unimportant things as well as life-changing things. But why wouldn't he? I was either sobbing or yelling all the time. I would lie to myself! I would ask him something, try to engage him, just so I could yell. The anger needed a place to go, and I unleashed it on Josh every time I caught wind of a lie. I was either numb and silent or raging all the time. I was a monster to live with. So, lying was the easiest course of action. Tell me what I wanted to hear and maybe I wouldn't yell. But he would never know. I didn't know! I was out of control, on the edge of exploding all the time. Or the opposite extreme, numb, ignoring him. There was very little in between.

As I started to get well again, as I started to see, I saw the ruin left in the wake of my last few years. Once again, my illness had severely damaged, if not ruined, a marriage. I didn't plan to leave, and I didn't plan to stay. I didn't plan anything. I just tried to survive. It was a long way back to a functioning level of well, and every ounce of energy went to work and my kids with very little leftover for Josh and attending to my marriage.

We were also adding to our family at the time. I was soon to be a gramma! My oldest son had married his high school sweetheart almost four years prior, had graduated university in mechanical engineering, and had secured employment in his field immediately. His job took him to a small town eight hours away from us, and they were about to have their first child. I was intensely focused on the new baby coming. My first grandchild!

The baby boy was born June first, and I couldn't get into my car fast enough to make the drive to see this beautiful bundle. My second son and my daughter were able to get time off to come with me. When I first held my grandson, I wept. Although I tried desperately to wipe the memories from my mind, I recalled how close I had been to missing this moment, how close I had come to ending my life. I felt a cold shiver run down my spine. Too close. I made a vow to myself that no matter what, if that ever happened again, I would call the mobile crisis unit or whoever I had to in order to be safe.

I cried as I left a few days later, having to return to work. I felt my heart physically aching. What was wrong with me? Why was this so hard? Then, without warning, I was in a full-blown panic attack. And an epic one to boot. All the bells and whistles. I was out of control. But nothing was wrong. In fact, everything was right. I had a beautiful, healthy grandson I had just spent time with. I was on medication. And yet here I was.

I continued to have panic attacks off and on, even on the escitalopram. The darkness and numbness had lifted, the anger was well in check, but the panic attacks continued. They were paralyzing and impacted my life. Out of the blue, my heart would race, I would have trouble breathing, and would lose my vision. The symptoms would arrive all at once and intensely, often with no warning, from zero to full-blown attack. If I were driving, I would have seconds to pull over while I could still see. If I were at work, I would try to get my door closed as quickly as possible, or if I was with others, I would run to the closest private space I could find, indoors or out.

One day, I was at the dentist, having my first-ever root canal done. I saw him and the hygienist leaning over me. I had a brief thought of suffocation, and then I found myself running down the street away from the dental office with the paper bib flying over my shoulder. I became aware that my mouth was held open with something and that I couldn't get any air into my body. I heard yelling behind me and somehow willed my legs to slow and then stop. The world slowly came back into focus, and I saw I was at least half a block away from the dentist's office. I saw people staring at me. I must have looked like a wild animal. I felt like one.

The hygienist had caught up to me, held my arm, and was gently turning me around to go back to the office. She led me down the street and down the walkway that led to the building. I noticed flower bushes on either side of the walkway. I hadn't seen that before. We entered the building and climbed two flights of stairs, stairs I must have just raced down. I had no memory of that. We entered the office and walked through the waiting room. Many were staring at me. I felt their eyes boring into me. "Crazy, crazy, crazy." I heard the chant in my head, mocking me.

I saw the dentist sitting on his swivel stool, waiting for me beside the chair I had occupied a short time ago. He was staring at me. Judging me. "Crazy, crazy, crazy." I was gently guided back into that chair. The dentist and hygienist were talking to me but I couldn't hear them. There was only a loud buzzing in my ears. They looked at me like they were afraid of me, afraid to work on me. Their lips were moving but their bodies weren't. I surmised they were expecting something of me. I nodded my head slightly, assuming they were waiting for my permission to begin again, forced my head back into the chair, and squeezed my eyes tightly shut. I felt tears dripping into my ears, but nothing else. I heard the buzzing in my ears but nothing else. I don't know how long I was there, but I do know after I paid I left, all in a blurred, dreamlike, detached state. I never returned. I was too embarrassed. I made such a scene. I never entered that office again.

54.

ONE DAY, THERE WAS ONE lie too many for me to manage.

In my marriage, I was drifting. I was existing. I was neither engaged nor not engaged. Josh and I circled each other, sharing our home, watching TV together, drinking coffee together, but didn't really connect. We were more roommates than husband and wife and I had no energy to address that. The panic attacks occurred about once per week, sometimes once every two weeks, and left me feeling like I had run a marathon. Any energy I had was focused on work and managing life. Cooking, cleaning, laundry, anything the children needed, and basic survival were all I could manage. Relationship wasn't in the needing attention queue at this point.

Then there was the lie that dragged relationship to the front of the line.

Josh had been promoted at his work and hated it. He hated being in a management role. He wanted to revert and return to his old job. I fully supported his need to do this. I always felt that contentment was more important than money and encouraged him to speak to his boss and share his needs. He did so, reverted to his previous position, and all was well.

A few months later, we attended a huge function for his work.

As we maneuvered through the crowds preparing to find our table for dinner, many people I knew from my fifteen years spent with Josh approached me and asked how I was doing. I was being asked in a pointed way, not a casual way as one would when catching up. I started to feel uneasy and a little suspicious after the fourth person, who happened to be Josh's direct manager, approached me, put her hand on my shoulder, looked into my eyes with very real concern, and asked me, "How are you doing? Really? How are you?" My mind was racing. Did they know about the panic attacks? I hope Josh hadn't said anything. I was dreadfully embarrassed by what happened to me without my control and didn't want everyone to know. Not in this crowd, not now.

My unease grew through dinner as others approached and asked.

I didn't ask Josh at the event what was going on; I wanted him to enjoy his evening with his coworkers, but on the drive home, I probed. What had he told people? Why was everyone so concerned about me?

"Oh, yeah, that ..." he started. "I should have told you, I guess. I told everyone your cancer was back, and that's why I had to step down from the management position. I told them I had to help you with doctors and stuff. You know?"

No.

I didn't know.

My body filled with emotions I couldn't readily identify. I stayed silent, trying to process what I had just heard. I felt the tears, always the damned tears.

I heard him say, "It's no big deal. I didn't want everyone to think I was a loser, so I told a little white lie. No harm done."

So why did I feel harmed?

I couldn't resolve this in my head as being OK. I tried to reason with myself; at least he hadn't told them about the panic attacks. Why couldn't that be enough for me? Why was I so upset that he would say I had cancer again? How did this impact me?

It made me sick. That's how it impacted me. I felt physically sick thinking about it. How could someone who loved me even pretend I had that illness again? That was such a bad time in my life. I was scared. I was told I might die. I felt completely out of control. What kind of human being would tell people I was in that place again? It felt wrong. Violating. Disrespectful. My crazy mind even worried that saying something, telling people something like that as truth could somehow make it happen again. Bad mojo. I couldn't make this little "white lie" OK. I tried but it had harmed me. It had broken trust. If he could lie so easily about something that bad, without even a passing thought, what else could he lie about? I don't know where my reaction fell on the continuum. Was I overreacting, being oversensitive, emotional, making something bigger than it was? Probably. But could I live with it? No.

I found an apartment, packed my and my daughter's things, she was my only child left at home, and moved out a month later. Crazy, unstable Nikki does it again. I knew what was being said about me. And did I feel I had done the right thing? No. Had I done the wrong thing? No. For me, I had done the only thing that I could do at that moment. Crazy? Healthy? What shade was this? I didn't know.

The day I rented the apartment, I told Josh early in the morning that I was leaving. I told him I had rented an apartment and that I would tell my daughter after work. When I got home that day, my daughter was furious with me for making a huge decision about our lives and not even telling her. Josh had told her when she got home from school. My daughter was livid and crushed. I was so angry with him for telling her before I had a chance to talk to her. But would it have made a difference? Once again, I had hurt the people I loved as my crazy couldn't manage life. She loved Josh, and ripping her away from him and that home seemed especially selfish and cruel.

As I continued to prepare for the move, Susan contacted me.

She asked me to please reconsider my decision to leave Josh. She stated she felt I was good for him. I told her I could not believe she would say such a thing after all the trouble she had caused us. And guess what? Shockingly, much of what I was told she had done, she denied. To this day, I don't know the actual truth, though I suspect it lies somewhere in between their two versions of events. We all have our perspective, and as I have shared, I can't even guarantee mine is a correct rendering of fact. I can say unequivocally that it is exactly how I recalled, interpreted, and reacted, but that is the best I can give.

Soon after the move, the panic attacks intensified to the point where they were almost unmanageable. I felt I was losing my mind. Once again, I dragged myself back to my doctor, and once again, my medication was increased to cope with the decisions I made. Bad decision? Here are more pills. Mistake? Here, this will make it go away. That's how I was starting to feel. I was forty-eight years old and I was still a mess.

I had stopped exercising. I had stopped eating well. I had completely forgotten all the tools Althea had taught me years ago. I had reverted back to all my old habits, and I couldn't blame the doctor for throwing pills at me. What was I doing to make things better? Nothing. I was as reliant on the pills to "save" me as the doctors were in giving them to me.

I had to do better.

I hauled my fat carcass back to the gym. I had reconnected with my dear friend, Carys, and as our friendship had started, we were full circle back at the same gym I had taught at many years prior. Her life had given her hardships as well. Mine were of my creation because I couldn't seem to manage my illness, but hers were outside of her control. She lost her husband, the man who had broken his neck those many years ago, to cancer. She too had gone through what must have been a very dark time. In our time together, we didn't talk much about the darkness; we focused more on survival.

We sweated and groaned side by side on our machines, and soon, the weight slowly started to come off. Along with that, the panic attacks reduced somewhat and my eating improved. I was living in a healthier environment with my daughter and her boyfriend, who had also moved in with us. Work was going well, and life was looking up. For a moment anyway. Until, one day, I stumbled onto a ghost of the past and made another damaging decision.

55.

FRANK. HE WAS STILL ROAMING the very same gym where I first met him. And the terrible cosmic joke of being drawn to the worst thing for me was well in play.

With Frank came unlimited quantities of alcohol and a complete disregard for any consequences from the intake. With unlimited quantities of alcohol came a numbness that annihilated all the darkness, panic, and feelings of worthlessness that still lurked under the surface. Oh, but that darkness rested, gained strength, and that panic refuelled while I was numbing my body and mind with the liquid magic, and the next day it would come back with a vengeance, stronger than ever. The panic would last the whole day after drinking, peaking off and on into full attacks but lingering at a buzzing level, constant throughout. The only solution was to get through the workday until I got home and downed that first glass of blood-red numbing juice. By the second glass, the ugliness would recede back to its hole somewhere deep in me, to rest and come back stronger the next day. But I didn't see this then. I had hangovers, but at the time, I didn't see the connection between the drinking and increased symptoms of my disease.

I was completely out of control. I was beginning to blackout, losing entire spans of time. I was causing incredible heartache to my daughter. She was concerned and disgusted at the same time. Her boyfriend tried to shield her from her toxic mother and was equally disgusted with me. I could see it on both their faces. I made them sick. Yet I continued. What was to be my new beginning was a disaster wholly caused by me. I was in a vicious cycle and didn't even try to get out of it.

A lifelong dream of mine had been to go to an all-inclusive beach resort. Josh and I talked of it endlessly but it was never the right time. With Frank, it finally happened. He told me he was going and I could come along if I could dig up the cash. I was so excited! And what better place for a drunk than a resort with an all-inclusive bar. Add to that endless food at my disposal. Check and check. All my vices were covered.

The vacation was not what I hoped. Frank and I did not get along. Add alcohol, the "fuel of reason," to our arguments, and things were just horrible.

When we got back, we went our separate ways for a few days to think. I certainly needed to; I needed to address my reckless behaviour.

A week after our return, we decided to go for dinner and talk. I had one glass of wine and it actually turned my stomach. I guess there is a max a liver can take before it screams "enough." Frank spoke of wanting to continue our relationship with the addition of a third party to our mix, the woman he had cheated on me with so long ago and had also been seeing at the same time as he was seeing me once again.

Frank had a weird hold on me; I can't explain it. But while we were together, I would do anything to make him happy. I would leave my needs, morals, and values at the door and give in to whatever he wanted. The need to keep him overrode all sense of reason. When we were apart, as in not in each other's lives throughout the many years that had passed, I would often think of him. I would romanticize our connection in my head, and he grew into a "one that got away" obsession.

It was not out of the question for him to ask for a polyamorous relationship; why wouldn't he? And truthfully, shamefully, in the past, I might have given in. I want to believe that would have been the line, but I can't say that for sure.

But that day, it was the line. I surprised myself by saying no. We drove back to my place, and I told him I was not prepared to do that, and in fact, this relationship was over. I knew we cared for each other, even loved each other in a sick and dysfunctional way. And I also knew that I had to clean up my life and I wouldn't do that attached to Frank.

I recall the conversation clearly. I was calm and had spoken my truth. And he was a cruel ass. He told me I would never be able to function on my own, and I would die if I had to be alone, assuring me that would be my destiny. He told me I would be alone the rest of my life, and I was too weak to manage that. He told me I was a burden on him. He told me my neediness was smothering. He told me I was a fake, a phony, a horrible human being, and no one would ever want me. He said I was an ugly, fat, drunk, and looking at me physically sickened him. He said he had to be drunk to even touch me. I cried silently listening to him describe me, exactly as I saw myself. He was right. All of this was true and I knew it.

He dropped me off and I walked into the apartment, went directly to my room, crawled into bed, and sobbed.

My grown baby girl tried to comfort me. I told her I was done with Frank, and I know she thought I was broken over that. But that wasn't the entire reason; it was only a small part of the anguish I was feeling. I knew Frank had spoken the truth. Everything he said was fact. I *was* garbage. I *was* a fat, disgusting, needy drunk. I *was* terrified to be alone and would die alone. I *was* a burden, and no one would ever want me. I *was* unlovable. I *was* a waste of skin. I *was* a mess. And I caused it.

I cried through the night and off and on over the next few days. I called in sick and stayed in bed. I didn't want to live, but I couldn't die. I didn't want to be. I was worthless. Frank had only pointed out what I knew.

Then, one morning, something shifted. Without warning, I decided I was done crying. My daughter's anxious face as she checked on me and cared for me filled my mind. What the fuck was I doing? I was being a sucky bitch! My baby, who was attending university full-time, working on assignments every night to the wee hours of the morning, going through her education on a full scholarship, and holding down a job to help me pay for this apartment, was now caring for a self-absorbed brat. A selfish, whiny suck. This was literally bullshit. Who the fuck did I think I was?

I was a mother and a grandmother to two beautiful little boys by this time. I was a manager of an entire region with the company I worked for. Was I everything Frank had said? Absolutely. But I was more as well. I had survived cancer and survived two divorces. I was a hard worker and climbed my way to the top position in my organization. I was a fucking YWCA Woman of Distinction for God's sake, an honour I had recently received in the area of Management and Leadership. I was making my way on my own, in my own apartment. And I was too fucking old to be acting like this! Fuck that! The pity party was over. All guests out.

So I had a mental illness! Everyone had something and I was done letting this illness control me. Words I had said over and over when I gave my talks to small and large groups about not being defined by your disability came back to me. I had said those words, passionately, to people who listened and applauded. People came to me after and said those words had moved them, changed them. But I didn't live them, not really. I battled mental illness. I was at war all the time. I didn't live with it. I fought the demon. I threw medication at it. I threw nutritional food at it. I threw exercise at it. I threw therapy at it. I argued internally with it all day, every day. And then I threw alcohol at it. I was constantly at war with it and with myself. I was done with the battle. Somehow, we, my illness and myself, needed to learn to coexist. It was here for the long haul and so was I. The war was over. I surrendered. I had mental illness ... and so what?

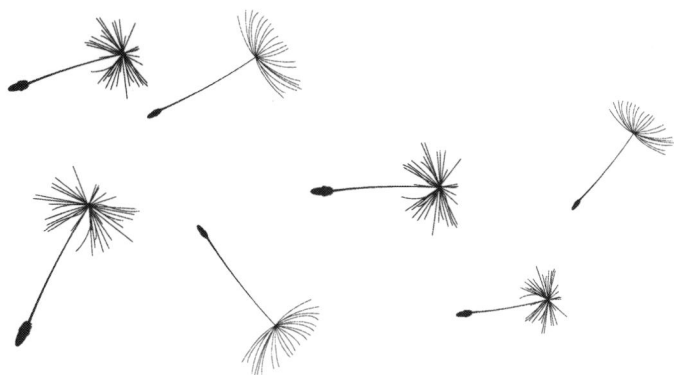

PART THREE
STEPPING INTO THE LIGHT
ACCEPTANCE

56.

REMEMBERED THE TIMES OF PEACE I felt while in a meditative state in Althea's chair. That was goal one, to learn to meditate. A friend of mine was also interested in learning more about the process and together we found a group to join. We didn't know, or I didn't know, that it was a Buddhist Sangha, a community of Buddhists who gather together to study the teachings of Buddhism. When I realized where I was and what I was actually attending on my first day, it didn't impact me or my decision to be there. I wasn't concerned about what they called themselves or what their gathering purpose was. In fact, I was intrigued; perhaps I could learn something that would help me on my quest to become a whole person rather than two divided beings in a constant war. Sick Nikki versus Well Nikki, the battle of a lifetime. A forty-nine-year war with no winner.

The group rented a room in a local church every Saturday morning. I was nervous entering, and my familiar feeling of being watched and judged accompanied me as I walked into the room. I had done my homework and knew I needed a cushion, comfortable clothing, and a water bottle, and had all that with me. My friend and I found a space on the floor and plopped onto our cushions.

A bell rang, everyone bowed, and we did the same. The leader told us to close our eyes and focus on our breath. The bell rang again. Everyone closed their eyes and I followed suit. I tried to focus on my breathing but my mind raced. I peeked several times to see if there was something more I should be doing, but everyone sat, eyes closed, breathing. We sat for what felt like an eternity; my legs were cramping, my back was aching, but I didn't want to shift and draw attention to myself. I tried a thousand times to return to watching my breath while my mind raced away, and it was frankly exhausting. All I did was return to the breath the entire time we sat. I never stayed with the breath. I was too busy reliving every mistake I had ever made, large or small, and making sure I felt the appropriate amount of guilt for each infraction.

Eventually, the bell rang again. We all opened our eyes and bowed. Then the leader spoke. She shared a story that resonated with me. It was about two monks who were walking and came across a woman standing next to a river. She wanted to cross but not get her finery dirty. One of the monks picked her up, carried her across, sat her down, and the two continued on their way. Three hours later, the monk who had not carried the woman spoke to the one who had. He said something to the effect that monks weren't allowed to touch women, and he had broken that rule by picking up the woman. The monk who had carried the woman responded, "I set her down three hours ago yet you still carry her." I realized, at that moment, the intense guilt I still carried over my destruction of my first marriage, and how my choices changed forever the trajectory of my children's lives. I still punished myself regularly for the wholesale damage I had done. I had sentenced myself to a lifetime of guilt and was making sure every day I paid my self-imposed penalty.

I continued to attend the Sangha every Saturday morning, and within a few months, I was able to mostly focus on just breathing or was otherwise able to return my wandering mind to breathing during the meditative time. I came to know that the meditation period was only fifteen minutes, but for those first few weeks, it had felt like an hour of constant wrangling with my brain. The stories spoke to me. Every week it was another version of how holding onto something, being attached to something, not letting go of something caused most of our grief. I listened intently and tried to see how each story applied to me.

This was all knowledge I was taking in. The knowledge would resonate with me on my brain level. Well Nikki thought it all made enormous sense. But Sick Nikki was resistant. What if I allowed myself to truly embrace this mindset? Although it made sense on one level, it didn't in the reality of my life. If I truly let go of suffering, would I continue to work hard? I felt pretty sure this acceptance business would breed nothing but problems. Hard work and struggle were life. That's how I got better. That's how I did things correctly. Even though I was working toward integrating my warring internal factions, letting things flow without constant management and attention didn't seem to be something I could effectively work into my existence.

57.

I BEGAN PRACTICING MEDITATION AT HOME. I had purchased a zafu, a cushion specifically for seated meditation, and that went a long way to helping my back and knees as I sat. Each evening, I would tell the kids I was going to meditate for a while, much better than going to my room to drink, and I would sit and breathe as long as I could and then return to the activity of the apartment. After several months of this daily ritual, my body adopted some sort of internal timer. I would bow, settle, breathe, and then naturally, twenty minutes later, I would slowly open my eyes, start to move my body, and wake up. I didn't sleep in the true sense of the word, but often the time passed without much conscious thought. I could hear, feel, and smell; I would watch my breathing, scan my body for tightness or discomfort, notice thoughts as they drifted in and out, and then magically, twenty minutes had passed. I felt more rested and revived after these sessions than I often did after a night's sleep.

I continued to go to the gym throughout this time, had an occasional glass of wine but nothing more, and focused on consuming nutritional food. I journaled every day, and with renewed vigor, I threw myself into my work toward expanding the region I was responsible for. I had two good friends I saw regularly: my gym friend, Carys, from years ago and a newer friend I had met through work. I continued to read self-help books voraciously but found

myself getting picky about what I read. I allowed myself to purchase
a book, read part of it, and then put it down if it didn't resonate with
me. I would never have considered doing that prior. If I bought a
book, I would read every page. You finished what you started, period,
no question. I wasn't making huge changes, but every day was a small
step. There were many days I was tired and didn't want to do the
work, days I felt my illness, days I felt the fear, and even had the
occasional panic attack. I wasn't healed; I was simply learning to
work with my mental illness and integrate it as part of a whole me.

On those bad days, my knee-jerk was to fight it. Make it go away.
Bring all the tools to the forefront and kick its ass until it receded,
and I often did that without thinking. But, occasionally, very very
occasionally, I encouraged myself to sit with the fear, or anger, or
numbness, or whatever manifestation the illness chose that day. I
would try to experience it, try to dialogue with it. It was so difficult
to just be ill. Everything in me continued to revolt against it. I still
believed somewhere deep within that if I ever did fully integrate all
those parts, my illness would win and I would be put away, locked
up, lost forever. I would lose the part of me that was reasonable and
instead be consumed by illness. I would forever and only be Sick
Nikki, and I had way too much to lose for that to happen.

I accepted my mental illness. I spoke publicly about it and my
journey. I often felt that this illness was a gift in that I survived
and was, in fact, doing well in my life, and I could share that with
people who were struggling. I could show them what mental illness
looked like, that it looked like me, and that there was hope. I shared
my strategies and tools and told them not everything worked all the
time and not everything worked for everyone. I made it clear I
wasn't a professional and they should always consult professionals.
I was simply a person with lived experience and it was different for
everyone. But I wanted to share that I was a survivor.

But accepting and integrating? Those were very different. I
accepted it as part of my life. I didn't hide it. I openly spoke to it.
But I still kept a tight leash on Sick Nikki and always would. She
could take it all away if allowed.

58.

I STUMBLED ACROSS AN APARTMENT FOR rent that I knew would be perfect for my daughter and her boyfriend. She was graduating with her degree in a month's time, and she had already received four job offers. She was ready—they were ready—to start their lives on their own. I knew it. But I was afraid. Frank's words came rushing back to me: "You will die if you have to be alone."

Should I share the information with them? Should I keep them with me so I feel safe?

I knew the correct decision and told them what I had found. They weren't sure it was the right move. They weren't sure if they were ready. I wanted to assure them they weren't and it wasn't the right move. They should stay with me forever. But I knew that was wrong. I convinced them it was the right thing to do, fighting everything in me, and soon they were gone, starting their life together as they should be.

The worst was going to bed and getting up in the morning. The silence and loneliness engulfed me at those times, and the fear filled me. I started to have regular panic attacks again. And the weekends. The weekends were brutal. The weekends became constant panic, punctuated by full-blown attacks.

I developed a routine to try to curb the attacks. During the week, I went to the gym every day after work for an hour or more. When I got home, I immediately turned the TV on and kept it on throughout the entire evening. I would prepare myself a light meal and eat it in front of the screen. I would go to my room and do my meditation but had to leave the TV on in the living room. And then, when I could hold my eyes open no longer, I would shut the TV off and go to bed. That's when the terror that had barely been kept at bay would pounce, and I would find myself struggling to breathe, heart racing, crying, crouched somewhere, unable to move. When I was finally able, I would crawl to my bed and drift off from pure exhaustion into a fitful sleep. I would then find myself running through my apartment, never leaving it thank God, filled with terror.

The weekends were the worst, so early every week, I made plans to fill those days with activities to mimic the hours of my workday. I would go to the gym every Saturday and Sunday morning for a few hours. I would come home, turn on the TV, have a quick lunch, and then go see my children, travelling to each of their homes in rotation. Then I would have a coffee date with a friend or have an activity such as a visit to a museum or park or something lined up. It couldn't be an event with lots of people attending. That would cause an immediate attack. But it had to be something distracting enough to carry me through to suppertime when I would engage in my regular weekday evening routine.

I was growing more and more exhausted and with exhaustion came increasing numbness and fear. I recognized this and knew I needed to see my doctor again. I was once again at the top dose of my antidepressant, escitalopram, and I wasn't sure how she could help me but I knew I needed help.

She prescribed clonazepam, telling me to take one as soon as I felt a panic attack coming. She said it was a small dose but advised me to not take it daily and only if that panic was bad. She said it was addictive and could cause other problems. She started me with seven pills and told me to see her in a month.

Her lecture about the addictive issues scared me. I was certain I was addicted to alcohol, even though it had only been for a short period of time. And if I wasn't a full-on addict at that time, I certainly had the ability to become one. I put the pills aside and vowed to only use them if absolutely necessary.

I continued with the daily panic attacks for two more days, not wanting to use the pills. The third day when I shut the TV off to go to bed, I felt the panic begin once again. I was too exhausted to fight any further. I needed relief, and in the midst of panic, addiction was the least of my worries. As the anxiety built, I ran to the pills and swallowed one quickly before I could change my mind. I brushed my teeth, the panic still within me. I got into my pajamas, struggling with my breathing. "Why isn't this thing working?" my mind raced. I tried to crawl into bed but couldn't. I had to pace. It wasn't helping! And the more I thought that the more the anxiety increased. And then, about twenty minutes later, I noticed my breathing had slowed, my heart rate had stabilized, and I was tired of pacing and was feeling a bit drowsy. I crawled into bed.

I awoke the next morning, still in my bed. I got up and felt the fear as per usual when I opened my eyes and remembered I was completely alone. I threw back the covers as I did every day, ran to the living room, and turned the TV on. I gulped air, knowing soon I wouldn't be able to breathe. And I waited. Within minutes, I knew today was different. The fear clung to me, ached in me. I cried and felt a very real physical pain in my chest. But it remained at that level. It didn't explode into a full attack. I remained terrified and I paced, but I could think; I was aware of where I was and was still seeing and breathing.

I cried as I made my coffee. I cried as I dressed. I cried as I drove to work but I didn't have an attack.

That night, I had another attack and took another pill. At this rate, I wouldn't last a month with seven pills, now five. But I couldn't obsess about that. I just needed to breathe.

Once again, I slept through the night, and although I was filled with the same achy, consuming fear, I didn't have my usual morning panic attack.

I used those seven pills in seven days and returned to my doctor. She gave me more. In the end, I needed twenty pills the first month. The next month, I took ten, and soon, I was down to about three pills per month. Was it the medication or my transition to learning to be on my own? Both, I would say.

I wouldn't say I enjoyed being alone, but I managed it. I wasn't as fearful at night and enjoyed reading my book before I slept. The mornings and weekends remained the hardest, but overall, I was managing and was once again, more or less, enjoying my life.

59.

M Y BEST FRIEND, GOOD WINE, and a tablet. What could go wrong?

Carys had recently met a wonderful man online and felt it was in my best interests to do the same. Two glasses of wine in, my self-imposed limit now, it sounded like a fun idea.

We developed a profile on a fish-themed dating site, and it was brilliant! Wine brilliant! Everything was determined to be perfect and complete with the exception of two things: my online name and a picture that showed me off to be the most desirable, yet not slutty, fun, yet serious, independent yet properly dependant, mature yet child-like, stable yet risk-taking, well-read, drama-free, well-travelled, financially independent, well-rounded person to ever exist. Surprisingly, I didn't have a picture like that handy. So we focused on my name. Every single good name was taken. I wanted something that described me. I had grown from an uptight perfectionist into a meditating, crystal-toting, incense-burning, hippie-like individual and wanted something to show that. We tried everything and were getting more and more out there. I glanced at the crystal in the ring on my hand, a lapis lazuli, and asked her to try that as a name. It worked. Shockingly, no one had taken that as their online name.

The next morning, reason and sobriety prevailed, and I decided to shut down the profile. I was just learning to be on my own, coming to terms with living with my illness, had developed a solid routine, and was actually enjoying life. I didn't do well in a relationship. My illness thrived in relationship. I hadn't learned to manage it when coupled, and I wasn't ready to do that yet.

As I hovered my mouse over the delete button, I noticed an option, a hide button, and for some reason, I clicked that one.

Over the next couple of weeks, I wondered, would it be so bad to meet people, find a few new friends to connect with, have dinner with, go to a movie with? I didn't want a relationship, but I was on my own and open to friendships. I was fascinated with what made people do what they did, and this was a chance to dig deeper into that interest.

Two weeks later, I decided what harm could come from just seeing who was out there? I had my co-workers take a couple of pictures of me that met zero of the above-described criteria and clicked the button to unhide my profile.

"Welcome back, Lapis Lazuli!" I cringed. That had to go.

Then I read the profile. It had dimmed in brilliance and needed revision to accurately reflect my truth. It never occurred to me to lie or exaggerate. There was no point. I was soon to be fifty years old and wanted to connect with people who might be interested in meeting me, people I actually had things in common with, not a wildly fictional character I created. And what happened if you actually met a person face-to-face and you weren't thirty pounds lighter and twenty years younger than the picture you posted? That had to be a problem. From my perspective, that would result in a brutal conversation that I had no interest in being involved in. I wanted fun, friends, people to go for walks with, go out to eat with, talk to. I didn't want a partner or all the strings and nonsense with dating. I was finished with that in my life. I had grown children who were all extremely successful in careers and relationships. I had two grandchildren. My career was thriving. I had my cute little apartment and I was doing great on my own. The panic attacks were rare. The darkness was present but it kept quiet for the most part. I lost close to forty pounds. I exercised and ate well and felt physically good. I meditated at least five times a week. I had a couple of good friends that I spent time with. I felt content. I didn't have any drama in my life and didn't want any. I was living a peaceful existence and had no need to mess with that.

First off, Lapis Lazuli needed to be changed. What a ridiculous name! What would best describe me? Truth was critical. I wanted something that would accurately reflect me and who I was if I was going to do this. I pondered. I loved the outdoors and nature. I was a bit of a hippie, a Type A hippie. I was small in stature. What one word could convey those things? Bingo! Woodnymph!

I changed my profile name at that moment. Perfect! Now we were cooking.

Then I uploaded the pictures. I made sure they were whole-body pictures, current, and in clothing I actually owned, with hair and slight makeup I actually wore. In the two weeks I had hidden my profile, I perused other profiles and saw lots of pictures clearly taken from a ladder, looking down from above, and capturing a face only. I understood why. Gravity pulled jowls and chins out of the camera's view. But what were they going to do with all that extra flesh when they actually met a person? Sit on the floor of some restaurant or coffee shop and gaze softly upward as they chatted? My pictures all looked exactly like me, flaws and all.

Then the series of questions to complete the profile needed to be addressed. Children at home—no. Longest relationship length—forever. Body type—fat wasn't a choice but I chose the closest to it. Smoker—long since stopped. Relationship wanted—I cringed a bit as I scrolled through "long-term relationship" to find the correct option for me, "just friends."

I rewrote the paragraph description, making sure it was painfully accurate, and then clicked save. I was proud of myself. This was a big step from the fearful person I had been only a few years ago.

I immediately texted my friend who had initiated this whole process and told her I had unlocked my profile and was ready to give it a whirl. She was excited for me. I also told her I changed my stupid name, and she asked what I called myself.

"Woodnymph," I texted.

"W … T … F?" appeared immediately in response.

Before I could respond to her text, I saw the icon flash on the dating app. I had mail!

"So you're a nympho who likes wood, huh?"

Fuck.

I went back into my profile to change my name. Any name would be better. Back to Lapis Lazuli would even be a step up. Anything but a "nympho who likes wood." It was locked with a cheery little note advising me that my name couldn't be changed after two weeks. I was woodnymph! Could I have made a whole new profile? Absolutely! Did I think of that? Absolutely not.

So I revised my descriptor paragraph to include why I had chosen my name—nature, outdoors, short—all my reasoning, hoping to clarify what the moniker really indicated.

Oh, and by the way, "just friends" is also an issue I came to understand. It means "no-strings-attached intimate encounters." Why that couldn't have been clearer on the drop-down menu of relationship choices is still a mystery to me.

Being able to open this profile, answer messages, engage in conversations showed me I was tipping toward well. I have always taken incidents, encounters, situations, actions, something outward, to show how the inward was doing, an indicator of where I fell on the wellness continuum. I was never able to be the one who could sit on the zafu for a time and emerge with a clear knowing of where I was in my life with mental illness. I hoped for the day that would become my truth, but at this time, that was not the case. I would skip or plod through my life and something I had done, or not done, a way I had behaved or not behaved, would indicate where I was on the continuum from my perspective. The day I was able to purchase my groceries, for example, that day showed me I was tipping toward a shade of well. The day Frank and I ended things, and how I laid in bed immobilized for days, showed me I was tipping toward illness. I never seemed to be pre-aware; I operated from hindsight.

As I reflected at the end of each day after wading through the dating fishpond, I felt I had achieved my goal. I was no longer battling mental illness. Mental illness was part of my life, my breath, just as my eye colour and my height. It was part of me, the fibre of me, and Well and Sick Nikki somehow agreed to coexist and work together as one. I know this story would be way more fun if I could isolate a lightning bolt incident when the two collided in a fiery mess, wrestled, and struggled, dark against light until finally, thunderously, they fused into one being. But the thing I promised myself when I sat to write my story was to be completely truthful. And the truth is that somehow over time, maintaining all the things I learned over the years of battling, the exercise, nutrition, spiritual connection through meditation, medication, seeing the doctor when I knew I needed, and then adding the final piece to the puzzle, the sleep, I finally found my level of wellness.

I still had very dark days. I still had the occasional panic attack. My staff would gently ask if I had been to the gym lately on days I was snappy and irritable for no reason, and without fail, the answer was I hadn't. If I had too many drinks one night, I would suffer from horrible panic attacks and uncontrollable fear for the next two days. If I drifted from my meditation and journaling, the symptoms would return. The fact was simply that I had a chronic disease, a disability, and I had the tools I needed to manage my symptoms to live a full life. Just as a diabetic has to take their medication, watch their diet, and exercise to be well, I was the same. It was no different in my mind, and if I developed symptoms from something I had done or not done, I was the one responsible for fixing it.

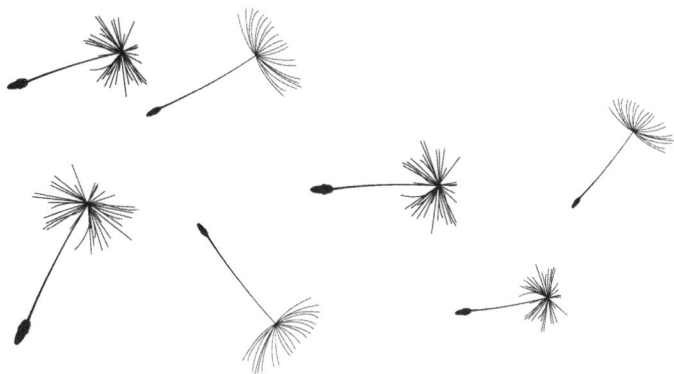

60.

SWIMMING IN THE DATING FISHPOND was a very enjoyable time of my life. As I wasn't looking for a relationship and was really just looking for friends at best, or a great story at the worst, it became incredibly exciting and just fun.

Each day after work, I would sign on and see what was happening. I had made a promise to myself at the outset that I would answer every single message I received, believing that if someone took the time to write something, no matter how off-colour, and some were, that I would answer them. I found out early on that I needed to set some limits on age groupings that could message me after I received a message from an eighteen-year-old who asked me to describe my favourite pair of boots. I thanked him for his message, said they were older than he was, and wished him luck in his search. Then immediately went to settings and set it such that no one under forty years of age could message me.

"I wish you the best in your search" became a go-to written and spoken sentence.

Most messages I received were answered as such, but I did engage in messaging back and forth with approximately thirty men. Over time, after several messages back and forth, I agreed to meet several of them face-to-face. I always ensured safety first; we always met in a public place, and my children knew where I was at all times. Some were a single meeting with my now well-used phrase wrapping up a quick coffee date. Some were a few meetings and then we just drifted to texting and then to nothing. And some became friends that I did indeed spend time with. Most importantly, I found each and every person I interacted with interesting in their own way. I was fascinated by humankind and thoroughly enjoyed messaging through the site and getting to know so many people. I even messaged with a few scam artists who were so obvious it was laughable. I would continue until we got to the "money ask" and then cut them off, but it was interesting to get to see a new side of humanity, and I loved every minute of it.

Of the ones I met face-to-face, a couple had forgotten they were married, a few posted pictures from many, many years ago, one apparently lost his high-paying professional job between our messaging and meeting only a few days later. One wasn't sure if he had children, and if he did, he wasn't sure where those children were. Some were looking for fun only; some were looking for a housekeeper and caregiver, but I have to say, most of the people I met face-to-face were genuine, good, lonely people. I marvelled at what the world handed to some. I was frustrated by a few who clearly enjoyed their victimhood. But could I really judge? Had I been a professional victim at some point in my journey to wellness? My perception says no, but I bet their perception says the same of themselves.

I found myself learning not to judge. I found myself trying to step into the shoes of another. Initially, I was appalled by the married men on the site looking for companionship, but did I know their lives and circumstances? Was I in any position to judge them? No, I was only in control of myself, and the few I met before they remembered their wives existed were nice people, and I enjoyed my visits with them. I chose not to continue an active friendship with them, but that wasn't a judgement of them. It was a boundary of mine.

I became aware that, somewhere along the line, I had become less rigid, less judgemental, and I fully believe that started internally with myself and then spread outward. As I started to accept myself, really accept all parts of myself, I started to recognize that I could make mistakes and survive. That was still a hard one to swallow but I was working on it. And as I grew, I extended that to others, and it circled back to making my life better. I became better at my work, better as a mother to grown children, better as a grandmother, better at being an ex-wife, better at being a friend, and just being a better person. In the past, I had been completely self-absorbed in the very true sense of the word. I had to monitor and battle my illness so intensely and for so long it absorbed me. But now, at this point in my life when everything was stable, I was able to grow and learn and experience life in a way I could never have allowed myself to do so prior.

Dating online also helped to practice setting boundaries. I had never been successful at that. I needed to please everyone first as my value, and therefore wellness, depended on outside approval. I wouldn't say I became skilled at it, but I was learning that I could set boundaries and feel OK. It was much easier to do with strangers but it was a place to start.

I also learned that I could start to trust myself a little more. Since my diagnosis, I hadn't really been able to trust anything. I couldn't fully determine or rely on my analysis of where things fell on the wellness scale. Everything was always shadowed, covered by illness. Was this an appropriate reaction or an illness-based overreaction? Was this normal fear or my out-of-control paranoia? What was correct? What did society say was normal? I never knew and spent hours in my head reliving and replaying conversations, scenarios, arguments, and actions over and over, analyzing, critiquing, and never coming out with an answer.

So I was on a path, nowhere near the end or success, but I was seeing small wins along the way. I still had many moments when my illness ruled the day, but I knew that was my life.

My meditative practice had also taken an interesting turn along the way. Now, as I settled onto my zafu and started focusing on my breathing, I would enter a deep state quickly and often felt I had "seen" things or "visited" places during my spiritual time. Very often, I felt myself "going downward" and would see myself and others around a fire at night. The light of the fire flickered over our faces as some danced and some sat. I felt warm and at home as I slid into this ... dream? Vision? Imagining? I couldn't share these experiences with many people in my life, as I knew it further substantiated my "craziness," so I kept them mostly to myself. My analysis was, real or not real, it didn't matter since how I felt after was most important. And I felt rested and renewed after visiting this fire with friends.

One night in my meditation, I saw, on my left side, a tunnel that was lit from the end furthest from me. It reminded me of the tunnel football players run through to get onto the field. I could see someone walking toward me along this tunnel but could only see that person's outline as the light was behind them. I couldn't see the face or any features. I knew it was a man but had no idea who or what the meaning of this held for me. I was pretty sure I didn't know the person but I may have. I vowed to pay more attention as I went through my days. Was this maybe someone I would meet through the dating application? Did this person have a message for me? Or was it just my overactive imagination? Any or all could have been true. I didn't know what to make of these new details that occurred during my meditative times and assumed most were just fantasy, dream, or imagination at work.

61.

ONE SATURDAY EVENING, I WAS meeting a person I had recently been messaging on the site. I hadn't messaged him for as long as some of the others, but I was planning a vacation and wanted to meet him before I spent two weeks away and lost touch, something that could happen quickly on the site.

He was a strong, broad-shouldered, long-haired, strong-armed, terrifying-looking human. He had pictures of himself on a motorcycle and in front of a semi on the site. He looked like he ripped phone books apart for shits and giggles and could and would do the same to a person if they slightly irritated him. So why was I meeting him face-to-face? Because his messages were engaging and fun and didn't match the pictures at all. I was curious to see what this dichotomy was about.

I was a little more nervous than I usually was prior to meeting a new person. The more I looked at the pictures, the more I wondered at the wisdom of this meeting. But I promised myself I wanted to stretch my comfort zone, meet all kinds of people I would normally never cross paths with, and step into new experiences. And nothing about this person seemed congruent and I wanted to find out more.

Being prudent and safety-minded, I had asked him in messages prior to our meeting if he was an axe murderer as he did indeed look as I perceived an axe murderer would look. He said no and his long-winded response to my question made me laugh. But my mind raced as I prepared for the meeting; would an axe murderer lie? And could they be funny? Yes and yes.

Best be prepared. I grabbed a steak knife and threw it in my purse. We were going to Boston Pizza, and it never occurred to me they may have protective cutlery on hand. As I was grabbing my keys, a realization dawned on me. An axe murderer would take my purse! I removed the knife from the purse and shoved it into my bra so I could readily grab it. And I sliced open my bosom. I saw the blood on my blouse and then felt the stinging wound my weapon of protection created. Great. I bandaged the wound and put the steak knife back in my bag. I would simply need to be lightning-quick, I surmised and headed to the restaurant.

I sat on a raised bar stool waiting and watched as the axe murderer drove up on his Harley. He took off a cumbersome-looking suit and then headed into the building. He didn't seem armed and dangerous. He approached me with the most beautiful smile I had ever seen, those broad shoulders and strong arms just as in the pictures, and he gave me a warm hug. I felt a little tingle. We visited for hours, drinking endless glasses of pop as I applied constant pressure to my bosom to stop the oozing from the self-inflicted wound. He seemed like a nice man, not murderous in the slightest, and I hoped we could develop a friendship.

A few days later, I celebrated my fiftieth birthday. I felt as well as I ever had and life was looking up.

I did see Jack, my biker, once more before I left on vacation. I had initiated the first meeting and he had the second. I had a very nice time once again, and I believed we could be on our way to a friendship.

As spring turned to summer, I was starting to see more of Biker Jack. All my dating friends had a descriptor and name. There was Icon Jeff, Weather Jim, Farmer John, Hippie Greg, Fixit Bill, Sad

George, Salesman Sam, and a few others. Biker Jack was slowly taking over part of my social schedule, but I continued to remain friends with many others. I was determined not to enter into a relationship. I didn't want to ever go back to sickness or even tempt it. I had just the right amount of stress, just the right amount of responsibility, and just the correct balance in my life to remain stable with all my wellness supports, activities, and medication in place.

I soon felt safe enough to visit Jack's home after dinner one evening and met his son and stepson, both of whom lived with him. He was a single dad and raised both kids basically on his own. That was something I admired deeply. He was an owner/operator trucker and had a massive Peterbilt in the driveway and more than a few motorcycles parked in front. On that visit, I also discovered he was an incredibly talented musician. In fact, he had made much of his living performing from a very young age and had been part of a very well-known country band. I saw CDs and promotional calendars and posters all over his home that were obviously professionally done, and I recognized the music from the radio. I was impressed. To be fair, he had told me at our first meeting that he was in a band, but seriously, who wasn't? I didn't know he meant a real band.

I also became aware after a few visits that they basically ate garbage. There appeared to be no real food anywhere in the home, and the garbage can was filled with takeout containers. I thought I could offer an occasional solution to that situation. Part of my wellness work, as I now referred to it, was making sure I engaged in hobbies I enjoyed. A couple of those were cooking on weekends and crocheting every evening while watching TV. Cooking filled those long, lonely weekends with joy and time would fly by. I always loved to cook; from the time I was twelve years old, I was making full, homemade meals for my family. I made everything from scratch, and my kids, along with their partners, were guinea pigs for new recipes. I would make up a large batch of a meal and a dessert, fill my car, and do my rounds. When my children were young, I was severely limited in my experimental culinary endeavours because of their fussiness. But now, my brilliant children had all chosen partners who enjoyed varied food, and my horizons were unlimited.

Jack and I could only see each other Saturday or Sunday due to his trucking schedule, so we would discuss mid-week if we were going to get together sometime over the upcoming weekend. One week, I made the mid-week call and asked if he was available for a quick visit Saturday afternoon. We set a time, and I showed up with cabbage rolls, perogies, and chocolate chip cookies, all made from scratch and with all the needed trimmings. Jack appeared shocked. My idea was to visit for a few minutes, drop the food off for their supper, and carry on with my day. They insisted I stay and eat with them. I witnessed what appeared to be starved wild dogs stumbling across fresh meat. It was a combination of flattering, shocking, and a little appalling. The next Saturday, I brought chicken cordon bleu, hashbrown casserole, Caesar salad (trying to slip something green into the mix), and homemade, fresh-out-of-the-oven cinnamon buns with cream cheese icing in tow. The following week, why not try BBQ ribs, garlic mashed potatoes, coleslaw, and apple pie?

My weekly visits became a new tradition, and I soon started to stay after the meal to watch movies with the family.

After a few months, we started seeing each other on both days of the weekend and were having tons of fun. We would go on motorcycle rides all over the place with his boys who also rode. We went to the beach and would travel to all the little towns around us to dine out once per weekend, but mostly just to go for the ride. Until I met Jack, I had never been on a motorcycle and I loved it. Well, that's not entirely true, but I'll get to that.

As good a musician as Jack was, his son was even better, and every weekend I was treated to concerts and endless fun. I was truly having a blast, and so far, there had been no major, lasting symptoms from my illness. I was still having some not-so-good days and still having the occasional panic attack. I was taking the largest dose of escitalopram I was allowed and relying on my clonazepam when needed, and for the most part, was stable, functional, and enjoying life.

62.

AROUND THIS TIME, I GOT a call from none other than Frank. We hadn't spoken since the night he said those terrible things to me, and I had no idea why we would need to speak ever again. He said he had something to talk about and asked me to meet him for lunch. I stated very clearly on the phone that there was zero chance of a foray into romance with us and if he understood that, I would meet him.

Why, dear reader, would I agree to dine with an ass? Excellent question, and I have a brilliant rationalization to share with you. I had a connection, a thing, an attachment with Frank that was clearly unhealthy but nevertheless a palpable thing I felt in my core, and it had lasted over twenty years. When he called or showed up, my heart would flutter a little and I would feel a little more alive. The few times that I fed that little flame, disaster would result. But the flutter remained, except for after that last horrible conversation. I had really forgotten Frank and, to be truthful, I hadn't really done that since we met at the gym all those years ago. But I wanted to tempt it. Test it. Confirm it. I had zero flutter when I heard his voice on the phone and hoped that would be the same for the face-to-face situation.

And it was. He gave me an awkward hug, and there was nothing.

Yes! My need was met for the meeting, but I chose to sit for lunch. I was curious as to what he had to say.

He opened with, "Are you seeing someone?" Hmm … I had expressed the boundaries on the phone; was he trying to suggest something? More than likely just conversation but I chose to be suspicious. I told him sort of and what was happening. I babbled about Jack, how he was a trucker, a musician, and a biker. I told him how I had never been on a bike before but loved to ride with Jack. I could tell I had hit a nerve, so I stopped monopolizing the conversation and asked him about his life.

To which Frank responded, "You have so been on a motorcycle. You were on mine." He sounded defensive.

True, he had a tiny dirt bike I had ridden a few times with him around his acreage. I answered, "Oh yes, but this is different. It's a real motorcycle that goes on the highway." This was not helpful.

And then, Frank stated he was also a trucker and did not believe I would be able to date a trucker due to my neediness. It was true that when I had been with him, I was terribly needy, but I was no longer. It was also true that while Frank had the required license, he never actually held a trucking job in his life, and I kindly just pointed that out without a care in the world. "True, but I'm in a different place now, and he is a real trucker, with a truck, and a job."

I realized how shitty I was sounding and apologized for not thinking before I spoke.

"Just like the last conversation we had," he stated.

"Excuse me?" I didn't know what he was referring to.

"When I dropped you off, the last time we saw each other. You were such a bitch. You said so many mean things."

"I didn't say anything, but you had a lot of harsh things to say," I responded, shocked.

"That's a lie," he stated very firmly. "You said so many cruel things to me and I didn't say anything to you."

"That is not true," I answered, trying to keep my voice calm. "In fact, the exact opposite is true. I remember that night clearly."

He told me what he believed I had said, things I would never have uttered in my life even when hurt, and I told him what I knew he had said. I couldn't believe how different our version of events was.

"Well," he said. "I'm not a drunk who blacks out and forgets things."

I was about to escalate the argument, assuring him I was nowhere near drunk that evening, and then I realized there was a reason for this. We both needed to hear what we heard to finally end the unhealthy attachment to each other.

I decided to let the conversation be at that point and let him have this one. "That is true," I said simply.

We finished our lunch with very surface conversation, and I never did find out what Frank wanted that day for sure. When I left that restaurant, I knew Frank was no longer going to be in my life in any form. And that was a tremendous relief.

63.

M Y "NO RELATIONSHIP" PLAN DISSOLVED right before my very eyes and, more or less, without my notice. In the last few years, as I was coming to terms with my illness and welcoming all parts of me into one being, I had developed a very "live in the moment" sort of attitude. Instead of over-analyzing everything, I consciously tried to under-analyze, and so without proper care and focus, I soon found myself firmly in a relationship. This was not the plan at all. When I realized this, I became somewhat fearful. I didn't feel my stability was such that I could handle a romantic involvement. As expectations developed, I feared I would slip back into the pleasing, boundaryless person of my past and that I would again develop symptoms of my ever-present illness. I promised myself to remain vigilant and aware but also to have fun as long as life was fun. If I found my symptoms developing, I would end things and retreat to safety and my original plan.

Over the next year, two more of my children were married, I was having fun with Jack and his family, work was exceptional, and life was good. I lost seventy pounds from my heaviest, was eating well, was committed to my fitness and meditation, and was drawn to different literature than I had been in the past. I alternated nonfiction with fiction and read voraciously. I pursued hobbies that interested me and tried many new things. I was developing a new relationship with life and with living. Belief systems long-held as indisputable were being challenged and found wanting. I don't know if it was the deepening meditations, or my readings, or the fact that I was able to now climb Maslow's pyramid out of the basic survival level, but things were shifting.

I became aware that my truth was that life is simply a soul putting on a human suit for a time. I believed life was much more than our seventy-plus years in the "classroom on Earth." I knew that before I arrived for this incarnation, I had chosen mental illness as my path for my soul to grow and learn a set of lessons I had decided on. I believed souls would decide on "curriculum" in their eternal state and choose, as in choosing high school or post-secondary classes, what they wanted to learn and experience. For example, a life of financial issues, relationship issues, persecution issues, or any of the millions of other lives humans experience. Then, the soul would connect with other souls who would join them during this diploma or degree in that chosen area, and then it would pop into a body, forget those decisions post their human birth and carry on with that set of "classes." I don't know how I knew this, but I believed it. Many would find this tipping to crazy on the continuum, firmly landing in a shade of unwell and delusional, and that may be true. But it is my truth, and I have no debilitating symptoms impacting my life as I carry on with this belief system, so I'm OK with it. In fact, it comforts me to know nothing is permanent and I can find learning in each life event. Somehow, that makes the hard times manageable for me.

I also got to know my soul as separate yet part of me. I could find that little flame inside my core that I originally stumbled on in Althea's office all those years ago, and I could communicate with it. I could find truth and guidance in this communication. I could feel a universal love when I slowed the busyness of life, sitting on my zafu. I found myself connected to the Earth through strong roots that I could actually "see" and "feel." I would experience a white light surrounding me, a universal love called by whatever name best suits each soul. I felt all my cells were, in fact, one with all beings, human, animal, plant, rock … everything as one.

I found myself once again living a "dual" type of existence but not of an adversarial nature. Where I once fought my mind, argued with myself, Sick Nikki versus Well Nikki in constant battle, I now had conversations on my zafu between Soul Nikki and Human Nikki. Again, you may find this still a shade of firmly unwell on the continuum, and I couldn't argue that. I just knew it didn't cause damage or chaos, so I decided not to treat it.

I also became aware while sitting on my zafu, well over a year into my relationship, that the person I saw coming down that backlit tunnel a few years prior was indeed Jack, and in keeping with my belief system, I was right where I needed to be at the time. I was to learn something in my connection with, Jack and even though Human Nikki was fearful that my symptoms would grow in intensity and cause problems, Soul Nikki was excited.

64.

JACK'S STEPSON AND HIS GIRLFRIEND, a beautiful young lady who was simply joy wrapped in human skin, decided they were ready to move out of Jack's home and live on their own, and they took Angel, their pit bull with them. Jack was quite upset. He loved animals and wanted a dog of his own desperately. He had pets throughout his life and his second wife had taken their dog when she left, so now with the loss of Angel, he was petless.

My sister-in-law bred Rottweilers for years, and coincidentally, they had a new litter ready for new homes shortly. I decided to buy Jack a puppy, having no idea how this simple decision would permanently change the trajectory of my life. This was not a well-thought-out decision.

Jack was on the road all week, and Jack's son had a busy life and did not sign up for puppy training or care. So who was going to take care of and train this puppy? Clearly this fell to me, and I wound up spending the weekdays at Jack's home and part of every weekend caring for Hanna, this new furry being. And for anyone who has ever owned a large breed puppy, you know training is critical. A tiny puppy can jump up on an elderly grandmother and it is cute, but a Rottie can knock them over and break their hip. Training was not optional, and someone had to take on this responsibility and that defaulted to me.

The last thing I wanted to do was give up my apartment. It had become my safe space, my sanctuary. I needed that space. My wellness felt anchored to that space. But paying for an apartment and basically living at Jack's seemed stupid, so three months after Hanna came to live with Jack, we decided I should move in.

I needed to somehow establish a boundary, a space that would mimic my apartment, so we agreed I would take over the basement of the home and set it up as my space. My children helped me clean and paint the space to create my home. Both our families moved me, using Jack's semi and a trailer he borrowed, with all of our children hauling furniture and boxes.

Jack's son wasn't happy with this move and I felt the tension. And I couldn't blame him. His father's history with past partners wasn't good. He and his dad had a strong bond and he didn't want any threat to that. I truly understood. I lived the same with my children. It's very hard on children when their parents date no matter what their age, dragging people in and out of their lives, expecting them to just accept this new person just because you, the parent, have decided they should. The whole single parent in a relationship thing is generally a mess, and how could I expect this to be different? He was seventeen years old, and he didn't need a "stepmother" or really anyone messing with his life.

Tension equals panic, and after all the boxes were unpacked and my area was set up, I had a massive panic attack. I hadn't had one that intense in quite some time and was rocked. I found my clonazepam, swallowed it and hid in the bathroom until it passed. Fuck. Had I made another mistake? What Human Nikki feared most had started on day one.

I tried to reason with myself. I tried to locate Soul Nikki. I reminded myself that this was a lesson and I had chosen it, and clearly, I had nailed last semester and this semester was a new challenge. This made perfect sense to Soul Nikki, but Human Nikki was fearful.

65.

I READ MANY BOOKS INDICATING THAT once one becomes enlightened, recognizes their soul as eternal and human existence as temporary, once one is able to connect with their soul within and can feel and experience the oneness of all, life becomes an easy, purely spiritual, entirely joyful, skip through wonderland. For me, that was a huge steaming pile of bullshit. I knew all that on one level, but I still lived in a body with a chemical imbalance that liked to fuck me over every now and again. Just to make sure I was paying attention and hadn't forgotten or missed a wellness step.

I set a few boundaries before I moved in with Jack and his son. One was I didn't ever want to live with another woman in the home. I knew I wouldn't do well with that, and part of my journey had taught me to acknowledge my needs and speak my truth out loud. I tried to do that years ago with Josh and Susan but never stuck to it. This time, it was non-negotiable. And it felt good setting some terms for myself. It strengthened my belief that I could be well in a relationship setting. They both didn't understand exactly why it was important or something I needed but agreed to my demand before I moved my entire life into their home. And that was all well and good until they both decided to do exactly what I had asked not to be done a couple of years later.

It was Josh and Susan all over again.

Jack's son had met someone and they had become very close very quickly. Jack was on the road the first night this young lady had a "sleepover." Neither Jack nor I had met her yet. I reminded both Jack and his son of our agreement. They both stated they remembered, and it was a one-time thing, and otherwise, the young couple would stay at her place when "sleepovers" were warranted.

Soon she was "just visiting" all the time. Her laundry was in the washer. Her food was in the fridge. She was there day and night. I sat all three down, Jack, his son, and the new girlfriend, and reminded them once again of my boundaries set out at the onset of our living arrangement. The young lady, to her credit, was appalled and upset. She hadn't been informed of an agreement that was being violated by her continual presence. Jack stated he thought I wouldn't notice and his son couldn't understand what the big deal was. It became clear to me in this conversation that this maneuver had gone on with Jack and his son's agreement behind my back, assuming I wouldn't notice or mind. My boundary had been violated and now I was in a situation.

I told them all we couldn't go on like this, and she could not live with us. Period. I stated this prior to moving in and it wasn't optional. Jack tried to appeal to my soft heart, telling me that the young lady was having trouble at her own home and couldn't live there, and they wouldn't bother me. And it made his son happy. He said he was OK with it, had told his son the same, and told me it wasn't going to be this way forever. Jack made his message very clear. His house, his son, his rules, and she stayed.

I felt trapped. We were over four years into this relationship. I had feelings for Jack. Did I leave? Move out? He had completely disregarded my needs. He didn't understand why it even was a need, and without discussion, had simply annihilated my known boundary. I was stressed by the whole situation and the more stressed I became, the greater my symptoms became once again.

In the meantime, while I took time to process and decide, I moved upstairs and left the basement to the couple "not really living" with us. That was Jack's descriptor of the situation. She was "just staying," not really living with us. In my past, I had always made knee-jerk decisions, and I had promised myself I would now process all sides of situations, meditate, journal, and really make sure I was deciding from a place of calmness and what was best for me, my growth, and my wellness.

My symptoms intensified, the panic attacks increased, and I started having trouble sleeping and having the nighttime attacks again. I was angry all the time and found it hard to control my irritability. I hated the anger and was continually suppressing that powerful feeling, and with that, the numbness began creeping in again.

I kept putting off deciding what to do. I didn't want to lose Jack but I felt so betrayed and violated. The longer I delayed, the more pronounced my symptoms became. What was entirely inside was beginning to manifest outside. I had two new granddaughters by this time, and even though I loved them dearly, I wasn't having the same feelings of joy when I visited or played with them. I was beginning to have that same past feeling of displacement, like I was playing with them but also watching myself play at the same time. I didn't feel the depth of joy looking into their innocent eyes, and I didn't feel grounded or connected as I once had. And I knew I needed to do something. I made a doctor's appointment and decided Jack and I needed to have a talk.

We were bickering much of the time. I was either angry or detached, my standard illness moves, and things were strained in our home. Jack and I decided to go away for the weekend together to try to connect once again. I thought this was a good time to have a conversation, and hopefully, he could fully understand my feelings and we could come to a resolution.

We had a nice time alone with each other, remembered our

feelings for each other, and agreed we would have a chat with his son when we returned home. Jack suggested that we ask his son and his girlfriend to split time between their respective homes. I felt it was a compromise I could try to live with, although I still felt wronged. But if Buddhism had taught me anything, it was that hanging on to such things, attaching to ideas and insults and pain, only hurt me.

We walked through the door feeling much more united, and then I saw the sink and counters overloaded with dirty dishes. That Zen Buddhism I just espoused? Gone! Vanished! I lost my shit. Jack's son and his girlfriend had stayed with our now two dogs all weekend and hadn't washed a dish, wiped a counter, laundered a towel, swept a floor, or located a vacuum. They had left it all for me. And why? Because I fucking always did it.

I started looking for apartments. Fuck learning and not hanging onto things. I was done with this bullshit.

And this is what I meant, dear reader, when I said experiencing the oneness of all, knowing and interacting with my soul, that which is one with God/Source/Universe, believing this was all passing experience for learning and growth did not indicate permanent peace and enlightenment. At least, for me, it didn't. And I do believe I'm not alone in this. I experienced all the above and was still completely pissed off and entirely attached to that feeling and the outcomes. I intended to pursue my spirituality and grow in it and also show people they couldn't fuck with me. I could be and was both. And yes, over a pile of dishes that indicated to me a complete disrespect for my entire personhood and existence. Again, dear reader, what shade is this?

66.

I SAW MY DOCTOR SHORTLY AFTER to try to deal with the mental illness symptoms I was once again experiencing, although I had a pretty good idea that once I was in an apartment alone again, those symptoms would subside. I didn't do well in a relationship and wasn't interested any longer in learning how to be. I had my children, the last one recently married. I had four grandchildren with another on the way and longed once again for that full life without drama that I had five years prior. I was ready to drop out of this semester of soul learning.

I had also been experiencing quite a bit of abdominal pain and thought I might as well get that checked at the same time.

I was on the highest dose of medication I could be on, and there was nothing more the doctor could do for my mental health, which further encouraged me to leave the drama I had created and find a quiet solace again. I had been well on that level of medication once and would be again. I truly believed the increased symptoms of my illness were entirely caused by the situation I created.

The doctor called me back in for a follow-up to my abdominal situation and told me my ovary, that lone soldier that had made four people and caused my numerous trips to emergency with random cysts growing and rupturing, was very sick. She said it might even be cancerous. At least she was a little better at sharing this information than my previous doctor had been. She was basing this information on the same diagnostic tool my prior cancer had chosen to show its presence. An ultrasound. However, this time, the ceiling hadn't opened above me during the procedure and showed me Heaven. I decided that had to be a good sign.

I was immediately booked with a gynecologist. Jack attended with me. The specialist agreed that the left ovary, and a tiny bit of the right one that had valiantly tried to grow back, were indeed sick, but he didn't feel they were cancerous. He said they needed to come out right away, and he would know after the tissue was analyzed by the lab. Now we were rocking. This is how the cancer diagnosis is supposed to go. I was booked for surgery, and within a month, had all traces of ovarian tissue removed. This time, I actually had a partner present after the surgery. Jack had been working and hadn't been able to drive me to the hospital, but he was able to be there when I woke up, as were my daughter and daughter-in-law. The gynecologist stated that he did not believe the tissue was cancerous and would have it analyzed, but from his experience, I was good to go. The relief was palpable.

I put all apartment hunting on hold during this time and somehow wasn't as angry as I had been prior. Jack's son and his girlfriend had apologized, realized they needed to take some responsibility for household management, and were, in fact, spending more and more time at her house. Jack was upset by this. His bond with his son was deep and he struggled not seeing him every day.

One would think I would start to get well now that some of the stressors that caused my symptoms to once again manifest were gone, but I didn't. In fact, I got sicker and sicker.

The depression was all-consuming. The panic was out of control. I was right back to my very worst times very, very suddenly. Without warning, I was as ill as I had ever been. I had night panic attacks again and the clonazepam wasn't touching them. I was unable to concentrate and was struggling with even simple things like showering and getting dressed. I managed to go to work most days, and that was all the energy I was able to muster. I would come home and crawl into bed, needing to slide into unconsciousness and knowing it would only last a short time, and then I would be running through the house in a panic and once again pacing and rocking and trying to get through life. I was completely unable to meditate; I was unable to sit still on my zafu, and concentration was out of the question. I would sit in front of the TV not watching, having no idea what I just saw, shoving handfuls of potato chips into my mouth. I tried to crochet, or colour, hobbies I had done constantly prior but was unable to do either. I wasn't allowed to exercise after my surgery but I wouldn't have anyway. I had no energy. I was completely numb and panicked all at the same time, and I felt I would never be well again. Fifty-four years old. All the work I had done. And here I was. I was ready to give up.

67.

M Y DAUGHTER DRAGGED ME TO my surgical follow-up. I didn't want to go. I didn't want to get dressed. I didn't care about anything except trying to sleep and not being able to.

I already put it off for a few weeks. What was the point? If the tissue came back cancerous, that was fine with me. A relief, in fact. I could just die and be done with this endless horrible life. If it wasn't, who cared? I certainly didn't.

I finally found myself in the specialist's office, and when he asked how I was doing, I told him. Shitty. He asked if I had been taking my hormones. I told him what I was taking and that it was doing nothing. He said no, not my regular medication, the hormones he had prescribed in the hospital. I told him I had no prescription from the hospital. Someone missed giving me something, apparently. I was supposed to have a shot and then a prescription to go home with. I had neither.

I left with yet another prescription in hand; my daughter made sure I filled it immediately, and I started taking yet more pills.

It took about six weeks for the deep depression to start to lift. I hoped for a full recovery, a full return to my former self. But something changed with the removal of my ovary, and even though the depression had lifted, I didn't feel as I had before. As the darkness started to slide away and the panic attacks were once again more or less managed with clonazepam, I started to live my life again. I longed for the level of joy and connection I had prior and hoped that, somehow, I could attain it once more.

I still felt numb much of the time. I found and positioned my mask back in place to keep the bouts of irritation from breaking through. I found the occasional glass of wine helped keep things more or less under control, and as long I didn't over imbibe and cause myself extreme panic and anxiety the following day or two, I managed. I joined a gym with my daughter and son-in-law and tried to eat well once again. I meditated sporadically but found I couldn't control my racing mind and so would give up easily. Then I just stopped trying.

Once again, I lost the ability to sleep. I saw my doctor at regular intervals as required to fill my prescriptions, and I basically plodded through life, always feeling right on the edge of tipping into complete madness and often waiting for it. Then maybe the pain would be gone.

Another doctor moved. One more new face that I had to explain everything to. I was so tired of the doctor rotation and being required to explain to each one in detail why I was prescribed the medications I was on. Why clonazepam? Did I understand what this drug was? And they would start me with five pills. Two weeks later, I would have to return, sometimes sooner, just to be able to manage the panic attacks. It was visit after visit, proving I wasn't an addict and did indeed have a mental illness. Why did this always have to be so hard? Did the diabetic have to prove themselves over and over? Why was my illness always questioned? Did these doctors think I liked living like this? That I loved having to take medication every day to just function like a normal person apparently did. The endless questionnaires, the weekly visits, how they, in fact, made it harder with the suspicion they cast. Did they have any idea how difficult it was to even leave the house just to sit in a crowded waiting room because they were always running behind? And then I had two minutes to prove to someone that I lived with this illness. The very best scenario, not for me but for them, was when I would have a full panic attack in their office. And being forced to sit in a crowded room with heightened anxiety often resulted in that. Then I was to be believed. But to repeatedly have to endure this was excruciating.

After several visits to my new doctor, after a few months of seeing her to get my allotment of medication, she said she believed that escitalopram did not work in menopausal women, and that was why I was having so much trouble. She immediately took me off that medication and prescribed venlafaxine. I expected the gruesome withdrawal as per last time I changed medication, but it had surprisingly little effect. That confirmed to me that she had been correct, and for months, the escitalopram had been doing nothing for me. About six weeks after I started the venlafaxine, I started to feel slightly better. I didn't feel as good as I had in the past and by now didn't expect to.

I developed a new norm: a norm where I was slightly irritable at all times and wasn't able to sleep through the night without a panic attack, but other than that, I was basically existing.

I enjoyed being a gramma who sang, danced, played games, coloured, and joined my grandchildren in "make-believe land." I continued to drink my glass or four of wine at least three nights of the week and was managing, not thriving but managing. I enjoyed my work, and my region was growing just as I hoped and worked toward. But I was still irritated much of the time. And much of that time was spent irritated with Jack.

Jack was a very talented person, a very hard worker, and was very sensitive and loving, especially with animals. He would help anyone who asked, and in fact, when my son became ill and there was a concern that he may have to be off work with no access to sick benefits, Jack, without being asked for anything, offered to pay all his family's bills until he got back on his feet. Jack was passionate and said the most beautiful and loving things to me often. Every day, I would get a kind and loving text from him. He had long-term, dear friendships, was treasured by his family, and I knew he loved me deeply. But Jack also loved to bitch. About any and everything. He was able to rant for hours on end without taking a breath. And something was always irritating him. Mostly the weather.

Jack hated the colder weather and all that came with it. And I got it. He was a trucker pulling a hundred and three feet of trailer through blizzards on snow and ice five nights a week. I fully understood how crappy this could be. But just in case I forgot, Jack would phone from the truck every single night and remind me for two to three hours how horrible it was. For someone teetering on the edge of full-blown unmanageable depression at all times, this daily negativity didn't help. I told Jack I couldn't manage his daily rants, but somehow that didn't register with him. I had been extremely forthright about my mental illness, and everything within, from our very first meeting. He said because he couldn't see it, he didn't get it. So I would go for bouts of time not talking to him when he was in the truck. Or I would end our conversations when the bitching became too much. Or I would yell and scream; that special power of mine was resurrected and flourishing. Or I would cry, not on purpose, but because I couldn't help it. Or I would become silent and removed, shutting down so I didn't have to listen. But none of this appeared to impact Jack.

Even in the summer months when the weather wasn't an issue, Jack would bitch about how short the season was, how soon the weather would be poor again, and how he simply would not be able to survive another winter on the road. But he never did anything about it, never changed his work, never took steps to make his life better. He just endlessly ranted and complained.

Now, this wasn't a new aspect to our relationship. In fact, Jack had shared prior to our first winter together how he would get in the winter and wanted me to know he could be a tad difficult through those months. But the blush of romance, me having my safe space in my own apartment, as well as having one poorly functioning ovary apparently shielded me from the impact of this never-ending negativity.

The shield was now off. I was barely hanging on to whatever level of sanity I was able to maintain, and Jack had upped his game. Shortly after my surgery, Jack's son moved. He followed in his father's footsteps and became a trucker, but unlike his father, he wasn't going to sit and bitch about the weather that he hated as much as his senior did. He decided to move to a warmer climate to pursue his career and moved first to the British Columbia interior and then to Vancouver Island. Two provinces away from his father. Two provinces away from the brutal winter season.

And now Jack had to move as well. To be fair, he talked about moving since we met, leaving winter behind, but within a year or two, I knew this was mostly talk and had no real substance. But now the conversations were more serious, and I was beginning to believe he would move at some point. He wanted to move the island. He would fiercely deny it had anything to do with his son living there; it was simply because he needed away from our winters, and it was pure coincidence that his son happened to live in the exact place that he needed to relocate to. And there was nothing wrong with this. I completely supported both his need to get off the winter roads and the need to be close to his one and only child. I felt the same about my children and grandchildren. I fully believed that if he wanted to continue his career in trucking, he needed to leave our climate and the dangers within. I believe everyone should seek out their dream and achieve their goals, and I wanted him to have his dream and move to wherever he needed to be to find his happiness.

The problem was I didn't want to move. My family was here, and with my mental illness, I desperately needed that support system.

I knew Jack didn't have the ability to support me. He couldn't see my illness and, even with me sharing tips on the kind of support I needed, he had no clue how to relate to me most of the time. He couldn't understand how his constant complaining and endless pressuring me could cause issues and exacerbate my symptoms. He was only able to project his needs. He knew he would feel better in a better climate, so therefore, I would also. He was sad and miserable all winter because of the weather, so naturally, that was what was wrong with me, and he had the solution if I would just listen. He was pressuring me for my own good. This conversion was daily, the argument would ensue, and soon it would come out that he wouldn't be OK without me. He needed me to move with him for him to be OK. But that wasn't all of it, he would quickly interject. It would also make me better. My mental illness was a location-based situation in Jack's mind. And he had the cure.

I really did understand that his intent wasn't mean-spirited. I remembered feeling exactly the same way in past relationships. If I wasn't with the person all the time, I felt like I would die. I knew how it felt to truly need a person with you at all times or feel like you did. I was able to put myself in his shoes and get it. But he wasn't able to put himself in mine and that was OK. That was his path. The problem was, even though I loved Jack deeply, I didn't know how much longer we could share this path, especially with me feeling the way I did so much of the time.

68.

My DAUGHTER-IN-LAW HAD JOINED A new gym and was trying to get me to try it with her. She had experienced some mental health issues as well and told me this particular gym was different, better, and it would help me manage my illness. She said it wasn't just a gym; it was a community, a philosophy. It was actually a hot yoga studio that offered many different classes, from stretching to yoga to hard-core fitness classes in infrared heat. It took her two full months until I begrudgingly attended a yoga class with her, and by the time the hour ended, I was hooked. I needed this in my life. My soul knew it and I listened. This would heal me. This was part of my path back to wellness.

It was a very calm, welcoming space. Every class began and ended in a meditative state on our mats. I felt it was my workout, not a competition, and I had never felt that way in a class setting before. Prior, I would constantly compare my performance, ability, and fitness level to those around me. Maybe it was a leftover from so many years of dance and then facilitating classes myself. But I didn't feel that way at this studio. We all stayed on our own mats and did our own workouts. I tried all the different classes but was very drawn to the fitness classes. I loved that feeling of sweat pouring off my body in the thirty-five degrees Celsius heat. I loved the feeling of my heart beating hard and my muscles working. And I loved how I felt both during and after class. It feels ridiculous to say, but it was almost like the space itself had "energy," and it was a welcoming, safe energy.

The instructors were amazing. They shared an unspoken warmth, a welcoming, and an acceptance of all that was actually something I could feel. Not just see on the surface and notice, but actually feel. My daughter-in-law was right. This was a community, a philosophy, and I had found my home.

Six months is my maximum attention span for anything, especially fitness-related. I don't know why, but then I get bored with whatever I'm doing. But this time, I didn't. At the time of writing this, I am over two-and-a-half years into regular attendance at the studio and am loving it more than ever.

The studio was a space of meditation, so we didn't visit much within the actual fitness room, but I did start to recognize people and we would chat before and after class. I started to make friends. I even started to see a couple of people outside of the studio for coffee, and that helped my life enormously. I had an outlet in the studio for my anger and tension and physically burned and sweated it out. I could feel it leaving my body in that daily hour on my mat. And I also had my new friends that I saw on occasion outside of the studio that shared some of the same things I found on my zafu years ago, and that felt good. I wasn't such a weirdo anymore ... or I was and had just found my tribe.

Even with these supports in place, I still became aware that my symptoms were continuing to increase. It had to be my relationship. What else could it be? I was on my new medication, exercising, meditating, eating well, spending time with my growing family, doing well in my work, and now socializing occasionally with a community that got me, and I was still unravelling.

I was about six months into my medication change and was back to the doctor again. And wouldn't you know it, it was another new doctor but the same clinic, so at least it was a much easier transition. And this doctor believed me. I didn't need to go through several appointments to arrive at the same diagnosis again. She felt I needed a higher dose of venlafaxine and prescribed it to me along with my clonazepam for the ever-present panic attacks.

I upped my dose and went through the usual adjustment and side effects, hoping to feel better, but even six weeks later, I didn't feel much different.

That confirmed for me that it was my relationship. I was so sick of going to the doctor and it seemed pointless; they had done all they could for me. I believed that I would never be as well as I had been prior to this relationship nonsense. As I suspected, no, as I knew, me, my illness, and romantic relationships did not mix. I longed for those happier, more peaceful times that felt so far away.

As we worked our way into another winter, my symptoms became more intense. I was struggling with depression, horrible panic attacks day and night, an inability to concentrate, and lost interest in everything. But as one does with mental health, I wasn't really monitoring. I share this more from hindsight than from being aware when I was actually living it. I just focused on trying to live each day. Without really noticing or monitoring, my alcohol intake was increasing. Where a bottle of wine had once sat on the counter, a box now sat. I would date it when I opened it, knowing it only lasted six weeks, and it never made it to expiration. If I had too much, the next day or two were filled with horrible panic attacks, but that didn't seem to stop me from doing it once every second week or so. I was losing control of my life and not even paying attention. I was just trying to get through the days.

It was in my interaction with my grandchildren that I really started to become aware of my advancing symptoms. I played and read and enjoyed my time with them, but not enough. There was a cloud, a veil that covered my brain that dulled the interactions. I knew it wasn't right but didn't know what to do about it. I needed to do something.

Jack's son flew home for Christmas that year, and the plan was for the three of us to drive back to the island together on Boxing Day. I knew I couldn't go. My anxiety was so high and the panic attacks so frequent that I knew I would be completely unable to get into a vehicle and drive that long way. I shared my situation with Jack, my feeling that things were getting out of control, but he was unable to provide support to me. He couldn't understand things he couldn't see, so when I was having a panic attack or would be numb for days on end, he would offer the timeless solutions such as "cheer up," "get up—you'll feel better," "why are you afraid? There is nothing to be afraid of," "just do something and you will feel fine." They were all the flawless solutions to mental illness symptoms that if only we, the ill group, would just think of and try, our lives would be bliss. He would not or could not acknowledge my illness as something that I couldn't just make go away, but on the other hand, if I were angry or short-tempered with him about something, he would readily attach that to my illness. And when you are actively in the throes of this illness, you believe that. And he could have been right. Everything was suspect.

So no matter how many times I explained to Jack what was happening, he couldn't understand it. I tried to share what I needed, but to be truthful, I didn't really know what I needed anymore. What I did know was that I couldn't manage my attacks in close quarters with others, and I knew I couldn't explain it to them. But I couldn't drive with them to British Columbia; I knew I couldn't even attempt it. And I reasoned, if Jack was the problem, I should start to feel better and less impacted by his moods while he was far away.

I knew they were both disappointed and didn't understand, but I had no ability to explain. I was completely unable to travel and that was all I could verbalize by that point.

They left, and I chose to spend lots of time with my family over the holidays where wine flowed freely, so I was able to manage since I was half-lit most of the time. My family are not drinkers, not the way I was. During celebratory days, they would have a few drinks, and during this time, my son and his family from Calgary were visiting and as we played games, we would imbibe a little. But I imbibed a lot.

I didn't have panic attacks when I was tipsy. But the next day? Brutal. And I missed Jack terribly. And with the alcohol abuse, the illness, and missing Jack, things slowly got worse and worse. I recall having a huge panic attack on New Year's Day after a night of drinking alone on New Year's Eve, feeling sorry for myself for my own choices, and staring blankly at the TV as I filled my glass time and time again. But I was not able to calm myself in any way the next day. It just wouldn't subside no matter what I did. The clonazepam didn't help; nothing did. It was horrible. It was then I knew that I caused this and I needed to get a grip on myself.

I cleared the alcohol out of my house and decided to get my head out of my ass.

69.

JANUARY WAS HORRIBLE. WITHOUT WINE, I had daily, horrible, uninterrupted symptoms. Jack was miserable because it was winter, and I was just miserable.

My daughter and son-in-law were planning to go on a vacation and asked if I wanted to tag along. They were going somewhere warm and beachy, and I hadn't been on a winter vacation since the disaster with Frank and longed to go again. Jack was too afraid to fly, would never agree to go on a winter vacation unless he could drive, so my kids asked if I would like to join them.

To be clear, though, Jack and I did vacation together, as long as we didn't have to fly. Every summer, we had one or two amazing, incredibly memorable motorcycle trips all over the southwestern United States ad those trips were beautiful and untouchable. I loved and soaked up every second of them until the last few years. That same cloud or veil I had with the grandbabies shrouded those last few trips as well. I had fun but not as much as I felt I should have or could have. Everything was foggy, hazy, and a little removed from me. Nothing was vibrant and real and alive as it had been in the past. I put it off at the time as just experiencing the same things we had done prior, but that niggling voice inside told me that wasn't it. Life was just getting more and more blah, more colourless. And maybe that was my life from now on, and I just needed to accept that and be grateful for what I had.

I pondered the invitation. I was nervous, with my anxiety being so high of late, but decided maybe it would be good for me. Maybe having something to look forward to would lift my mood and minimize my symptoms. Maybe getting some sun and being away from anything stressful would give me a much-needed reset. And my daughter and son-in-law knew all about my anxiety and were an incredible support for me. They knew just how to help me and I knew I would be safe with them.

So we booked it. I was excited and did feel a little lighter.

Then something came up and my daughter and her family couldn't go. We decided we would all postpone the vacation and take it the following year. The travel agency agreed to hold our money and transfer it to any vacation in the future so we wouldn't lose anything.

A few days later, out of the blue, a very clear thought came to me: "You need to go on your own." I knew it was Soul Nikki speaking. And I also knew we hadn't communicated for a long, long time. In fact, I had forgotten her. But I knew she had spoken and I knew I would do it.

So I rebooked my vacation. I needed to go a different week and to a different resort, but with the travel agent's help, I was soon booked for an all-inclusive vacation to Mexico. I booked excursions at the same time so as to minimize any stress I may find when there and was soon set up for what I hoped would be a relaxing time. I was quite nervous but had travelled alone to Sedona six years prior and had a wonderful time hiking and dining and touring around all by myself. Jack couldn't join me as I flew for that trip, but I really had a memorable and amazing time all on my own. I had not just managed but actually excelled on my own. But that was when I was feeling much better. That was before my ovarian removal and my slide into darkness. But if I could do it once, I surely could do it again. And maybe this is what I needed to reset myself and begin an upward climb to wellness again.

My trip was booked and I was ready to go. I was leaving on March 7 and returning on March 14, 2020.

We heard that there was a new virus out and had been told to wipe surfaces down, wash our hands regularly, and use hand sanitizer, but that was the extent of it and travel was not impacted besides wiping down the airplane seatbelts and trays. I packed my wipes and my sanitizer, my medication, five novels, several sundresses, shorts, and bathing suits, and was good to go.

I had an amazing time, and for the most part, was able to keep my anxiety at bay. I toured Chichén Itzá, a bucket list goal, and afterwards rappelled seventy feet down into a type of water-filled cave basin called a cenote. There were no walls to bounce off of, and I was essentially dangling from a string in the centre of a massive opening in the rock. Being both terrified of heights and unable to swim, I felt pretty brave doing this. My anxiety was high, but I had taken a clonazepam before and reasoned I would be angry with myself for not trying, so I did. I needed to do things that would force my brain to reset, and this certainly seemed to be one of those things. I made it with only one little hiccup. We weren't allowed to wear life jackets while rappelling, so when I got to the bottom, I grabbed at and clung fiercely onto the poor young man whose job it was to catch me. I heard him trying to tell me something, but I had just rappelled seventy feet and did not intend to drown, so I dug my fingers into him with everything I had. I was a tad out of control! He was finally able to get my attention as he struggled to breathe through my suffocating grip and told me to put my feet down. Apparently, there was a raised bottom where I landed. I put my feet down on something solid and was waist-high in water. He got me out of the harness, put me in a big tube, and pushed me toward the deck where I could get a life jacket and continue to bob around in the cenote. I should have been quite embarrassed, but I had just overcome my fear and rappelled. I was elated! Maybe this was the reset after all.

I went to Tulum; I attended a traditional Mayan dinner with ten couples; I was blessed by a Mayan priest; I went on a catamaran tour; and I literally looked many fears in the face and stepped out on my own in a foreign country with crippling anxiety lurking around every corner. I used my medication as needed. I did have a few drinks each day but closely monitored my alcohol intake. I did everything completely on my own. I ate every meal alone. I navigated my resort and tours alone, and I enjoyed my own company for the first time in a very long while. I felt my symptoms throughout but was able to manage them. I had survived!

Until two days before I was to return home.

COVID-19 was declared a global pandemic on March 12, 2020.

My boss was texting me, unsure if I would be able to return to Canada. Resort staff seemed unconcerned. I wasn't sure what was happening. I had to remain as calm as possible as I had only me to count on to get me safely home. I struggled to contain my panic.

I caught my shuttle to the airport on March 14 to fly home with the same group I had flown to Mexico with. We had all stayed at different resorts, but all flew in and out together as per our travel company arrangements. But something was wrong. We waited hours, and then we were all loaded back onto buses and taken to a different resort. We were given rooms with no information. I was well into panic mode but had to keep myself as stable as I could. I was two clonazepam in just seven hours after I was supposed to have left Mexico. I tried to find food in this new resort and couldn't figure anything out. It was way larger than the one I had vacationed at. Golf carts had to take us to our rooms. I wandered around trying not to get lost searching for food. I couldn't find anything, returned to my room, tried to keep breathing, and searched my space once again for a map. I felt the panic rise and turned the TV on to try to distract myself and found a room service menu scrolling across the screen. One problem was solved, and I was able to calm a bit.

Two hours later, we were all gathered up again and taken back to the airport where we waited some more. We left Mexico at three a.m. on March 15, and I arrived safely home five hours later.

I was required to be isolated for two weeks, and the next day, our offices were closed, and we were all immediately to work from home for the next two weeks. As the manager of the region, I was scrambling to make sure we transitioned effectively into working remotely. I tried to support my staff as best as possible with the unknown playing out before us and the world.

Well, we all know how that first two weeks ended. We did not return to normal operations as expected when we shut down. We were to continue to work from home for a then-unknown extended length of time. I was thrown into managing a new situation with the added responsibilities of ensuring our funders were informed, coming up with a plan on how to continue to meet our contractual requirements, and how to keep my region afloat in an unprecedented situation. What was normally a stressful job became immediately and exponentially more stressful.

I continued to manage my mental illness symptoms throughout, knowing I had staff and clients who needed me. I just couldn't allow myself to become ill. I was the leader and many were looking to me for guidance. I was responsible for my region, and I needed to show up every day, work hard, be creative, think on my feet constantly, make sure we navigated a situation new to the entire world, all while offering an ear and support for my staff. And I do have to say that all of my employees were incredible throughout this time, and I couldn't have managed any of it without them. But in the end, I was the final say and it was a lot of responsibility.

But, somehow, I was managing and each day did what was needed.

Until I didn't.

70.

M Y DAUGHTER WAS EXPECTING HER second child just off a miscarriage, and we were all terrified of what this disease would do to her and the baby if she caught it. My grandchildren were all so young; what if they got it? My parents were in their eighties; what if they got it? What if my children got it? They all had young kids to take care of. What if we needed to shut down our offices and we couldn't work? How would my staff survive? How would I survive? Every day, the news and information was changing, and the world had no real idea what was going on. And we were all scared.

I lost my ability to visit my support system, to connect with people. I lost my fitness when my studio closed. I lost the ability to shop properly for food. I felt like I lost my footing, as did many many others. But we were able to maintain our employment and I fully recognize how lucky we were. Now I had to make sure we continued. My staff needed that from me.

I was having daily panic attacks. I wasn't sleeping, but I was still working every day to do what was needed. I had to keep our jobs.

Then, two months into shutdown, Jack said he was going to go visit his son in British Columbia. Travel was not recommended, and we didn't know how to stay safe except for washing our hands and using sanitizer. I begged him not to go. His travelling against the recommendations could cause me tremendous implications with my work, with my family, and my entire life. I was terribly sick with my mental illness. My anxiety was getting worse and worse, and the panic attacks were getting bigger and harder to manage. I struggled so much with being alone when he travelled over Christmas, and that was just a few months earlier, even before COVID. I wasn't using alcohol anymore and was trying to get through each day but doing poorly. I begged him not to leave me. I cried and pleaded. I knew I wouldn't be able to manage my symptoms on my own. I implored him to stay with me, to put his trip off for a few months, to help me, to be with me. I knew I was too sick to be alone and I was terrified.

But he simply stated he was going. And he left.

The day after he left, I was pacing at four a.m. I hadn't been able to rest at all. I hadn't even been able to lie down. I had to move my body. My mind was racing, and soon, I was in a full-blown panic attack. I simply couldn't go on. It was one attack on top of another, and they continued throughout the night and into the morning. I couldn't breathe; I couldn't see; I was sobbing. At one point, I found myself running down the street in my housecoat and slippers, screaming and wailing. I don't know how I got back to my house, but I somehow did. I told my staff I was sick and was barely able to text that message. My vision was blurred with tears and panic. It took me several minutes to just send a simple message.

I was able to come in and out of complete non-functional terror as the morning wore on, and when I could catch my breath, I started phoning my support system. I called my daughter first and couldn't form words for the sobbing. Then the attack intensified again and I had to hang up. When I was able to breathe again, I was going to call my daughter again but felt a terrible guilt wash over me. She was struggling herself, with her pregnancy, and staying safe, and I was stressing her. What a horrible person I was!

When next I could breathe, I tried my daughter-in-law, who is a social worker and works with people with this illness. She tried her best with me, but the panic was so far gone she couldn't help. As the terror engulfed me once again, I had to hang up.

The next time the overwhelming fear receded slightly, I didn't make any calls but did send my daughter and daughter-in-law texts so they didn't worry. I said I was better and needed to work. I knew they would want to check on me but I wasn't able to speak.

The panic continued, ebbing and peaking.

At some point when I could breathe for a few minutes, I remembered that some people used cannabis. When I was able to speak, I called a nearby store that was open and asked if they had CBD oil. I heard or read somewhere that helped. They did, and I drove to the store as soon as I was physically able and bought some. I took my first dose in the parking lot. I took two more as the day wore on.

I had also taken three clonazepam over the last seven hours.

I don't know what eventually stopped the attack in its full force, whether it was the medication or the CBD or a combination, but as the afternoon wore into the evening, I was finally able to breathe. And I collapsed onto the couch. I was exhausted. I felt beat up, bruised, and in pain. My muscles were all pulled and strained. I ached everywhere. And I was still crying. This time, not from panic as such, but because I had given up. I couldn't survive that again and I knew it. For the second time in my life, I considered suicide.

I thought I could just go out for a walk and step in front of a car when they didn't have time to stop. Or maybe it would be better if I rode my bike and turned into the path of a large oncoming truck. That might be more effective. I couldn't live like this anymore. I couldn't survive another attack like that and knew there would be more. There was always more. This was my life. I was trying to process thought with my exhausted and now well-drugged brain.

What would be the best way to end all of this? I was so tired I didn't think I could even walk or ride a bike. But I had to do something.

Then I thought of my children. And then I thought of my grandchildren. Or maybe Soul Nikki popped in just for a second and thought of all these beautiful beings in my life. I felt the little arms of my grandchildren hugging me. I saw their clear, innocent eyes looking into mine with unconditional love. Somehow, even in my exhaustion, this was all very real. And that made me cry even harder as I knew that ending my life was not the answer. I was to be stuck in this miserable existence, always on edge, waiting for the next panic attack for the rest of my life.

But something had to change and change immediately as I wasn't sure this feeling would last. I was alone and very, very ill with symptoms, and I had to do something before those suicidal thoughts returned and I harmed myself. I needed to go to the hospital. I believed I was far worse than when I was taken to emergency before, and I felt that was where I needed to go to make sure I was safe from myself. I got my keys to drive myself to help, to safety.

Then I remembered I was alone with two Rottweilers, and I had no one to care for them with the COVID restrictions in place. My niece and one of Jack's friends would care for them when we travelled, but that was pre-COVID before we were locked down. No one could come into my home, which meant I couldn't go to get the care I felt I needed. So I searched my mind. What was the next best thing? What could I do to make sure I was safe, or as safe as I could be?

I took a paper and pen and wrote a promise to myself.

I will not harm myself until I have done all these things:

1. Use my CBD oil—take two, three, even four doses back-to-back if needed

2. Take up to three clonazepam a day if I need to

3. Physically speak with a member of my support group once a day, not just text

4. Talk to my doctor again

5. Exercise in some way every day

6. Get some outside time every day

7. Eat whole-wheat toast and peanut butter once a day

I wrote this down six times in large print and posted it all over my house. I posted it on the front door so I could see it if I was running outside. I posted it on the mirror in the bathroom. I posted it right below the TV. I posted it right next to my laptop. I posted it on the microwave and I posted it right beside my bed.

And then I called to make a doctor's appointment.

It took four weeks to set a phone appointment with my doctor. COVID had changed everything, and doctors were backed up and only doing phone appointments. I used CBD oil once a day before bed, and I needed to take two clonazepam a day for a couple of days. I talked to at least one of my children on the phone or via video conferencing every day to connect with the outside world, and I went for a walk or a bike ride every day. I made sure I ate at least one good meal of toast and peanut butter every day, and I made myself put check marks beside the lists all over the house to ensure I didn't miss a step.

I also connected with Jack by phone or text every day, but this wasn't uplifting or supportive. He was irritated with me. He said I was ruining his vacation with my mood and attitude. I wasn't happy enough, and I knew talking to me was difficult and I was bringing his mood down. I understood that completely. When he called from the truck to complain every night, he brought my mood down, so I knew what he meant. I knew he wanted me to be supportive of him travelling and seeing his child, but I was barely hanging on, and as such, was unable to fake happy in the state

I was in. This upset him. In hindsight, we shouldn't have been connecting while he travelled. I made things worse for him and he did for me. I vowed in the future to remember that lesson.

I had at least one panic attack a day, but never as bad as the one the night Jack left and somehow, I was able to survive.

Jack came home and things had changed between us, or maybe had just changed with me. I lost a level of trust with him. When someone can walk away from someone who is very ill with no looking back, someone they say they love very much, trust is impacted.

I asked him why he did it. He stated we were fighting all the time before he left. True. And he felt that we needed a break. Undoubtedly true. Even though I told him I needed him with me, he felt that his decision was right for the longevity of our relationship. I understood the reasoning; I got how miserable it is to live with someone with mental illness and how one may want to just get away. I know how very ill I was and how very hard I must have been to be around. But I needed him. He was all I had access to, and he walked away.

Right or wrong, my feelings for Jack were forever changed the day he left me in the height of my illness. I couldn't trust him to be there for me when I needed him. My brain understood that caring for or loving someone with mental illness could be too much sometimes. My brain understood that he wanted to see his child and that was his focus. I was able to put myself in his shoes, and I really did get it on an intellectual level. But my heart was broken. My heart didn't get it. My brain reminded me that no one could really manage my illness, and this eventually happened in all my relationships. The day always came when the illness was too much to manage, for us both, and then the relationship was the casualty. On one hand, I truly believed that I would never have done that to another person, certainly not one I said I loved. But I never lived with someone as profoundly ill as I was and am.

I shared my feelings of abandonment sometime later with
Carys. I shared how hurt I was, how alone I was, and how angry
I continued to feel when I remembered. She said something that
really impacted me. She told me that over the thirty-plus years she
had known me, since shortly after my diagnosis, that she had never
really seen any symptoms of my mental illness. I was completely
shocked! I thought it was so apparent to everyone! I was certain it
was written all over me in bold letters! But she said no, it wasn't.
She said I managed it and hid it extremely well, so people close to
me couldn't actually see it. She knew what I told her, but I guess
from a lifetime of managing and hiding this disability, I had grown
so good at it that maybe people in my life really couldn't see it. She
told me she understood my hurt, understood my feelings when Jack
abandoned me with my illness at such a bad time, but said, "maybe
he really couldn't see it." She agreed he should have listened to me,
believed me, and stayed with me because I asked. But she did open
my eyes with her words. Maybe my illness wasn't as apparent as I
assumed. And was that a good thing or a bad thing? What shade is
that, dear reader?

71.

AFTER HIS RETURN, WE HAD a few discussions about how alone and sick I was when he left, but he stood his ground and all of my energy was directed to managing my illness or working, and I just didn't have anything left to argue with him. He believed he had done the correct thing and would stand on that, so I just left it. He had his perspective and I had mine. So life continued as it had been with the added bonus of complete lockdown in my home for fourteen days as I was in direct contact with someone who had travelled against recommendations. I continued to work and adhere to my list.

One day, I became aware I felt better. My symptoms notably decreased. With my illness, I didn't notice changes when they occurred but did notice when there was a pronounced difference in how I felt, and that was almost always in hindsight. This is true for both ends of the continuum. I could gradually get worse and worse and not notice until my symptoms are quite pronounced, and in the same way, I could get gradually better and better and not notice until it is quite obvious. This time, it was better and better, but to be truthful, I don't know how much worse it could have gotten. I knew I should have been in the hospital, but times were strange and things that would have happened pre-COVID just didn't anymore.

But now something had shifted, and I felt a little better. I tried to think of what had changed. I needed to identify the thing that helped me. I tried to isolate what made things different, lighter. I wrote down everything I had been doing. Was it the CBD oil? Maybe. Started to exercise again? Possibly. My meds were the same ... Wait ... Whoa ... My meds.

I realized at that moment that I had been so distracted, had so much difficulty managing the minutiae of life, had been isolated and unable to go anywhere for the past fourteen days that, in that time, I had completely forgotten to get my prescriptions refilled. I hadn't taken venlafaxine in over a week. And I felt better. That was the biggest change. And I had no brutal symptoms of withdrawal. I had literally stopped taking the maximum dose allowed, cold turkey, and was feeling better. How was that even possible?

A few days after this discovery, I had an appointment with, once again, a new doctor but was at the same clinic, so I didn't need to go through mountains of history as I had so many times prior. I openly shared every detail with the new doctor. I told her about my suicidal thoughts. I told her about the panic. I told her about the CBD oil. I told her the change when I accidentally stopped taking venlafaxine. Everything poured out of me. I hoped that there was some sort of help for me but didn't really believe it was possible. I had been in this position so many times before. I just felt exhausted.

She said to stay away from the venlafaxine and put me back on escitalopram. I was disappointed. Had I been able to gather more feeling in my numb body, I would have been so pissed off. But I was just sad. Were there only two medications in the world? Only two options for me? And out of the two neither worked? Fan-fucking-tastic. I was out of strength to advocate, reason, discuss; I just wanted to be better. So I said, "OK."

Then she asked when I had last seen a psychiatrist.

"Thirty-some years ago," I answered.

There was silence on the other end of the line.

"Hello," I queried, "Are you there?"

"Yes, yes. Sorry, did you say thirty as in three zero?"

"Yes," I replied.

"You need to see a psychiatrist," she stated. "I'm writing a referral and you will be called soon."

"OK," was all I replied.

Four weeks later, I sat in a psychiatrist's office filling in paperwork. I felt hopeless in the truest sense of the word. I had been taking the escitalopram and wasn't feeling any better. I didn't believe that anyone could really help me any further. I felt I would simply continue as I was, functioning but not much more than that, for the rest of my life. Was it my relationship? Likely that was a big part of it. But I had no energy to consider leaving it, and with COVID, the last thing I could consider was moving. And I just didn't care anymore. I was basically a numb blob of flesh that had panic attacks. Actually, a part of me felt sorry for Jack having to live with me.

The psychiatrist came to get me from the waiting room, and I decided immediately, for no reason in particular, I wouldn't like him. I made the decision just as he called my name.

I followed him to his office, and for the next hour, he asked questions and I answered, staring at the floor. I told him about my history, the years of illness. I told him about constant panic attacks. I told him how I would fall asleep from exhaustion every night, and without fail, ten to twenty minutes after I fell asleep, I would wake in complete panic. I told him I couldn't concentrate, that I was numb, that I didn't feel functional, and I told him I had recently considered ending my life. I told him all this in short choppy sentences as that was the best I could do. At one point, I saw him smile at something I said, and I changed my mind in that second. I decided I did like him after all. And, even in my state, I was impressed with how much information he was able to acquire from my muddled, exhausted brain.

He asked me if I had ever heard of Transcranial Magnetic Stimulation (TMS). I said I actually had, that one of my clients shared they had tried it, but I really knew nothing about it. He explained to me that it was a therapy he felt may help me. He told me that magnets were used to stimulate nerve cells in the brain and help with depression and anxiety when other methods had failed. He said a magnetic field is used to cause an electric current in a certain part of the brain. I asked if it was like the shock therapy my grandpa had had so many times so many years ago. He said that it was less invasive, required more treatments, and had fewer side effects, but the stimulating the brain part was similar. I said yes immediately. I would have said yes to electric shock therapy as well. I needed to get better and was prepared to do whatever I needed to do.

He increased my escitalopram and told me to take a clonazepam every night before bed. I asked about the addiction issue, and he assured me it would take a very long time to become addicted to the tiny dosage I was taking.

He spent time with me. He didn't make me prove my illness. He made me feel he cared and he gave me hope.

And I wondered to myself ... Why had I not seen a psychiatrist for over thirty years? Was it because, for all those years, mental illness wasn't really taken seriously? I had a specialist for my cancer; why didn't I have one for this illness that had consumed so many of my fifty-eight years on this Earth? I was ill in the sixties and seventies. I had horrible postpartum depression all through the eighties and was finally diagnosed in the very early nineties. And in all that time, I had seen two psychiatrists, one initially and one briefly in emergency. But being angry about the past wouldn't help my future, and all I can say is, I am glad that this illness is now taken more seriously. I am grateful that, if this runs in my family, if my children and grandchildren experience the things I did, that they can now get treatment that wasn't available to me.

Four weeks later, I was in another psychiatrist's office. We met, and he asked me several questions to determine if I was a good candidate for the magnetic treatment. He told me the potential side effects. Then he asked if I wanted to proceed and I did.

Two weeks later, I was having my brain mapped. I sat in a chair with a cotton cap that fit snugly on my head. The doctor started shooting pulses of magnetic energy into my brain and watched my hands, resting on my lap, palms up, for some sort of twitching that was to be the indicator to him that he had the right area that needed stimulation and the correct intensity of pulse that was required for me. This went on for several minutes, and finally, the cap on my head was marked with a red marker, and that would be the spot where the magnet would be placed.

The following week, I started my therapy. I went every weekday for six weeks straight. It was a time commitment, but I was committed to trying anything to get better.

It was uncomfortable but not really painful. My spot was on my upper left-side forehead, and the magnet was heavy as it rested on that spot on my head. Sometimes my jaw or eye would twitch with each pulse. One of the instructions was to keep my tongue in the middle of my mouth so I didn't bite it during treatment. It was a weird zapping of ten pulses, a little pause and then ten again, for a total of two hundred pulses per session. I could hear the buzzing outside and inside my head. It sounded like an electrical shock but didn't hurt like one. It felt like holding a birthday sparkler. The tiny pricks of burning were not really painful but were prickly and tingly. It was as if someone was pressing a really heavy birthday sparkler into my head and that prickly, shocky feeling was focused on that spot, pulsing into the brain. The whole treatment took two to three minutes per session.

By week three, I was no better and was getting frustrated with the time and energy this took. The technician was very encouraging and told me to give it until week four and promised I would see a difference, if it was to work for me, that is. My psychiatrist, who saw me every two weeks, said the same. He was very forthright and stated it didn't work for everyone but to give it the full six weeks and see. And really, I had nothing to lose except a few minutes out of every weekday.

Week four was a miracle. Week four, I felt different. I felt human. Week four was the magic week. Nothing was ever the same after week four.

It's hard to explain the change as it was subtle and huge at the same time. Midway through my fourth week, I was chatting and joking with the technician. I was taking my eyes off the ground as I walked and smiling at people I passed. Everything seemed a little brighter, the colours a little richer. I was able to pick up medications at the pharmacy and pause to look at makeup or grab a box of hair dye that I actually used. I wore earrings. I heard myself laughing on more than one occasion. By this time, some COVID restrictions were lifted, and I was able to go see my children and grandchildren, just go get in the car and go, and was excited to do so. I could pick up the phone and call people. I could concentrate on my work. I had new ideas. I started making macrame hangings and dream catchers. I wasn't angry all the time. I wasn't numb any longer. I felt like I was alive. I felt hope. I knew things had changed for me. I was getting better, really better, for the first time ever. I knew it and I trusted it.

72.

B Y WEEK SIX, JUST BEFORE Christmas of 2020, the darkness was gone. It was like putting on a brand-new pair of glasses with the correct prescription. All of a sudden, I could see. I could think. I laughed. I sang (poorly). I danced (epically, in my own mind). I became alive. I felt joy. I felt excitement. I felt emotions. I felt all emotions, the good and the bad, but at least there was good sprinkled in now. I wanted to try new things. I was excited to work. I had ideas. I had plans. I didn't have to argue with myself or force myself to do things every single moment of every day. Things were interesting. Things needed to be explored. I had to read. I had to study. I didn't dread meetings or interacting with people on video calls. I looked forward to it. I learned to curl my hair. I bought makeup and used it.

And I prepared for Christmas. I put up a tree. I know this doesn't sound like much but it was huge. Because I despise Christmas. I have, for as long as I can remember, literally hated everything about the season. I hated the shopping, the decorating, the cooking, the baking, the celebrating, the disgusting movies, the cards, the music, the wrapping, the entire season made me want to curl up and go to bed and not move until the miserable time was over. It was an excessive amount of work for nothing and then a huge letdown. I had to steel myself every single year to get through it. I tried not to act like the Grinch and ruin it for everyone, and for years, I was successful. I made the season fun for my kids and extended family, at least I felt I had, but the last few years, I had been unable to hide my despise for the season, and I knew I spoiled it for others. So I added a nice dose of guilt to the festivities.

Christmas 2020, after six weeks of magnetic therapy, I found myself, really without thinking, cranking up the Christmas music and digging out the Christmas tree. And I did this knowing I was alone for Christmas! I did it because it was pretty, and I wanted to turn off the lights and look at it while I watched sappy movies.

What had happened?

Jack was leaving for the third time since COVID was announced, still with travel not advised, to see his son for the holidays. We shut down again and couldn't see anyone but our own households and I was alone, but I still set up the tree.

I saw my psychiatrist just before Christmas Day and shared how I was feeling. I was still waking with panic attacks ten to twenty minutes after I went to sleep but was able to get back to sleep within an hour or two. I had some bad days still but nowhere near the number I had throughout most of my life. And I had some feelings of happiness, some joy. I could live like this forever! This was so manageable for me! But this was not enough for my psychiatrist. He believed that I could live without a weekly panic attack or waking up every night. He believed I could live without having to argue with myself in order to function in my world. I was content with my progress; I was better than I ever had been, even in my best good times. But he felt I could still do better. He increased my escitalopram and said if that didn't eliminate the attacks, we would perhaps add another medication to it.

He asked me what my Christmas plans were, and when I shared I would be alone, he was concerned. He told me to contact him if things took a bad turn.

Christmas was hard alone but I didn't spiral as I had prior. I did have panic attacks but smaller ones that only lasted at most an hour and only once a day or every second day. But the difference was, I was able to pull myself out after that hour and the intensity was less. As I was considered a single-person household with Jack being gone, I was able to stop in and see my children for brief visits and would do so as needed. And sometimes, I just needed to cry, and I allowed myself to do that.

I can see where you, dear reader, might think I wasn't doing all that well, but I can assure you, I was incredibly well compared to what I had been prior. Having one, one hour-long panic attack a day and being able to focus on an entire shitty romantic Christmas movie was a massive improvement.

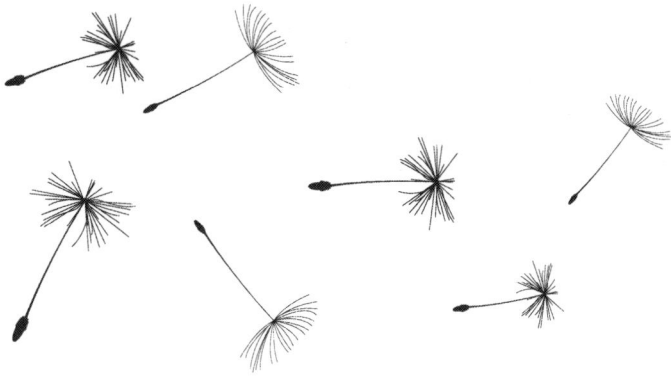

73.

THE FIRST WEEK IN JANUARY, I found a noticeable decline in my mood and function and an increase in my anxiety and panic attacks. Part of my TMS therapy included a monthly maintenance week, which means once a month, every day for a week, I received the same magnetic pulses into my brain. I noticed the decline in function the week just prior to my maintenance therapy. I suppose this is why maintenance treatment exists. I reported this to both the technician and my psychiatrist. My psychiatrist increased my escitalopram to above the highest recommended dosage. I had come to trust him, so if he recommended it, I was prepared to do it. And that worked for me. The increased dosage seemed to be just enough to keep the panic attacks at bay.

As of this writing, I am in the middle of my fifth month of maintenance therapy.

I still feel anxiety in that my heart speeds up a bit, and I struggle with breathing deeply. My chest tightens as if I am being painfully squeezed, and I feel my pulse pounding in my head. But anxiety and a panic attack are very different, and for me, the anxiety is manageable. It may even be normal, whatever that means.

I still feel anger and irritation much of the time. I have sadness; I have fear. I feel lonely, and sometimes, I feel all those for an entire day or two at a time. But it doesn't consume me the way it did prior. When I feel those things, I can usually find a thought or reason behind them. They aren't consuming waves that will crush me. I am able to breathe and feel sad. I am able to breathe and feel anger, or fear, or loneliness. I can cry, and it does not turn into loss of vision with the feeling that my heart will explode. I still wake up every night after ten to twenty minutes of rest with my heart pounding, but it is not a full-on panic attack. I am awake and very often can fall asleep again within the hour. Sometimes my mind races with ideas, but I think most people experience that. I am able to read and actually concentrate and focus on what I read until my eyes are once again heavy, and then I can rest through the night.

Some days, I don't feel like getting up and going to work, but again, I feel that is universal. I don't feel that painful, physical dread when I open my eyes every morning, knowing I have to face another day. I occasionally feel the panic begin, the feeling that would lead to a full-on attack, but I can usually circumvent it. In fact, today was such a moment as I picked up prescriptions and bought some groceries. We are still deep in COVID, and where I live is once again fully locked down due to variants of concern. I felt crowded in the grocery store, and my anxiety started to build, and I simply grabbed what I needed, paid, and left the store and was able to head off a full-blown attack.

I know I don't feel the impending doom hovering, just waiting for me to drop my guard. I don't have that constant vibration inside that makes me bounce or shake my foot at all times. I feel balanced. I feel stable. I feel like I can trust myself, which is very new.

Things have definitely changed with me. I am still me with all my quirks, my over-sensitivity, my thoughts, and my illness. But I function and don't feel that I need to wear a mask or hide myself any longer, and that is an indicator of edging toward a shade of wellness. I am growing comfortable showing me, the real me, all of me, without hiding or being ashamed of a huge aspect of me.

As for Jack and my relationship, I can't say what our future holds. Now that I am feeling much better, I am able to step back and see things more objectively. I realize that Jack is not able to understand or support me in my illness. But I also feel that is not his job. It is my job. It has always been my job. I can't expect a partner to be a caregiver when I am in the throes of symptoms. My anger toward him was, in fact, anger toward myself, toward my illness. I was furious that I had battled this for so long, felt that brief reprieve of wellness, and was back to worse than ever and that anger had to go somewhere, so I dumped it on Jack. Should he have stayed with me when I was that ill? I still believe he should have with all the external things going on, but that is past, and I can't focus on that and continue my growth into wellness.

Jack also still plans to move in the next several months and speaks about it often. And he is still pressuring me to move with him. That's not an option for me at this time. I support him entirely, encourage him to go, and fully understand his need to. He suffers living here, and no one should suffer if they have the option to change that suffering, which he does. I just can't go with him, for two main reasons. Firstly, my support system is here, and he is unable to provide the support I need when in a flare. Secondly, my TMS treatment does not exist where he wants to live, and I need my monthly maintenance.

I am open to a long-distance relationship, and we may try that, or this relationship of nine years may have run its course. Only time will tell. I do know that I still struggle often with Jack and being in a relationship in general. There is no doubt I love him deeply, but I feel tension and irritation much of the time. At this point, I am still not able to discern what the issues and core of the dissension are. I am still not entirely sure where I am on the wellness continuum, and because of that, don't want to make any decisions on this relationship and its longevity. I question this all the time. Is my constant irritation my illness? Is it COVID? Is it my illness and COVID combined? Is it that Jack and I are not well-matched? Would I be able to have a relationship with anyone? Am I just too sensitive and too impacted emotionally by things to be coupled? I was so good on my own and have never been truly good and solid and well in a relationship. Is that because my partners hold me to a standard of normal behaviour, and I can't attain whatever normal is? Or is it my lesson for this lifetime? Do I need to learn to manage my life with mental illness in a relationship to pass this class? Or, heaven forbid, retake it yet again as I have so many times already in this incarnation? That is not an option for me at all! Not at this time. If I feel I just can't manage my relationship with Jack, then I need to find that beautiful peace I had on my own and live out the rest of the days in this lifetime that way.

With the addition of the TMS therapy, I fully believe I could manage well at this time and live a happy, fulfilled life. I would miss Jack, and some of the things a partnership offers, but would never learn to manage my illness in a relationship, and in some ways, I feel like that would be the same as not rappelling in Mexico. I could have taken the stairs down into the cenote and not faced the uncomfortable and the fear induced by rappelling into it. And I could do the same now, not face the uncomfortable and just take the easy path. But is that best for me? As I get better and better in therapy, will I be able to manage relationships? As long as those questions remain unanswered, I will stay where I am, at least for today.

I now understand through the care of my psychiatrist that having my ovary removed and losing those hormones did, in fact, cause my rapid decline into active illness once again. I was stable before that but still always had underlying symptoms that I was masking. Looking back from this point, I can see it wasn't true wellness, but it was pretty damned good.

I have no idea what normal is. I am, sadly, one of those people who takes polls, asking others I trust how they would feel and react in situations I find myself in, and have done this throughout my entire life. I know that isn't healthy, and we all need to find our own path, and I now do make the final decision on things, but having never been able to trust myself and my thought processes, I have no normal measure. I expect as you read this, you may feel I reacted normally to some situations and not to others. I expect many will even disagree on what those situations are. It's very possible I have lived more normally than I think I have, which I can assure you is through years of practice keeping a mask well in place. As my friend shared, she never really saw the illness and that may be true of many in my life. But I can assure you that the endless internal turmoil that I have had since I can remember ruled my life, and even if I could hide it, I was never able to escape it. Until now. I now feel true wellness. I feel a clarity in my mind that I have never had before. I feel able to think and focus and even relax as I walk through my days. It could last forever or may not. If I need to, I will have ECT treatments. But that is a future problem. For today, my TMS is working wonders for me and I am content.

I will always have a mental illness. That is part of the very fabric of me and I like me, finally.

Thank you, dear reader, for accompanying me along this journey. Till we meet again.

Namaste

NOTE FROM THE AUTHOR

I WOULD LIKE TO TAKE THIS moment to share a few thank yous:
My family, my kids, my grandkids, my parents, my dear aunt
and uncle, my extended family (including the beautiful family Jack
has brought to me), and a special shout out to the father of my
children and his beautiful wife as well as all the other grandparents
to my perfect grandchildren who share the same love I do for those
magical beings. You all support me by supporting them and I love
you all.

My eternal thanks and gratitude to a caring friend who didn't
turn away from an ugly situation. It would have been much easier to
just leave me believing I was functioning. But you, my brave friend,
were in the right place at the right time doing the right thing.
You loved me when it was hard and messy and took responsibility
in a situation that wasn't yours to fix. You fought for me when I
couldn't. You know who you are! You are an angel. I thank you and
I love you!

Carys. What started in a neighbourhood school gym with the
agreement that the wisp of a human leading our exercises had never
consumed a cookie and grew into over thirty years of love, support,
and unconditional acceptance. Your consistency in my life, being
there to laugh with, cry with, raise our children together, and now

crocheting grammas together. You always allowed me space or connection, honouring wherever I was and whatever I needed with zero judgement. Our souls are woven together and I love you very very much.

Oxygen Yoga and Fitness thank you for providing me a safe space to find all levels of wellness. I have become physically strong, but not just that. I have found emotional, spiritual, and mental growth in this commUNITY as well. The warm smiles every day, the hugs when allowed (COVID), the consistent encouragement and support of all. The complete lack of judgement within, the energy of peace ever present in the studio, and the daily mantra, "I love my life" has become part of my soul. Thank you for being there and offering this to anyone who knocks on your door.

And last but not least, Catherine Milos and her incredible team, who took a manuscript from a woman about her life, filled with misspelled words and zero understanding of something called "an oxford comma" and led it from that point to what you hold today. They took a frightened fifty-nine-year-old woman who decided to bare her soul by hand and led her gently through the entire process to become a published author. Simply—you rule!

ABOUT THE AUTHOR

Nikki Langdon grew up on a farm in rural Saskatchewan in a time when mental illness was profoundly stigmatized and kept well hidden. For years, she knew and heard she was "too sensitive" to survive in the world. She believed she was born broken. If she could just fake "normal" and keep the darkness hidden, she would survive. With her own diagnosis, she began to understand that she could not only survive but coexist with her darkness.

As a motivational speaker, sharing her story with others helps tear down the stigma of mental illness in our society and remind those struggling with similar challenges that they are not alone.

Nikki holds a bachelor's degree with great distinction in Adapted Physical Activity Studies (Kinesiology) and has been awarded the YWCA Woman of Distinction award in Leadership and Management. She holds the Registered Rehabilitation Professional Certification form the Vocational Rehabilitation Society of Canada and the Certified Vocational Professional and Return to Work Disability Manager designations from the College of Vocational Professionals. She also holds certifications in the Strong Interest Inventory and Level II MBTI Assessments.

She has worked with people with disabilities for over 23 years and has sat on many related committees.

Nikki is a mother of four grown children, all married to amazing talented partners, and a grandmother to eight perfect little humans that are the centre of her world.

Nikki can be contacted through her website **nikkilangdon. com** or email at **nikkilangdonauthor@gmail.com** or Facebook at **Nikki Langdon Author.**

DISCUSSION QUESTIONS

PART ONE
PRE-DIAGNOSIS
THE DARK

W HAT "SHADE" WOULD YOU ASSIGN to Nikki's firm belief that there was a demon in her apartment. Can there be "bad energies" or "evil spirits" in a location, and is it possible that there was something there with her, or was that all mental illness?

Discuss the need for perfection. Is that a sign of a mental illness? Can someone be a perfectionist and not have a mental illness? Is there a shade on the continuum where perfectionism becomes illness? Is our society focussed on perfection more or less than in years past in your opinion?

Nikki developed an eating disorder when they were not recognized as such. Do you believe there is enough understanding of eating disorders in our current society, and do you believe eating disorders are more prevalent in all children in our society at this time than in the past?

Nikki obviously had postpartum depression after the birth of each child. The depression after each child, however, manifested differently. Do you think medicine and society in general have a full understanding of all shades of postpartum depression?

Although never diagnosed with Seasonal Affective Disorder (SAD), Nikki did have worse symptoms in the winter months before her diagnosis. What are your thoughts of SAD and its treatment in our society?

PART TWO
DIAGNOSIS
THE PATH

WHAT DO YOU THINK ABOUT Nikki's friend's forceful intervention at the beginning of the section? Have you ever been in a similar situation where you felt you had to do something very uncomfortable as it was the "right" thing to do?

Do you believe that Nikki's relationship with her husband was an issue as her counsellor alluded to?

What do you think about the fact that Nikki doesn't remember much of her childhood or teen years? Is that normal? Do you remember your childhood and teen years?

Nikki struggled finding something to do that was solely for herself. What do you do that is just for you?

Do you believe Nikki acted out more in her 30's, seeing friends, going for drinks after work, as she missed that in her teen years? Or was her behaviour normal for a woman in her 30's?

Nikki did not set healthy boundaries as far as entertaining guests/relatives in her home and in many other areas. What healthy boundaries have you set to maintain wellness and minimize stress in your life? Do you need to set more boundaries?

When Nikki was taken to the hospital with her mental breakdown, she was told she should be admitted but there were no beds available. What do you think of mental health support available in our society?

What are your thoughts on Nikki's trip to Edmonton with Josh. Was she so self consumed she couldn't see what was going on with Josh, did Josh "play" her, or was it a combination of both?

What role did Nikki's self esteem or lack thereof play in her relationship with Josh?

Nikki started journaling to help sort her thoughts. Have you ever tried journaling and would it be something you would consider trying?

Nikki had an urgent need to leave Frank's place one night in the middle of a date. Have you ever experienced an overwhelming need like that, as in a need to leave a place or do something immediately?

Have you ever used an outside "sign" to make a decision as Nikki did with the sale of her house?

Josh and Susan's dysfunctional relationship impacted Nikki severely. Have you let or are you letting others' dysfunctional relationship(s) impact your feelings of wellness? If so, what is one step you can make to change that?

Nikki was completely shocked by her weight gain. Has something similar ever happened in your life? Have you experienced a change so gradual that when you became aware you were in a far different place than you realized?

Managing a blended household can be very stressful. Have you ever had to manage this? What was your role in the household (parent, child, partner or ex-partner of a member of a blended household)? What was your experience?

Do you agree with the counsellor who told Nikki to leave Josh after the counselling session where he stated he would not help Nikki with necessities after her surgery? Should the counsellor have tried more solutions or did she behave correctly in that situation?

It takes two people to dissolve a relationship. What do you think were the biggest factors on both Nikki's and Josh's side that caused their marriage and blended family to come to an end?

What do you think about Althea's counselling techniques?

Nikki found she had a guardian angel in the form of a wolf. Do you believe you have a guardian angel? What form does it take?

Nikki didn't want to experience anger so she suppressed that feeling. Have you ever felt the need to strongly suppress a feeling and did you find all feelings were subsequently suppressed?

Take a moment to ponder and discuss parental guilt. Do all parents seem to have some feelings of guilt around raising their children? Do you and how does that manifest?

Nikki revisits relationships previously ended several times throughout her life. What are your thoughts on this? If a relationship doesn't work the first time, can it work a subsequent time?

Was Nikki's decision to leave Josh after she found he lied about her having cancer again an over reaction?

PART THREE
STEPPING INTO THE LIGHT
ACCEPTANCE

NIKKI FALLS INTO THE HABIT of using alcohol to manage her symptoms, do you think people with mental illness sometimes self prescribe for similar reasons?

Nikki takes up meditation. What is your experience with mediation?

Nikki feels she can't manage wellness within a relationship. What do you think of that statement?

As Nikki starts interacting with others through a dating site, she finds herself releasing judgement of others, and subsequently, she becomes more accepting of herself. Do you judge yourself? In what areas? Can you take a small step today toward releasing that self judgement?

What do you think of Nikki and Frank's wildly different memories from their "breakup" conversation?

Have you ever had your boundaries challenged as Jack and his son challenged Nikki's boundaries? How did you handle that?

How do you feel about having to explain health issues to new doctors who come into your life? Do you think explaining invisible chronic illness, including but not limited to mental illness, is difficult every time you see a new doctor or practitioner? How do you manage this?

Have you ever travelled alone? Did you enjoy the experience? How was it different from travelling with others?

COVID-19 severely impacted Nikki's mental wellness as it did with many others. How did COVID-19 impact your mental health and wellness?

Do you think Jack should have left Nikki alone to travel to see his son when she was completely isolated and travel was not recommended? Would she have found her way to the wellness she eventually did if he hadn't left?

Nikki shares several paranormal events she believes she experienced in her life throughout this work. What are your thoughts on events like this? Do you believe people can experience situations or events that can't be explained?

Can two partners have very different lifetime goals and still maintain a committed romantic relationship? Jack plans to move; Nikki does not. Do you know of a couple or do you yourself have a relationship with someone who has different life goals in some areas, and how have you and your partner worked it out?

Nikki comes to believe that her mental illness can not be controlled through medication alone. She realizes, for her stability, she needs to incorporate fitness, nutrition, proper rest, and aspects of spiritual and emotional health into her lifestyle. Do you attend to all these facets of wellness in your life? What is missing? What can you add? Is there something you would like to eliminate?

25913190R00182